1925

10ᶜ

SILENCING THE SELF

DANA CROWLEY JACK

SILENCING THE SELF

WOMEN AND DEPRESSION

Harvard University Press
Cambridge, Massachusetts
London, England 1991

Library of Congress Cataloging-in-Publication Data

Jack, Dana Crowley.
    Silencing the self : women and depression / Dana
Crowley Jack.
        p.   cm.
    Includes bibliographical references and index.
    ISBN 0-674-80815-0 (alk. paper)
    1. Depression, Mental.   2. Women—Mental
health.   I. Title.
RC537.J26   1991
616.85′27′0082—dc20   91-15472
                                                                        CIP

Designed by Gwen Frankfeldt

To
Rand, Darby, and Kelsey
and to my mother
Dorothy Beach

CONTENTS

SILENCING THE SELF

PREPARING
TO LISTEN

. 1 .

Even though I can objectively say, okay, I am above average in looks, I have been very successful with my art, I have been very successful at singing, I'm gregarious, I make friends easily. I can say all that, and still there is this, "You are no good, what's the use."

I always feel the failure of my marriage was my fault, because I wanted a career, and didn't know how to manage being a professional with being a wife.

I'm a liar and a cheat and I'm no good.

I'm afraid to get back into a relationship because I will lose my sense of self.

I don't know how to work through this feeling of I'm not quite good enough or something. I mean, somewhere along the line I have got to drop that or I'm going to be fighting that the rest of my life.

These are the words of women diagnosed as depressed. The rate of depression is twice as high for women as for men in the United States and in most Western societies.[1] What is it about women's inner and outer worlds that creates this vulnerability to the hopelessness and pain of depression? I think that these women are telling us. To understand, we must prepare to listen in new ways, unobstructed by prior assumptions.

Depression is a complex and multi-faceted illness. By current consensus, major depression results from an interaction of biological and psychosocial factors; no single cause can be isolated. Given that psychosocial stresses translate into biochemical changes within the brain, the distinction between physical and social factors may be artificial; psychological and biological factors are simply different sides of the same coin (Beck, 1983). Though aware of possible biological influences on depression in women, in this book I focus on psychosocial factors.

Since no existing theory adequately explains the complex phenomenon of female depression, a return to depressed women's own descriptions of their experiences and feelings becomes critically important as a means to gain new insights. Yet, as depressed women tell their stories, we immediately encounter obstacles to our ability to understand what they say. As the feminist critique has taught us, traditional theories and concepts of psychology have not accurately represented or measured the experience of women, and therefore women's depression cannot be understood within traditional categories. The very words—dependence, autonomy, passivity—used to describe what a woman is or should be reflect the male experience. Particularly where women's interests and experiences vary significantly from those of men, the tendency in psychology has been to consider women's patterns deviant. From the stance of psychoanalytic or cognitive theory, it may be impossible to hear what a woman is trying to say about her life, her loss, and her sadness.

For years, as a therapist, I listened to depressed women through a filter of theories that told me how to understand and interpret their conflicts. I was constantly dissatisfied with my comprehension of recurring themes such as loss of self, self-condemnation, and hopelessness. My difficulty in understanding depressed women's experience did not reside in the hollows or silences of their narratives; the difficulty arose because what they said was so familiar and I had already been taught how to interpret it. Depressed women, I had learned, were too "dependent" on relationships for a sense of identity and self-esteem; they needed to develop more autonomy and self-reliance. These formulations did not help me distinguish between healthy attachment needs and what clinical theory describes as women's overdependent and often pathological need for relationship. Calling women "dependent" contributed little to my comprehension of the meaning or the forms of relationships in depressed women's lives. As I began to hear more clearly with the help of recent developments in the psychology of women, it appeared that major concepts used in theories of depression—attachment, loss, dependence, self-esteem—required reexamination from a depressed woman's perspective.

The proposal to return and listen carefully to depressed women in order to formulate new insights and concepts is particularly appropriate now, because emerging theoretical frameworks about women's psychology provide us with a new standpoint from which to hear their narratives. Psychologists who are listening to women from a developmental perspective, a clinical orientation, or a psychoanalytic viewpoint all agree that women's orientation to relationships is the central component of female identity and emotional activity.[2] This relational, connected female self differs significantly from the autonomous, bounded self described by Western psychology and presupposed by most theories of depression.

If the "I," the subjective organization of ongoing experience that we commonly call the sense of self, differs for women, then the experience of depression, as well as its causes, may also significantly differ. There has been an upsurge in biological and epidemiological studies of depression in the past decade, but a startling lack of basic research on the psychology of female depression remains. We have an increasing supply of information on the externals of depressed women's lives—the violence directed against them, the money they earn or fail to earn, their ages and marital status—but very little knowledge about aspects of their internal worlds, such as their imaginings, feelings, and patterns of thought. While depressed women have been *observed* by researchers, their experience has been filtered and distilled to fit within existing concepts. We rarely hear depressed women's own words; instead, we are commonly given summaries and vignettes created by the interpreter and ordered by concepts that may obscure women's own representations of their lives. Our lack of direct knowledge about depressed women's inner worlds is of particular concern given that the majority of people seeking treatment for depression are women.

If we listen to how depressed women define and devalue their own orientation to their relationships, the need for new concepts takes on even greater urgency. In a first interview with Susan, diagnosed as depressed by her referring therapist, the following interchange occurred minutes into the interview. Susan was 30, had been married for seven years, and was the mother of two young daughters. I asked her, "What, in your own mind, led up to your depression?" She said she felt she had "lost a lot of myself" through being a wife and a mother. In her self-reflection, the issue of dependence was central and problematic: "You know, I'm basically a very dependent person to start with. And then you get married and tied down to a home and not working . . ." Asked what she meant by "dependent," she responded:[3]

> I like closeness. I like companionship. I like somebody, an intimate closeness, even with a best friend. I was always so close to my mother . . . I was used to that all through my childhood, having an intimate closeness . . . someone that shared my feelings, my fears, my doubts, my happiness, my achievements, my failures. And I've never had that with my husband. I can't talk to him on those levels . . . He lives in a very concrete, day-to-day, black-and-white world. But I've always been used to channeling a lot of my energies into more deep levels of intimacy with people, and sharing . . . And so I guess when I say I'm a dependent person, I guess I mean that I

like having a closeness. I have need for a deep intimate level of friendship with somebody.

(*How is that dependent?*) Maybe it isn't. But I do have that need for closeness, and I've always, sometimes I've, sometimes I get frustrated with myself that I have to have that, you know. I look at other people that seem so self-sufficient and so independent and so—I don't know—I just have always needed a closeness. And maybe I identified that as dependency.

(*Does that have a negative kind of connotation to you?*) It never used to, but since I've been married I realize it's kind of a negative thing to be that way. Because I've tried to bury that. And so I guess that has also contributed to a lot of my frustrations.

Susan "had been feeling that my need for intimacy and my need for that kind of a deep level of friendship or relationships with people was sort of bad," and she began "to believe there was something the matter with me."

In Susan's narrative, we hear how women use the language of the culture to deny what, on another level, they value and desire. Susan tells us that she cannot ask for what she wants most—an intimate closeness. Hidden from her description is the reason why she cannot ask: inequality mutes her ability to communicate directly about her needs. She does not feel entitled to ask to have her needs filled, nor does she feel they are legitimate. Explaining how she must bury part of her self in order to relate to her husband, Susan reveals the activity required to suppress the self, to try to live up to self-alienating images of the autonomous adult.

We see how this woman's healthy capacity for intimacy, a hallmark of adult maturity and health, has been held up to her by the culture as a weakness. Susan judges her feelings against a standard that says needing closeness makes one dependent, that one should be able to be self-sufficient and autonomous. She reflects upon her own experiences, her capabilities, and her needs not from the basis of who she is and what she wants, but in terms of how others see her. She denies and devalues her desire for relationships, considering it "a negative thing to be this way." This process of self-alienation is often deepened in therapy when a woman's problems are cast as inadequate separation, as excessive dependency. Her capacity for closeness and intimacy goes unacknowledged as a strength and is presented to her as something that she must overcome in order to adjust to her marriage. Rather than a failure of the husband's response, the problem is identified as the woman's "neediness."

From this example, we see the critical necessity for new concepts to replace the traditional equation of a yearning for closeness with dependency. The prevailing cultural norms that value self-sufficiency and independence contribute to the lowering of a depressed women's self-esteem. Ego strength has come to be equated with a lack of reliance on others for emotional support; self-reliance is seen as mature and reliance on others as immature. Thus women come to label their own needs and desires for relatedness as "neurotic" and "dependent." A woman is caught in a double bind: society still pushes her to define herself through her relationships, but then it invalidates her wish for connection by derogating the importance of attachments, but if relationships falter or fail, a woman often considers it her own fault. And in fact, a woman's striving for achievements often does threaten her relationships (Miller, 1976).

How should we understand depressed women's focus on their relationships? Let us delve further to examine some basic assumptions about the nature of the self, attachments, and loss that provide the basis for thinking about dependence and depression in women.

VISIONS OF THE SELF

Depression resembles grief because, in both, feelings of loss and sadness dominate the emotions. Depression, however, is distinguished by a fall in self-esteem and a syndrome of specific symptoms that affect thought, sleep, appetite, energy level, and behavior. Women and men typically respond with depression to different types of losses. Women most often become depressed over disruption or conflict in close relationships, whereas men respond with depression to the loss of an ideal or an achievement-related goal, or over performance issues.[4] For years, one prevalent clinical view has been that these differences between the sexes indicate women's greater dependence on relationships, their difficulty in achieving individuation and autonomy.

Whether a woman's depression in response to the disruption or loss of relationships is interpreted as dependent rests on the interpreter's understanding of the role relationships play in psychic life. Therefore, assumptions about the self and the function of attachments in adulthood are crucial to theories of depression. Such assumptions guide interpretation of the depressed person's words as well as the understanding of what constitutes health and healing. Two visions of the self underlie thinking about the place of attachment and loss in psychic life: the separate self and the relational self.

The Separate Self

Standing in the philosophical line of individualism, the view of the self that dominates psychology starts with the premise that "man" is intrinsically separate: "Normally, there is nothing of which we are more certain than the feeling of our self, of our own ego. This ego appears to us as something autonomous and unitary, marked off distinctly from everything else" (Freud, 1930, p. 13). In Freud's drive theory, development progresses from the infant's "oceanic feeling" of unbounded connection to the delineated autonomy of mature adulthood.

To explain how relationships become so important to these autonomous individuals, Freud relies on the "cupboard love theory of object relations" (Bowlby, 1969). Drives, such as sex and aggression, are satisfied by people; thus people become important emotionally as the objects of drives. Attachments to others are secondary to the economics of drive theory in this fundamental sense. The growing child becomes less dependent on the "supplies" of comfort, closeness, security, and self-esteem from another person as these are moved to inner locations (and become parts of the self, as introject, identifications, superego). Maturity implies self-sufficient autonomy; immaturity means a childlike dependence on others.

The psychological notion of the separate self dovetails neatly with dominant ideologies of the United States—individualism and its fraternal twin, capitalism. Capitalism requires autonomously functioning, independent individuals making economic determinations in their own self-interest. Mirroring the paternal matrix out of which it arose, the mature, separate self has its own internal economics: it owns itself.[5] Such self-ownership implies control, self-direction, independence, and the capacity to participate freely in economic structures that often require an autonomous adult's undivided commitment of time and energy. Adam Smith's legacy suggests a moral justification of this self-interested, economic self: "By pursuing his own interest he frequently promotes that of the society more effectually than when he really intends to promote it" (1937, p. 423). The intermeshing of ideas from political theory, philosophy, and cultural legends—of the lone cowboy, the hero, the warrior—has supported the psychological theory of the separate self to make it look "right."

The concept of the self as separate and autonomous determines the vision of what kind of relationships we have with others:

> If you are not responsible to anyone but yourself, it follows that relationships with other people are merely there to be exploited when (emotionally) profitable, and terminated when they cease to be profitable. The primary assumption is that each person in a relationship has a set of emotional, sexual, or other "needs" which he or she wants met. If they are no longer being satisfied by a friend or sexual partner, then that bond may be broken just as reasonably as a buyer would take his business away from a seller if he found a better price. The *needs* have an inherent legitimacy—the *people* are replaceable. (Ehrenreich and English, 1979, pp. 274–275)

These ideas add up to an individual for whom relationships are primarily functional, who should not "need" relationships, but merely have them. Objects can be replaced; therefore, relationships are not valuable in and of themselves, but only as they serve to satisfy basic drives or needs. One's beliefs about the role of relationships affect the way one views commitment to them, the consequences of losing them, and how much should be done to preserve them. If relationships are functional in this economic sense, then the deterioration or loss of a particular relationship should not strike the individual to the core, and the goal should be to replace the lost relationship with as little disruption as possible.

Many of these contemporary assumptions regarding the nature of the self and the healthy response to loss continue to bear the imprint of Freud's thought. In "Mourning and Melancholia," Freud concluded that depression reveals a failure to separate from a problematic love relationship. When a love relationship is shattered, instead of separating and attaching itself to a new object, the "free libido" withdraws into the ego and serves "to establish an *identification* of the ego with the abandoned object":

> Thus the shadow of the object fell upon the ego, and the latter could henceforth be judged by a special agency, as though it were an object, the forsaken object. In this way an object-loss was transformed into an ego-loss and the conflict between the ego and the loved person into a cleavage between the critical activity of the ego and the ego as altered by identification.   (1917, p. 249)

In Freud's view, this alteration of the self through identification with the lost object lays the foundation for the inner division, harsh self-judgment, and sense of loss characteristic of depression. His formulation reveals two basic assumptions: first, that the structure of the healthy adult self exists independent of and unaltered by current relationships; and second, that depression is created by an inability to detach from a lost relationship rather than by an inability to connect with a loved one. In Freud's view, a person falls into depression because of an inability to remain within the boundaries of the autonomous, separate self, as when the self becomes "altered by identification" with another.[6]

Today, many therapists treating depression still consider the origins of depression to reside within the problems of the individual personality. Even when an interpersonal event has clearly upset the person's emotional balance, the focus of treatment shifts to the individual and the deficits—cognitive, developmental, or behavioral—within the individual that perpetuate the depression. Sliding into depression after an interpersonal problem is thought to reveal the individual's unhealthy dependence on the relationship for a positive sense of self. It exposes an inability to be an autonomously functioning adult, an inability to stand on one's own two feet.

The Relational Self

Relational theory offers a radically different perspective on the self and the issues of relationships, attachment, and loss in depression. From the relational viewpoint, the self (in both women and men) is part of a fundamentally social experience. We all spring from a relational mold: "There is no 'self,' in a psychologically meaningful sense, in isolation, outside a matrix of relations with others" (Mitchell, 1988, p. 33). Attachments are not simply functional, but provide the foundation for self, mind, and behavior. Striving for relatedness replaces sex and aggression as the motivation for behavior; attachments are the soil from which cognition, emotion, and behavior originate.

Relational theory considers attainment of a sense of basic human connectedness to be the goal of development. Research on infants contradicts the psychoanalytic assumption of maturational change out of symbiotic union toward separation and individuation. Daniel Stern, as well as other researchers who have systematically analyzed interactions between infants and caregivers, finds that infants come into the world ready, eager, and equipped for social interaction. According to this contrasting view of development, the goal of infant behavior is to become securely attached to the caretaker, not to separate from symbiosis with her or him. Connectedness, from this perspective, is not "the result of a failure in differentiation; . . . it is a success of psychic functioning" (Stern, 1985, p. 241). According to relational theory, not only children but adults as well have this basic, biosocial motivation to make secure, intimate connection with others.

Shifting to look at depression from the relational perspective requires a change of focus from the intrapsychic to the interpersonal, to the quality and nature of attachments. If relatedness with others is of primary importance, it becomes clear why a person will go to any lengths, including altering the self, to establish and maintain intimate ties. Despair arises when a person feels hopeless about the possibility of emotional contact with others: "In most forms of depressive disorder, including that of chronic mourning, the principal issue about which a person feels helpless is his ability to make and to maintain affectional relationships" (Bowlby, 1980, p. 247). From the relational perspective, depression is *interpersonal*.[7]

THE PSYCHOLOGY OF WOMEN

Remaining within assumptions about the social nature of the self, a growing body of work on the psychology of women delineates the origins and development of women's orientation to relationships. Through this work on women, we see how the issue of gender redraws the outlines of the relational self in a way that is critical for understanding female depression. Carol Gilligan and her colleagues at Harvard University provide a developmental framework for listening to women's different ways of speaking about self, relationships, and morality, particularly for understanding how women's moral thought bears on their self-assessment and on their resolution of conflicts in relationships. Clinicians at the Stone Center, who examine the development of women's "self-in-relation," offer insights about ideal and problematic pathways of maturation. Writing from a psychoanalytic viewpoint, Nancy Chodorow presents ideas regarding women's subjective experience, development, and interpersonal orientation. Though these writers have important theoretical differences, they all agree that interpersonal intimacy is the profound organizer of female experience and the key to understanding women's "different voice." They also agree that gender differences in ego capacities, vulnerabilities, and strengths arise from the different social contexts and cultural norms that affect male and female development in characteristic ways.[8]

Women's Orientation to Relationships

The processes of forming a gender identity diverge for women and men and result in different senses of self, ego strengths, and emotional concerns. The female orientation to relationships arises out of culturally arranged, and therefore contingent, contexts of female caretaking and male dominance. Chodorow (1978, 1989) finds differing consequences for girls and boys of the near-universal fact that women take care of infants. Forming a gender identity in relation to a female caretaker forces boys to separate from femininity and to define masculinity through differentness: to be male is, in part, to be not-female. For girls, the process of forming a gender identity does not require this same kind of separation from the primary caretaker. Daughters bring to adolescence and adulthood more aspects of the original, closely bonded mother-child relationship, whereas boys must relinquish the closeness of that relationship to form a gender identity based on separateness from the mother.

Because of an unbroken identification with a primary caretaker, girls come to experience themselves as "less separate" than boys, and have a stronger basis "for experiencing another's needs or feelings as one's own" (Chodorow, 1978, p. 167). Further, because girls do not repress or completely give up their earliest identifications with the mother, they not only reproduce mothering but also are prepared to repeat the specific behaviors, attitudes, and values of their mother's nurturing role and to take on the cultural devaluation of her female gender. Out of this primary attachment with a mother, females' gender identity comes to be based on continuing connection, males' gender identity on separation (Chodorow, 1978, 1985; Gilligan, 1982, 1990).

Female Development

The developmental pathway for women appears to be characterized not by successive stages of separation and individuation but by differing forms of connection within relationships (Gilligan, 1982). Changing and developing one's own talents, abilities, and initiative *within* attachments, rather than separation, leads to a more mature, complex sense of self in relationship to other selves. Empowerment, vitality, and self-knowledge arise from the experience of "mutual empathy," which Miller (1986b) describes as the cognitive/emotional activity of experiencing the self's feelings and thoughts while simultaneously experiencing those of the other person, including the effects of the emotional interchange on both self and other. In this schema of development, "Differentiation is not distinctness and separateness, but a particular way of being connected to others" (Chodorow, 1985, p. 9). That is, one is differentiated not by a separateness that emphasizes *difference* from the other but by the assertion of one's agency—one's needs, feelings, capacities—within relationships.

Thus, one need not separate from attachments in order to develop one's own self. Aspects of self-development such as creativity, autonomy, competence, maturity, and self-esteem develop within the context of one's closest ties to others. Developmental arrest occurs not because of failure to separate but as a result of an inability to remain connected while forming or asserting a distinct sense of self (Gilligan, 1982, 1990).[9]

For women, positive connections are essential for a sense of well-being and for continuing healthy development. Self-esteem is tied to the *quality* of attachments (Brown et al., 1986; Surrey, 1984); feelings of guilt, shame, and depression are associated with the failure of intimate ties (Gilligan, 1982; Jack, 1987; Kaplan, 1984). With these ideas in mind, it becomes easier to recognize women's desire for connection and intimacy as healthy and thus to perceive how specific social contexts and certain forms of connection serve to distort and disturb this desire.

Because of differences in development, women and men arrive at adulthood with differing fears and needs regarding relationships. Women perceive danger in interpersonal situations that pose a threat to connection, while men are threatened by situations that impinge on autonomy: women fear isolation;

men fear entrapment.[10] For example, in female development, adolescence is a particularly vulnerable time, marked by an increase in depression and in eating disorders.[11] At adolescence, girls must struggle to reconcile their wish for continuing connection with the cultural command for separation. Adolescence is

> a time when girls' desire for relationship and for knowledge comes up against a wall of cultural prohibition and girls must make a series of disconnections—between psyche and body, between voice and desire, between self and relationship, between the inner world of thoughts and feelings and the outer world of public knowledge—if they are to enter, without disrupting, the world they are to live in as young women. (Brown and Gilligan, 1990b, p. 3)

In the wider social world, women's orientation to relationships encounters social structures that devalue and deny the contribution of such an orientation (Belenky et al., 1986; Jack and Jack, 1989).

Gender Norms

Gender norms profoundly influence interpersonal interactions and affect the experience of the relational self, including basic anxieties, self-esteem, and sense of prerogatives in relationship. Though John Bowlby and other theorists detail the interpersonal nature of depression,[12] their writings reflect a startling omission. They do not examine the effects of gender, either on the experience of self or on the experience of relatedness. While stressing the social nature of mind and experience, they overlook the fundamental patterning of gender on consciousness and behavior.

If the self is relational, then that fact compels us to examine how the interactional world (and thus the self) is affected by gender norms. Clearly, gender influences the forms and the quality of relatedness from birth on. In childhood, through interactions with others, a person learns the acceptable ways to make and maintain connection—through empathy, listening, sharing, feelings, the nuances of glance and touch. From the beginning, parents tend to respond differently to male and female children;

in general, they discourage the expression of attachment needs in boys, pushing them to be independent, while they allow girls to ask for closeness, reassurance, and support more overtly. These gender-specific patterns of interaction encourage the development of certain traits: independence, exploration, and achievement in boys; proximity, nurturance, and responsibility in girls. Evidence from numerous studies shows that males tend to have more activity-focused relationships than do females, while females at all ages maintain more emotionally intimate relationships than do males.[13]

A person's body carries social meanings that profoundly affect the sense of self. We come into relation with people through a body whose sex, size, and shape elicit responses from others that enhance or diminish our feelings of confidence, self-esteem, and safety. A woman's body operates as a trigger for certain types of social interactions that are integrated into her sense of self-in-relation. Walking into a room full of people creates a different social experience for a woman whom others judge as physically attractive than for a woman whom others regard as unattractive. In general, the cultural sexualization and devaluation of women can create an internal feeling of low self-esteem and worthlessness (Westkott, 1986). And the high incidence of sexual abuse of girls and rape and violence against women fosters feelings of helplessness, rage, and shame.[14]

Social expectations about gender express themselves most clearly in interpersonal behaviors. Even the qualities used to describe masculine and feminine stereotypes—strong, independent, assertive, gentle, sensitive, compassionate—are made up of behaviors that take place within interpersonal contexts. Thus, to examine female depression without considering the social context and gender norms is bound to lead to a distorted understanding of the dynamics that produce depression.

A woman forms images of self (what psychologists call her "cognitive schemas" or "representational models of self") that directly reflect her interpersonal experiences—as able to give and receive love, or as unable; as worthy of care and support from others, or as unworthy; as free to be herself while maintaining connection, or as unfree. A woman's social context, both in particular relationships and in the wider world, fundamentally affects these images of self. Because women's core sense of self is more relationally based than men's, and also is affected by norms that stress affiliation and interpersonal sensitivity, then the qualities of current relationships—not just the relationships experienced in early childhood—may more deeply influence the female than the male self.[15]

This perspective on women's interpersonal orientation, female development, and the gender norms that govern social interactions recasts the issue of relationships in women's psychology. According to the relational point of view, depression arises from the inability to make or sustain supportive, authentic connection with a loved person. If the separate, autonomous self no longer serves as a model for health, then "standing on one's own" does not mean standing alone but implies that one feels securely attached and confident that a trusted person is available in times of need. The focus shifts from searching for the developmental deficits in the individual that create dependence to examining the forms of connection that result in a "loss of self" and depression for women.

THE OBSTACLE OF DEPENDENCE

Why does the concept of dependence create such an obstacle as depressed women try to name their experience and as therapists and researchers attempt to understand it? This concept, which contains a fundamental bias against women's orientation to relationships, has influenced thinking about depression since Freud and Abraham. In all major theories, dependency is considered either to predispose a person to depression or to be characteristic of depression: "Pathologic dependency is perhaps the one characteristic of the depressive that has been unanimously emphasized in the psychiatric literature" (Arieti and Bemporad, 1978, p. 163). Dependency is commonly defined as an inordinate attachment to a person, cause, or organization, so that self-esteem is derived from the external object and not from an internalized source or from autonomous actions. More generally, as the opposite of independence, dependence has signified helplessness, indicating either regression to an infantile state or developmental arrest at the earliest stages. Dependence does not imply a specific or discriminating tie to another person, but rather a state of childlike neediness; what is sought and received matters rather than the person from whom it is received.[16]

Not all people become clinically depressed over problems in relationship; those who do are considered to be excessively dependent on the relationship for self-esteem and a sense of identity. We read about the depressed person's "desperate cry for love . . . patterned on the hungry infant's loud cry for help" (Rado, 1968b, p. 98), or we are told that depressed persons "cling to their object like leeches . . . and feed upon them, as though it were their intention to devour them altogether" (Rado, 1968a, p. 74). Or we read that

> Depression prone people are inordinately and almost exclusively dependent on narcissistic supplies derived directly or indirectly from other people for maintenance of their self-esteem. Their frustration tolerance is low, and they employ various techniques—submissive, manipulative, coercive, piteous, demanding and placating—to maintain their desperately needed but essentially ambivalent relationships with the external or internalized objects of their demands. (Chodoff, 1972, p. 670)

In the current literature, dependency has lost its tie with Freudian psychosexual stages and has become synonymous with exaggerated needs for affection and support. An example of how much the concept has blurred the distinction between normal human needs and "pathology" is evident in the 1980 *Psychiatric Glossary* definition of dependency as "vital needs for mothering, love, affection, shelter, protection, security, food and warmth; [which] may be a manifestation of regression when they appear openly in adults" (p. 28). Since most adults could not survive without most of these "dependency" needs being expressed and met, the attitude revealed by the definition is telling. Mental health coincides with the dominant values of the culture: autonomy, independence, power, wealth.[17]

Most writing about depressed people's dependence on their relationships overlooks evidence from the work of John Bowlby, who has examined how people form significant bonds with others and how they behave when these bonds are threatened or broken. Bowlby argues that the terms dependence and independence should be replaced by the concepts of attachment, trust, reliance, and self-reliance. He defines the attachment bond as necessary for healthy functioning throughout life and notes that the requirement of adults for this "secure base" tends to be overlooked or disparaged in theories of development. His evidence suggests that "human beings of all ages are happiest and able to deploy their talents to best advantage when they are confident that, standing behind them, there are one or more trusted persons who will come to their aid should difficulties arise" (1979, p. 103). Attachment behaviors—crying, calling, following, clinging, searching—are part of a repertoire of interpersonal responses that ensure the development of affectional bonds. Attachments and reliance on them should not be seen as dependence, but as a healthy, normal human need, and, in fact, a source of valuable strength.

Looking at responses to life stress, researchers find that people function best when they have at least one close attachment to another person.[18] Uncertainty about the reliability and availability of support creates what Bowlby calls "anxious attachment behaviors" such as clinging, fear of separation, and requests for reassurance, in adults as well as in children. Further, Bowlby outlines a predictable sequence of protest, despair, and detachment behaviors that arise in response to threatened or actual loss of an important attachment. These behaviors can be observed across species, and occur at all ages of life.[19]

Given research findings regarding the importance of relationships to mental health, as well as theory regarding the central role of attachments throughout life, why does the concept of dependence continue to be so influential in the understanding and treatment of depression? First, the word connects depression to a wider ideology of gender stereotypes—that women are immature, weak, helpless, *dependent* on their relationships, and that men are strong, self-reliant, independent.[20] Second, the term dependence covers a variety of meanings—economic, political, social, psychological—but as used in clinical writing on depression it designates only one, the psychological. Yet all the other meanings are unconsciously present, and feed into the power of the word.

The label of dependence obscures the perception of external situations, such as poverty, economic dependence, physical illness, a partner's hostility, naming them instead as an internal trait, considered to be an immature need for others. Thus it focuses attention on the fault or developmental deficiency of the person, and eliminates the need to search for the specific cultural conditions that serve to create what is perceived as a dependent stance in relationship. In part this is why, though theorists have long recognized the fundamentally interpersonal nature of depression, they continue to focus on its individual, intrapsychic, or cognitive aspects. The familiar dichotomous oppositions of dependence with independence, strength, maleness, and freedom, along with the cultural abhorrence of any display of vulnerability in men, makes dependence seem more "naturally" true of women than men. Since conceptual frameworks construct our perceptions of reality, systems of meaning attached to dependence have inhibited the creation of new ways of seeing.

If a researcher or a therapist interviewed a depressed woman like Susan with the traditional notion of dependence in mind, it would be easy to see her as confirmation of the prevalent view that depressed women are "overdependent" on their relationships and need to develop other sources of self-esteem. But such a judgment adds little to our understanding. The crucial issue, as we begin to listen to depressed women talk about their relationships, is how to distinguish between healthy, mature interdependence and debilitating forms of connection. As it currently exists, the concept of dependence hampers our ability to perceive this distinction; it labels women's orientation to their relationships as weakness or pathology. What encourages one person to abandon the self in order to form some type of relationship with another, giving to that other the authority to define personal identity and self-worth? What lies behind women's yearning for connection or their personal sense of failure? How do the shapes of their relationships, the quality of their connections with others, contribute to their depression?

We live in a time when gender roles are in flux and many women would like to emulate the autonomy traditionally assigned to men. The demands of relationships can swallow up the self and steal possibilities for creativity, goal-directedness, expression of unique capabilities. Having been forced into economic dependence through female roles, many women long to rid themselves of constraints and join the male world, which appears to offer freedom and power. In Catherine Keller's words, for women, "The cleanness of masculine separation, in the vacuum of alternative models for maturation, exercises an undoubted appeal" (1986, p. 132). Margaret Thatcher, when her twins were born, resolved, "I am not going to be overcome by this," and immediately began studying for admission to the Bar.[21] The plethora of popular books with titles like "Women Who Love Too Much" and "Love Addicts" show the deep desire to extricate oneself from the tangles of "love," to relate to men as "Just Desserts," that is, as pleasurable but not necessary. What is missing in these books—and in the trend they exemplify—is a vision of relatedness that does not imply either the rigid boundaries and separation of the traditional male model or the yielding openness, nondifferentiation, and "dependence" of the traditional female model. For women struggling to find their own point of view, there has been neither a language nor stories to portray the nature of healthy, mature interdependence in heterosexual relationships.[22]

As we listen to depressed women, we are led to a reexamination of loss itself, commonly considered to be the trigger for the onset of depression. Traditional theories cast the depressed person's problem as an inability to let go after a real or imagined loss, as a failure to separate, as excessive dependence on the lost other for self-esteem, as inordinate concern about relationships. But if we shift ground to stand with depressed women and listen to their words, we begin to question what is lost: the other or the self. When depressed women talk about their experiences in unsatisfactory relationships, the most common phrase that recurs is "loss of self." Listen: "I lost myself in that relationship." "I was losing my sense of who I was." "I put myself as a person out of the picture." "I'm afraid to get back in a relationship because I will lose my sense of self." Far from a transformation of object loss into ego loss, this common female language suggests a diminution of self that occurs *within* the context of unsatisfactory relationships.

So too, different lines of research are converging to the inescapable conclusion that women's vulnerability to depression does not lie in their "dependence" on relationships or in their depressive response to loss, but in what happens to them within their relationships. For example, studies have identified conflict and disruption in intimate relationships as critical factors in women's depressions. While problems in relationships are strongly associated with depression in women, other research indicates that supportive intimate relationships protect women against depression. The presence of an intimate and confiding relationship with a partner, even in the face of stressful conditions such as poverty, inadequate housing, young children, or illness, shields women from depression.[23]

Thus, in women, depression exposes the faltering lines of attachment, the fraying of the relational tapestry into which the experience of female self is woven; it highlights the *quality of a woman's relationship to her partner*. Missing from most accounts of depression are the entanglements that result when intimacy occurs within a context of inequality. Yet women's experience of adult attachments continually intersects with issues of dominance and subordination, as we shall see in later chapters. As Jean Baker Miller observes:

> Women have played a specific role in male-led society in ways no other suppressed groups have done. They have been en-

twined with men in intimate and intense relationships, creating the milieu—the family—in which the human mind as we
know it has been formed. Thus women's situation is a crucial
key to understanding the psychological order.   (1976, p. 1)

What happens to a woman's psychology when social norms
dictate that her adult heterosexual attachments repeat a childhood position of inequality? What sense of self does she develop
to accommodate to this position, and how does that accommodation contribute to her vulnerability to depression?

As we listen to the words of depressed women, we will
necessarily interpret them. There is no such thing as truly raw
data; even the collection of data requires a framework for understanding and ordering reality. But we are at an awkward stage,
when old theories are being set aside or are under suspicion
as biased against women, and new ones are still emerging.
We must therefore be especially attentive to the influences that
shape what we hear and how we interpret. Otherwise, we may
repeat the errors of oversight, underestimation, exclusion, projection, and devaluation made by our predecessors, or we may
fall into new errors of exaggeration, distortion, and overestima-
tion (Lauter and Rupprecht, 1985).

While I am guided by new theories on the psychology of
women, depressed women themselves serve as correctives to
these theories, modifying concepts when necessary and creating
new ones where needed. Paying careful attention to women's
own experience of depression enriches our understanding of
traits associated with femininity, and helps prevent the idealization and reification of such traits by revealing their historical, socially situated aspects. For example, while traits associated with
female development—empathy, flexible ego boundaries, the
disposition to care for others—are positively valued as strengths
by relational feminists, they carry with them a vulnerability, as
witnessed by the large numbers of women who experience depression. Carol Gilligan (1982), Jean Baker Miller (1976; 1986a),
and Marcia Westkott (1986) have identified the vulnerability of
caring for others within a culture of inequality, but the intricacies

of such vulnerability within an individual personality and its tie with depression have not been closely mapped. The traditional female social role, particularly the cost of caring for others without receiving support oneself (Belle, 1982a), has been implicated as a cause of depression, but we do not know how social role manifests itself within a woman's inner conflicts or within her intimate interactions.

DEPRESSED WOMEN AS GUIDES

Since the traditional theories of depression do not adequately take into account women's relational sense of self or the effects of gender norms and inequality between the sexes, we face the need for a search—a search for better insight into the nature of depression in women, a search for new concepts that more adequately reflect women's emotional realities. The people best able to guide us in the search are depressed women, because they are the ones who know about their paths into depression as well as the ways that lead out of it.

In human relationships, "objective reality" is unfathomable, since multiple points of view exist regarding whatever happens. In order to understand how a woman's external and internal worlds affect and depress her, we must learn about how she sees and interprets them. What affects her is not some clearly perceptible, objective actuality, but experience as *she* perceives it. To learn of it there is no better source—indeed no other source— than the woman herself.

In this book, I take a phenomenological, descriptive approach that assumes that women are reliable witnesses of their own psychological experiences. Considering depressed women to be the best informants about their illness goes against a long tradition that has elevated the distanced observer, whether researcher or therapist, as the one best situated to describe the problem. Clinicians and researchers have been hesitant to rely on depressed persons' own accounts, for at least three reasons.

First, the psychoanalytic emphasis on the unconscious and

the defensive maneuvers of the ego suggests that people's own explanations for their behavior or emotions cannot be trusted. This stance holds even more strongly in the case of psychopathology. The clinical view is that the disturbed person represses painful, threatening material and cannot give an accurate explanation of his or her psychological state; the person's behavior and emotions must be explained by experts. Thus others become the necessary interpreters of a depressed person's experience; these interpreters come to hold a monopoly on the perception of what occurs in depression.

Second, depressive illness is seen as causing a person to exaggerate the negative aspects of experience (Beck, 1967, 1976). A pessimistic view of the self and the surrounding world is one of the symptoms of depression, and such cognitive distortions are thought to give a negative shading to the picture of reality presented by a depressed person.

Third, the positivist approach in empirical research joins with the clinical emphasis on inner conflicts to lead many researchers to engage in "context stripping" (Mishler, 1979), and to ignore the situation within which a woman's depression occurs. According to this view, attempts to discover causes of depression require objective measures of outside events, or some means of independently verifying the truth of the depressed person's subjective report. This search for "objective truth," along with the clinical suspicion of self-report, has supported a tendency to disregard the depressive's own perspective on her illness.

These objections to listening to women's own voices have been undermined by new evidence on the reliability of self-report. Several studies comparing accounts of external events by depressed women with descriptions of the same events by outside observers indicate that the women are more accurate in their reporting than previously believed.[24] However, my interest in depressed women's self-reports stems less from their accuracy in identifying external reality "correctly" than from their ability to inform us about interpersonal and subjective experience. They are the ones best situated to provide a clear picture of the intersection of female personality with culture.

In the spirit of anthropologists seeking knowledge of a culture, then, let us view depressed women as informants from women's sphere (Bernard, 1981), trusting them to locate and describe the stresses that render them vulnerable to depression. Listening to the "I," the subjective experience of self and relatedness, is a necessary step toward disentangling the threads of female depressive experience from a fabric of theory primarily woven by male structures of thought and psychological preferences. The knowledge we are gaining from epidemiological and biological research can point to risk factors associated with depression, but such research cannot explain why, in similar social and relational contexts, some women become depressed while others do not. To know the response a woman has to her context, we need to know the meaning she makes of that context— how she interprets her actions and evaluates herself and her worth within her culture and her relationships. Listening to depressed women's reflections about themselves, paying attention to their words and recurring themes, can help us to restore their experience from invisibility, to bring it out from behind the screen of traditional interpretations.

The depressed women who appear as guides in this book participated in a series of studies investigating the nature of women's depression.[25] Initially, I wanted to immerse myself in listening to depressed women's descriptions of their experiences, to keep an ear out for an idiom, for a pattern of discourse. To make this possible, I designed a longitudinal study of twelve clinically depressed women. Before being referred to the study, the women had been diagnosed as depressed by physicians and clinicians according to DSM III (1980) criteria for depression. Reflecting the population of the rural county from which they came, the women were Caucasian. They ranged in age from 19 to 55, with socioeconomic status from poverty (on welfare) to wealthy. Eight of the women had children, and only one woman was not married or in a heterosexual relationship when first interviewed. (See Appendix A for more details.) I interviewed the women when they were actively depressed, and then reinterviewed them approximately two years later in order to observe changes in their depression and accompanying social, cognitive, and emotional changes.

I used intensive, semistructured interviews to inquire about women's experiences and attempted to phrase questions so they did not supply categories to frame responses. Allowing women to speak in their own terms, I listened to their conflicts and concerns, and derived concepts from their descriptions.

To test the ideas gained from the longitudinal, exploratory study in larger samples of women, I designed an instrument, the Silencing the Self Scale (SSS), to measure women's beliefs about self in intimate relationship (see Appendix B). To date, this scale has been used in three very different populations of women— college students, residents of battered women's shelters, and new mothers who used cocaine during pregnancy.[26] Intensive interviews of five of the battered women, as well as a questionnaire item eliciting respondents' written thoughts, provide further data from which I draw.

The observations from this study are suggestive and cannot be generalized to all depressed women. Because the initial guides for the ideas were all Caucasian and heterosexual, we do not know how race or sexual preference affects the experience and language of female depression. Concepts presented here need to be taken to different social, racial, and ethnic groups to inform our understanding about the diversity of female experience. But all women must come to terms with the bias against their gender and the pervasive sexualization and devaluation that accompany femininity. The concepts formulated in this book take account of this baseline of female experience and include it in explorations of women's depression.

As we listen to depressed women, current collective ideas about femininity form a constant background. Cultural images of the female are impoverished and devalued, stripped of their ties to deeper, archetypal symbols. Today, women face the nearly impossible task of breaking through the glass ceiling of invisible barriers to achieve like men, while simultaneously curbing the self to fit into the traditional glass slipper that promises blissful relationship. These superficial images exist within a harsh day-to-day existence, for many women, of poverty, violence, lost anchors of religious or ethnic communities, and increasing divorce. Cultural myths or images of how to be a woman offer little guidance for how to be strong, for how to be authentic in relationships, or for how to combine self-development with intimacy.

In order to hear the message of these depressed women, we need to take into account their social context, which includes the lived reality of women's subordinate status as well as a cultural history that has demeaned women's orientations. This context fundamentally affects the language and the concepts women employ in thinking and talking about themselves. Though women and men both use the same language to represent their experiences, they use that language to convey different meanings (Brown and Gilligan, 1990a). We must become bilingual, in a sense, to understand the idiom of women's speech about their lives. We need to be aware of how women employ negatively valued words—dependent, passive, insecure, immature—as they attempt to represent aspects of a subjective reality that, as yet, have no other names. So to become bilingual means to listen for the patterns and meanings behind the negatively valued words, and then to translate those meanings into less negative terms that more accurately reflect the experiences the women are trying to convey.

Depicted as enmeshed in dependence and hanging on to relationships like "leeches," depressed women describe themselves as isolated. They fear not loss of other but loss of self. The clinical literature says depressed women have a problem with separation and self-esteem because they are dependent on their relationships; the women cast their problem as one of establishing and maintaining connection. Women describe their depression as precipitated not by the loss of a relationship, but by the recognition that they have lost themselves in trying to establish an intimacy that was never attained. For most depressed women the sense of hopelessness and helplessness stems from despair about the possibility of bringing their own needs and initiative into their relationships, and from their equation of failure of attachment with moral failure. Since the causes of depression are interpersonal, it is essential to inquire closely into a depressed woman's understanding of her intimate attachments. To understand a woman's disappearance into the "we" of heterosexual relatedness requires analysis of gender, personality, society, and the particularities of individual experience.

LOSS
OF SELF

. 2 .

I have always wanted the approval of my husband. And I still do, and yet, I know that isn't everything we should be working for. I know that part of the problem has been the lack of communication where I did not express my real feelings. I was just wanting to do certain things and not wanting to do what he wanted me to do, but not telling him the reasons I did not want to. I've ended up feeling like I've lost myself in my marriage; I'm not even sure what my real feelings are any more.

As women describe the pervasive impact of depression, they most frequently call on the metaphor "loss of self" to describe their inner experience. Metaphor, the use of a word or phrase in some new sense, comes into speech to remedy a gap in the existing vocabulary. Much has been written about the difficulties women encounter as they struggle with a male language that will not say what they intend (Heilbrun, 1988), but this language is all we have. It is what women must use to convey the stories of their depression, the shape of their pain and loss. Careful attention to the metaphors depressed women use can help take us behind accepted notions to hear their own perspective on their descent into desolation.

For example, since one cannot literally lose oneself, how

does this phrase serve the expressive purposes of women who employ it? What does it tell us about a woman's inner world and her interpersonal interactions? Is the loss of self she portrays temporary or irreversible? When we listen to depressed women rather than to psychological theories that tell us what to think, what can we learn about the self that becomes submerged, excluded, or weakened to the point that a woman mourns its loss?

With the exception of loss of self, the metaphors commonly used by depressed women refer explicitly to the experience of self in intimate relationship. Even loss of self, when followed as a thread through women's narratives, implies a relationship within which this loss occurs. Given research findings regarding women's connected sense of self, the central importance of these relational, interpersonal metaphors to women's descriptions of depression should not surprise us. One would expect women to invent phrases or use words to express a subjective reality different from the autonomous, individualistic "I," the self of Western psychology. Depressed women's distinctive use of relational metaphors not only alerts us to the contours of their subjective terrain but also compels us to explore how certain gender arrangements, which structure the experience of self and intimate attachments, create women's vulnerability to depression.

LOSS OF VOICE

Depressed women use the phrase "loss of self" as they depict their experience in marriage or in intimate relationships with men. They employ this language with striking similarity from woman to woman, regardless of age or education:

> For three years that has been my focus, holding this marriage together, for three years and being a parent for my children who are young . . . I felt, I can say that I lost myself in those years of marriage. But I didn't really because I don't think I could have sprung back as quickly or as fast. I think I went pretty low but I still had the ties

and the roots that could enable me, finally, when I was ready to grow, not to shrivel up and die. I don't want to fall back into a relationship where I would lose myself quite that way . . . I think that's my worst fear, that I'll fall into that pattern again of trying to be the way that other person wants me to be instead of the way I am. *(Linda, age 39, masters degree, separated after fifteen years of marriage)*

I was just so despondent and so depressed at the situation that we had gotten ourselves into [the lack of intimacy and communication], and I thought, if this is the way—it just seemed like I didn't count any more. And I thought, I've just, I've just had enough. When I'd be in the barn was when I'd have the most time to think, it seemed like. It was probably four hours, morning and night, milking and stuff, and I just thought, boy, to spend the next thirty years like this, I'm just not going to do it. I mean, could suicide be worse than suffering the next thirty years going through this empty marriage? Every day I'd just die a little bit more inside, another emotion or fraction of an emotion was just kind of freeze-dried. I'd just lose a little bit of myself all the time. I tried to cover up, and that's why John was so shocked when I left him, I finally left him. *(Therese, age 32, high school graduate, separated after fourteen years of marriage, no children)*

And I do know that in the seven years we've been married, I've lost a great deal of myself, as far as, well you know, when you put so much of your energy and you're so consumed physically and emotionally and mentally with babies and being a mother and a wife and a homemaker, and you're involved with other mothers . . . You tend to kind of put off your own goals and your own achievements and your own talents and your own self,

in a way. And I feel, this sounds very cliché, but I feel
that in the seven years I've been married, I have lost a lot
of myself that gave me some confidence. *(Susan, 30,*
college graduate, married seven years, two children)

In these examples, loss of self becomes a verbal shorthand
that conveys a number of things to the listener. First, as the
women present it, the loss of self coincides with a loss of *voice* in
relationship.[1] Voice is an indicator of self. Speaking one's feelings and thoughts is part of creating, maintaining, and recreating one's authentic self. As these women fail to hear themselves
speak to their partners, they are unable to sustain the convictions and feelings of "I" and slip, instead, into self-doubt about
the legitimacy of their privately held experience. For example,
fearing that expression of negative feelings would lead to catas-
trophe, Therese "freeze-dries" her emotions. She puts her silenced, feeling self on ice, to be preserved indefinitely, while the
duty-ridden "good self" controls her interactions with her husband. The wider the gap between outward presentation of self
and inward experience, the more likely that a woman will feel
anguish and despair over her inauthenticity and her self-
betrayal. At the same time, her interpersonal goals—love, acceptance, intimacy—are pushed farther from possibility by the
removal of a vital part of her self from dialogue.

Second, we notice that women lose themselves as they try to
fit into an image provided by someone else—the husband, parental teachings, the culture. In Linda's words, through the
process of "trying to be the way that other person wants me to be
instead of the way I am," women dissolve their own outlines in
order to form a self acceptable to the intimate partner. Certainly
we all have many possible selves, created to interact in different
social situations, and necessary for self-protection. But the self of
intimate interaction is, as research shows, the most important to
women's self-esteem and to their vulnerability or resistance to
depression. If the self of intimate interaction is contrived—that
is, constructed to accord with someone else's image—the pos-

sibility of attaining authentic relationship diminishes, while the probability of losing one's voice and self in the quest for intimacy increases.

Third, in their narratives, the women indicate that they refrain from speech not only to avoid conflict but because they fear they may be wrong. Talking about interactions with her husband, Cathy, quoted earlier, says, "I just had a lot of questions about why he always got his way. But this was from my point of view, and I felt it might have been wrong." This common feeling that she may be "wrong" relative to her male partner grows out of a woman's social position, not just her individual psychology. In a very real sense, a woman goes up against the masculinist culture—physically, economically, morally, and epistemologically—if she questions why her partner "always [gets] his way." Standing in his position of maleness, her husband or partner has the force of Western civilization behind him, a force that has consistently justified and elevated males while it has correspondingly discounted and demeaned females.

To be willing to risk arguments and explore difference, one has to believe in the legitimacy of one's own point of view. Others who have listened closely to women's voices describe how the culture prepares women to abdicate their own perspectives and values in order to adopt the prevailing male-oriented view. Mary Belenky and her colleagues (1986) present evidence that women become alienated from their own "ways of knowing" through formal educational processes and structures. Carol Gilligan (1988) traces the way adolescent girls lose confidence in their own perceptions as they notice the absence of their gender and their perspectives in supposedly authoritative texts representing human experience. Research in social psychology shows that women's opinions are still considered less important than those of men: men talk more often while women listen, and the products of women's minds are devalued.[2] Through the process of accommodating to cultural standards and practices, women absorb the male practice of discounting femininity itself—its knowledge, its perspectives, its values.

Listen, for example, to Alison, age 35, married thirteen years with two children, who works as an administrator for a major company in Boston:

A friend of mine said, "Gee whiz, Alison, when you were first married, you'd give these dinner parties and everything would be perfect. And you would sit there, you'd smile, and you'd listen to everything Steve said no matter how boring it was or how tedious it was. And you would listen to everything that everybody else said and then you would recede into the background and you'd wash all the dishes and you'd clean up and everything would be perfect. And everybody would go home and you'd smile the entire time."

And she said recently, "You know, I came to your house when you were talking to people and you were communicating." And I think that I did feel that I did. The expansive side of me was somewhere lost along the lines. Because I had no confidence in what I had to say and what I had to think. And, and when I married Steve, I was 21 and he was 36 and I thought that he knew all these things that I didn't know anything about . . . you know, how to think and everything that he thought was fit to read, and he, he traveled extensively and he had seen a lot of things and he was more worldly and cultured and knowledgeable . . . So I played this little role of the Boston matron and went to the symphony, did all these things, and entertained people, was loving wife and loving mother, and entertained all the time and cooked and did all these things.

When it comes to as simple yet critical a matter as maintaining and voicing her own perspective in relationship, a woman can hesitate—Is this legitimate? Am I wrong? What is at risk? Is it worth it? Reinforcing her hesitation is women's exclusion from social and economic power, the awareness that for many women, divorce leads straight into poverty. Though the awareness may remain in the background of women's minds, such a social reality encourages a psychological attitude of seeing "themselves as subject to a consensus or judgment made and enforced by the men on whose protection and support they depend and by whose names they are known" (Gilligan, 1982, p. 67). Once a woman has adopted such an attitude, it becomes hard for her to assert her own perspective for fear of the consequences that may follow.

Though it is too simple to posit a direct translation of cultural values into individual consciousness, it is also inadequate to point to a woman's family background as the primary cause of her difficulty in asserting her voice in relationship. Cultural patterns of gender prerogative powerfully shape family background and personal history. When these cultural patterns of male superiority and female inferiority are reinforced by parents, who, after all, represent the culture to the child, they are difficult to break as a woman tries to create and sustain adult relationships with men. Even if a woman is close to her partner, when she differs from him on significant matters it is easy for her to feel "my point of view . . . might have been wrong."

A fear of being wrong and a loss of voice in relationship also occur strongly in response to a man who uses force to assert his "gender prerogative." My research with 140 depressed women in three battered women's shelters (Jack and Dill, in press) indicates that depression corresponds with a woman's being silenced by an abusive partner. Sue, age 47, with three children, came to the shelter to escape a five-year relationship with a man who made it dangerous for her to say anything.

It's been such an insidious thing that's come along in such little pieces, that by the time I've come to this realization right now, the part of me that should be totally enraged isn't even there . . . He would start out by saying belittling things. He would say "You're crying around again, why are you always crying around again like a little kid," and "No woman's going to tell me what to do. No goddamn woman is going to tell me what to do and control my life," and "I'm going to do what I have to do here. You're going to make me have to tune you up. You want me to stomp the shit out of you." Reactions like that, and it makes you back off. And over a period of time, like two or three years, you become accustomed to not voicing anything. And you come to believe that that's all life is. Not intellectually, you don't believe that. But inside there is a part of you that believes that this is your place.

Counselors at battered women's shelters affirm the research findings that battered women use the idiom of a "loss of self" and link it with a loss of voice in relationship, with a loss of self-esteem, and with unexpressed rage.

Dialogue with an intimate partner, the interactive movement of speaking and listening, hearing and being heard, emerges in women's narratives as critical to the experience of connection and to the ongoing life of the self. When dialogue dies, as it can with either person's failure to speak, to hear, or to acknowledge the other, then part of the self also dies. Depressed women, in and out of abusive relationships, recount how their attempts to insert their voices (selves) into the relationship are accompanied by their partner's power to thwart them, and by a sense that to push too hard leads either to further isolation or to violence. Susan says,

> If I don't back out and walk out of the room or let him have the last word, and begin to ignore him, he gets angry. And if I continue to keep at the issue, then he gets extremely angry and goes into an uncontrollable rage, and—gets quite violent. Now he has never beat me up, so to speak, where he's had to take several swings at me and hit me and punched me. But he has come after me and thrown me against the wall and put his hands around my neck like he was going to strangle me, to the point where I nearly passed out. I'm afraid of him. I am afraid of him. And that's why it has made me tend to

keep my opinions to myself, so to speak, or not feel like I should interfere or ask questions or make suggestions or do any—you know, in other words, I have to walk on eggshells dealing with my husband, in just about any area, whether it be our children, or our personal relationship, or his business.

Though Susan monitors her arousal and display of emotions out of fear of her partner's aggression, other depressed women report just as vigilant a self-censoring process out of fear of losing the relationship through their partner's dissatisfaction. This process of continually monitoring feelings and censoring oneself, of being disconfirmed within a relationship that promises intimacy and identity, is part of what leads to the existential sense of loss of self and to depression.

THE FORMS OF CONNECTION

Let us turn again to metaphors women employ as they talk about their relationships, and listen for other themes that reveal the ways they connect with their partners and, at the same time, lose themselves. As three clinically depressed women state the imperatives that guide their behavior in their marriages, they situate themselves within a hierarchy of importance:

In terms of my priorities, I would have to say first comes my husband, well, my home and my husband and then me. I've thought a lot about—you asked me last time what's good for me, and maybe I don't consider that enough. Because, you know, I apply the word selfish to that. (Diana, age 30, pregnant with her second child)

I just put everybody else first . . . You know, I was just busy with raising a family and looking after my husband and I guess I just put me back. (Anna, age 55, married thirty-six years, two grown children)

I just tried to adjust to whatever he gave me to adjust
to. You know, he climbed mountains, and I didn't like it,
but I adjusted to it. Had good meals. And I just . . . I was
just trying to go along with what he wanted, I guess, as
much as I could. *(Betty, age 32, married fourteen years, two
children)*

These women place the husband at the center of their life stories
as the actor, the "hero," while they take the part of supporting
characters, inventing a self that will fit the particularities of the
man. They actively remove themselves—"I just put me back"—
in order to love their partners in ways learned from the culture. Their narratives echo myths that portray women waiting,
women preparing themselves for the knight in shining armor,
women being rescued, women being chosen while male heroes
stride out to find identity, adventure, romance, and manhood
through outer action. Like Penelope weaving at her loom, these
women occupy themselves faithfully with the repetitive, everyday tasks of a life woven around someone else's exploits.[3]

When depressed women describe more specifically how
they care for their men, we hear again the absence of self, of an
initiating, active "I," except as responsive to the husband or
partner. What matters within their relationships is pleasing the
man, keeping him happy, even at the expense of their own
identity.

I guess you please them, you look after them, you love
them, you do things to make them happy. I guess I don't
really think about myself, I put myself as a person out
of the picture and I just accommodate other people.
(Anna)

I read a lot of marriage books and how to keep your
husband happy and I thought I would try it. And I was
always very careful not to seem hurt but to protect
his ego, and I just always kind of worked around his
wishes. *(Cathy, age 36, married seventeen years, two children)*

This has always been my baseline, that is, to please my husband, to—well, I guess to turn it around, to be a good wife would be a wife who's cherished by her husband, you know. Just, "she's the living end, she's a great cook, she keeps the house clean and she holds a fifty-hour-a-week job and we've got ninety-nine kids, yeah, she's just great." Then I guess it would snowball. He would tell other people how neat I was, and then it would snowball. *(Jan, age 24, married one year, no children)*

These women try to accomplish their goals—to keep their husbands happy and thereby secure the attachment—through fulfilling the role of the traditional "good wife." Because they measure their effectiveness from the perspective of others (being there for others, nurturing others, pleasing others), they listen to others' demands and requirements more than to their own feelings and needs. When this occurs without mutuality or reciprocity, they experience a loss of self—they feel disconnected, unsupported, and alienated from themselves.

Compliance in Relationship
The symbolic act of marriage carries with it the promise of intimacy and a new family. Entry into a committed relationship, particularly into marriage, kindles a woman's deepest desire to support and enhance the relationship, to nurture it and work for its development. Marriage also strongly arouses a woman's ideals and images about intimacy, learned early within her family. Exploring the meaning of the word "intimacy," Stephen Mitchell observes that "the language reflects a sense of interiority—a gap or space between oneself and the other which one strives or longs to overcome" (1988, p. 105).

To bridge this gap or space in order to become intimate with another is a very complex, subtle process. Each gender learns certain behaviors—verbal, nonverbal, sexual—that are appropriate to span the gap.[4] As depressed women talk about their relationships, we hear a pattern in the ways they try to overcome distance in order to connect intimately with their partners: a pattern of *compliant relatedness* that is culturally dictated, damaging to themselves, and limiting to the possibilities of intimacy.

Compliance in relationship derives from both inner and outer factors. John Bowlby describes how feelings of security about the reliability and availability of close ties fosters confidence, self-reliance, a sense of freedom and curiosity within intimate relationships, while insecurity about such ties elicits anxious attachment behaviors. In adults, close relationships that are characterized by high levels of mutual affection, communication, affirmation, support, and availability create feelings of emotional security and satisfaction with the relationship in both partners. Such relational qualities "are most likely to be associated with personal characteristics of trust and openness, balanced by healthy self-reliance so that the separateness of each and connectedness of both are simultaneously maintained" (Kotler, 1985, p. 305).

Compliant relatedness, characterized by restriction of initiative and freedom of expression within a relationship, looks like an anxious attachment behavior and stems from an underlying fear that the loved one will not be available unless one hovers close and tries to please. As Bowlby tells us:

> of the many fear-arousing situations that a child, or older person, can foresee, none is likely to be more frightening than the possibility that an attachment figure will be absent or, in more general terms, unavailable when wanted. Not only must an attachment figure be accessible but he, or she, must be willing to respond in an appropriate way . . . Only when an attachment figure is both accessible and potentially responsive can he, or she, be said to be truly available. *(1973, pp. 201–202)*

The cultural pattern of a man's unresponsive, more distanced interactive style stimulates a woman's anxiety about the availability and security of her attachment. Like an insurance policy designed to protect against the possibility of loss, compliance in relationship is one way a woman attempts to guarantee that her partner will be "accessible and potentially responsive" in times of need.

Apart from these factors, women as a group are less secure about their attachments than men simply because of their subordinate social position. Though the rules have relaxed somewhat in recent years, women must still "attract and hold" a mate. Men usually have more economic freedom to come and go, as well as the prerogative of selecting younger partners when they enter middle age. More social support still exists for men to move through numerous relationships; there is no equivalent for men to the "damaged goods" syndrome that exists for women. The enormous amount of money and attention women spend on appearance, from clothes to cosmetic surgery, reveals how seriously they regard the importance of their looks to relationships. It seems fair to speculate that this overarching social reality contributes to a diffuse feminine sense of insecurity in relationship, and that women resort to compliance and other safe-keeping behaviors in the hope of securing the lines of attachment.

Power imbalances within heterosexual relationships also directly influence women's tendency to fall into compliant relatedness as a means of ensuring connection with their partners. Women are the most frequent targets of male violence, and they learn from an early age that one defense against hostile male attention is "sweet compliance" (Westkott, 1986). Depressed women describe their outwardly acquiescent behavior as occurring directly in response to violent partners, but more complex reasons underly it as well.

Take, for example, the expression of anger within a marriage. Anger is aroused when a significant relationship is threatened, and its goal is to promote, not to disrupt, the relationship. Anger "acting in the service of an affectional bond" has the goals of removing obstacles to a reunion and discouraging further separation (Bowlby, 1973). Anger toward a loved one is frequently accompanied by anxiety about the attachment, since these feelings are evoked by the same circumstances. For example, situations of sexual disloyalty within marriages provoke both anxiety over the security of the relationship and hostility toward the partner.[5]

Inequality further complicates the expression of anger in

such a situation. Within unequal relationships, the dominant person has more freedom to communicate anger directly than does the subordinate. As Jean Baker Miller (1976) observed, subordinates have to resort to covert communication of anger, a requirement that significantly increases the double bind accompanying anger's expression. When, for example, a woman is furious with her partner for his affairs, or his emotional unresponsiveness, or his threats to leave, she may be afraid that if she makes her feelings known he will retaliate with even greater anger or by acting on his threats to leave. Yet her inability to convey her feelings directly leads to hopelessness about the possibility of changing an unsatisfactory situation. In such a double bind, a woman can feel that any action she takes carries the threat of loss.

A study examining the display of emotion in thirty couples found strong differences in the ways women and men communicate negative feelings. John Gottman and Robert Levenson used measures of physiological responses, self-report, and video data to look at interaction in unhappy couples. At first glance, it appears as if each partner receives and gives back negative feelings to the other. Yet the wife and the husband are communicating different negative emotions: 78 percent of the husband's negative affect is anger and contempt, while 93 percent of the wife's negative feelings are expressed as "whining, sadness and fear" (1986, p. 43). The data reveal "a clear dominance structure . . . He reciprocates her anger, but she does not reciprocate his; instead she responds to his anger with fear, which leads back to his anger" (ibid.).

Not only do couples exhibit this structure of dominance in the emotions they express, but the communication of certain feelings corresponds with changes in marital satisfaction or dissatisfaction. Examining patterns of interaction that predict change in marital satisfaction over time, Gottman (1990) found that positive verbal behavior and compliance from wives created positive feelings in the husband in the short run but that the marital satisfaction of these couples deteriorated over time. When the wife expressed contempt and anger, it correlated positively with increases in her (but only her) marital satisfaction. A wife's expression of fear predicted deterioration in her marital satisfaction, while her sadness predicted a decline in both partners' marital satisfaction.

Unless conflicts can be openly communicated and resolved, a woman's anger may predict the husband's withdrawal. Thus, women face serious dilemmas about the display of emotion within marriage; they seem to be in a no-win situation. Research shows there is a basis to women's fears of negative consequences to the relationship if they express either anger and dissatisfaction or fear to their partners. These restrictions on self-expression and dialogue can make a woman feel hopeless about the possibility of bringing her full self into the couple relationship.[6]

Though the institution of marriage is in flux, it continues to institutionalize inequality between women and men, and this inequality contributes to the pattern of compliant relatedness and loss of self associated with women's depression. Recent research by Philip Blumstein and Pepper Schwartz on more than six thousand couples shows that once marriage is entered, its basic framework takes over to shape the relationship and the behavior of the partners within it. The researchers point out how difficult it is to change the "one model of how to live as a couple":

> the institution of marriage, at least until now, has been organized around inequality, and attempts to change this framework have not yet been very successful. The traditional married couples in our study often laid their solid foundation on roles that stabilized the relationship but gave the woman some of the less pleasant responsibilities, such as housework, and assigned her duties, such as the buyer role. If tasks were allotted on the basis of efficiency or affinity, we would expect that married couples could reassign household chores and have the institution remain as durable as ever. We have found, however, that when roles are reversed, with men doing the housework and women taking over as provider, couples become dreadfully unhappy. *Even couples who willingly try to change traditional male and female behavior have difficulty doing so.*

They must not only go against everything they have learned
and develop new skills, but they have to resist the negative
reaction of society. Thus we have learned that while the institution is bigger than the individuals within it, it may not be
bigger than the assignment of roles by gender. (Blumstein
and Schwartz, 1983, pp. 323–324, emphasis added)

As an institutionalized aspect of human relationships, the
role of wife continues to reflect the economic and hierarchical
arrangements that created it, even when a woman earns an
independent income. Historically the man's economic obligation
to support his wife and children allowed him rights of control
and access to those he supported; the woman, as recipient, was
obligated to provide services, both physical and interpersonal,
to him and to children.[7] The core of these services was the
requirement that the wife be a caretaker, which meant she was
required to put the needs of others first. Though the current
focus on equality, love, and partnership in marriage masks the
nurturing imperative present in the wife role, that imperative
remains alive (particularly when the woman is economically
dependent) to assert its claims on the woman's consciousness
and actions.[8]

Marriage is so effective at reinforcing gender roles because it
functions as a powerful myth, the "most persistent of myths
imprisoning women" (Heilbrun, 1988, p. 77). As a myth, it
promises intimacy, identity, and a well-marked life path that
even young children know by heart. Yet traveling its distance
without veering from the conventional path leads not to an
expansion of self through relatedness and mutuality, but to a
reduction of confidence, of possibilities, of "self." When women
try to fit their relational capacities and desires into the roles of
"wife" and "good woman," they run the risk of adapting to the
needs of those around them and becoming alienated from themselves. Rather than changing the wife role to suit themselves and
their relationships, they deny vital aspects of their personalities
in order to squeeze into its narrow confines; in doing so, they
lose, as Susan says, "your own goals and your own achievements and your own talents and your own self."

As a myth and as a social reality, marriage creates a conundrum for women and men: how to attain intimacy within a relationship based on inequality. The complications of this puzzle become clearer as we consider how pieces that are meant to interlock become misshapen by gender and by culture. Carol Gilligan and Grant Wiggins draw a helpful distinction between two dimensions of a child's experience of relatedness with loved ones that shape the child's sense of self-in-relationship and lead to the development of differing sensitivities and moral responses. The first dimension, inequality, arising from the reality of the adult's greater strength and authority, brings out the child's feelings of powerlessness and dependence on others. Morality within this dimension focuses on justice and rights, with the goal of placing parties on a more equal footing. The other dimension is attachment and the awareness of love, which creates a different consciousness of the self in relation to others—as capable of moving and being moved by others, as able to affect the emotions and the actions of loved others. "In the context of attachment, the child discovers the patterns of human interaction and observes the ways in which people care for and hurt one another. Like the experience of inequality, although in different ways, the experience of attachment profoundly affects the child's understanding of human feelings and how people should act toward one another" (Gilligan and Wiggins, 1988, p. 115).

Within marriage, where intimate attachment and inequality are mingled, one dimension of relationship—inequality—comes to overshadow the attachment dimension or to alter its meaning. Depressed women detail how they shape their attachment behaviors—their communication, their ways of caring for others, their responsiveness—to correspond with the perimeters set by their position of inequality relative to the partner. From the example set by their own parents, from the wider culture, and from their partners' expectations, women draw the belief that the way to connect to a man is through a sieve of "feminine" behaviors that filters out part of the self. The requirement that a woman always be "very careful not to seem hurt but to protect his ego, and . . . just always . . . [work] around his wishes" not only shows a compliant way of relating, but points to the underlying power imbalances that influence such attachment behaviors. Compliance in relationship is one way of solving the conundrum of how to attain intimacy within a relationship based on inequality: alter the self in order to connect in ways believed to be pleasing to the man.

Women commonly strive to overcome the gap between self and other through dialogue. If the partner is repeatedly unresponsive, then one possibility of connecting in a way that circumvents gender roles and inequality disappears. Emotional unavailability of the partner increases a woman's feelings of insecurity about the attachment. It also increases her anger and anxious attachment behaviors, such as clinging demandingness, which may drive the partner further away. The more he pushes her away, the more angry and anxious she becomes and the tighter she clings; the less secure she feels about the relationship, the less self-reliant she feels and the lower her self-esteem falls.

Depressed women explicitly portray this cycle of interpersonal interactions as they talk about being unable to connect with their partners through the give and take of dialogue. Betty talks about her husband's unwillingness to enter into discussions of central importance to her emotional life:

> If I do tell him how I'm feeling about something I'm shot down. I just, you know, he thinks it's just stupid. Because I've told him that I—well, let me see if I can think of an example. Well, like if I'm afraid, he'll just tell me that's stupid. That he's safer there [mountain climbing] than in an automobile, you know, and he just won't acknowledge that maybe there is a reason or try to understand why I might be afraid.

If we define mature interdependence as consisting of the ability to give support as well as appropriately ask for and receive support from another, we see Betty's concerns not as dependent, but as part of normal attachment behaviors. Her husband's

way of dealing with those concerns increases rather than miti-
gates her fears about the security of her primary relationship,
and this leads her to more anger and anxiety.

Susan also describes her husband's response to her expression of feelings:

> I have expressed my needs to him, and he'll come right
> out and say they're stupid or silly, or it's just not him to
> be that kind of person and not to expect it of him, you
> know. And he'll come right out and say to me, when I
> need to be close, even physically when I go over to him
> to hug him or just say, "Sit down with me for a minute
> and let's talk," he'll say, "I'm too busy right now," you
> know, kind of like, "You're a bother."

Susan's attempts to further intimacy through dialogue are
stopped short by the cold shoulder of her husband. The partner's refusal to listen, or his contempt for the woman's attempts
to share her feelings, closes off one way of achieving either closeness or change in the relationship. While these two women try to
affirm their relationships and know their husbands through dialogue, their partners refuse either to reveal themselves or to
engage with their wives' concerns. This is the essence of inequality: one person's reality governs the relationship, and the other
person's feelings are ignored. A woman whose partner, aligned
with the language, values, and power of the culture, rejects her
attempts to communicate may come to judge her own needs and
feelings as *he* does, as not worthy of consideration, and as in-
valid.

The tension between inequality and attachment, which converge in conventional marriage, is also evident as women talk
about the difficulty of being themselves in relationship. Therese,
for example, tells how she thinks her view of marriage contributed to her depression:

> I was absolutely stymied in the situation. I could not
> be myself—I didn't think—because he would find my

rough edges unacceptable and leave, and I was not enough of what he believed to become him, so I was trying to be someone that I wished I could be, I knew damn well I couldn't be or would not be happy being, and I did it for a long time. It wasn't me and it never will be me.

These women undertake such massive self-negation as part of their search for intimacy, a search that constitutes one of the organizing aims of adult life. But establishing intimacy is only one of the tasks of the adult years. The other lifelong goal is to develop and express one's unique capacities and interests: to be authentic, to be a self. The adult years bring the full development and integration of intellectual and physical capacities that enable people to express their abilities through purposeful, organized activity. Gender, the immediate family context, and the larger social environment all affect the individual's possibilities.

The tasks of intimacy and identity coincide when one is able to be a growing, changing self within ongoing relationships, when intimacy facilitates the developing authentic self and the developing self deepens the possibilities of intimacy. In our culture, women often experience these necessities for healthy adult development—intimacy and authenticity—as in conflict. Depressed women fear that if they try to be themselves they will lose their marriages; yet they describe having lost themselves in an unsuccessful attempt to achieve closeness. Striving for intimacy through the traditional female role constrains and compromises their own continually developing sense of self while it also limits the possibilities for honest connection. Conversely, their capacity for intimacy is diminished by their compromised self-development. Part of the feeling of hopelessness and helplessness in their depression stems from the sense that moving toward one major life goal forecloses the other.

When a relationship is troubled by lack of intimacy, by disruption and separation, a woman may feel her basic sense of identity to be threatened. At the same time, observing herself from the perspective of the culture, she may judge herself to be a failure according to the social standards of adult independence and achievement. In addition, her mother may have modeled selflessness as a wifely ideal, a standard that is unattainable and self-defeating. When being "selfless" in relationship is linked in the woman's mind with "goodness" (morality), with femininity (out of identification with a mother who was "selfless" in relationship), and with intimacy (providing safety from abandonment), a woman must deny whole parts of herself, including negative feelings and direct self-assertion.

But the willingness to give to others does not necessarily lead to self-alienation and depression. Critical is the context within which the giving occurs, and the giver's ability to *choose* when, how, and in what form to give. If caring for others in a compliant manner is seen as a necessary prerequisite to making and maintaining intimacy, then the woman becomes subservient to others' needs and grows increasingly angry, resentful, and confused. In addition, these women hold an ideal image of self as one who is loving and loved, who is competent in relationships. Faced with unsatisfactory relationships, they blame themselves for the difficulties, reflecting the cultural norm that women are more responsible than men for maintaining the emotional climate of intimate ties.

From the outside, such a woman's behavior may look "passive," "dependent," and "helpless." But from the inside, the compliant role, adopted in the hope of securing attachment, requires tremendous cognitive and emotional activity to curb the self. The woman must actively silence her negative feelings, which she (and society) considers unacceptable. Such self-silencing leads her to experience self-condemnation, inner division, and depression.

Covert Rebellion

While depressed women appear outwardly compliant in relationship, they talk about their indirect, everyday rebellions that add to the mix of anger and anxiety present in depression. Covert rebellion offers a sense of safety to a woman because it allows a surface appearance of harmony, an illusion of intimacy.

Depressed women describe learning from their mothers not to confront differences directly in marriage. Anna talks about how she never makes time during her day to enjoy herself, to do her watercolors or weaving. Asked if she feels she has to be available to her husband, she replies:

> I feel I am. But I just am, I don't feel that I have to be, because he doesn't expect me to be. But my father expected my mother to be. She'd go out to play bridge with somebody and she'd come home and have to change clothes and have to put on her work dress so that he didn't know that she had been out.

Such an incident, one of countless others occurring in daily transactions, conveys to the growing girl unwritten rules for interaction with one's husband. These rules, present in family patterns, prescribe how needs are to be expressed and met and how conflicts are to be resolved. Cathy tells how she solved a longstanding conflict, not by directly confronting her husband, but by what she calls a rebellious act:

> My husband said "No, you can't pierce your ears, that's terrible. If you want to pierce your ears I'll do it with a pitchfork." But, so finally I just went out and got it done. But I waited for years and years, you know, because I thought he disapproved.

Cathy goes on to observe the effect of her indirectness on her daughter.

> I just rebelled. I don't feel bad about that, but then . . . you know, I teach my daughter to do that too, kind of indirectly. So I guess it really isn't so good.
> *(You teach your daughter to do what?)* To rebel, I guess. Not directly, I mean. I don't say "do this" whether he says so or not, but then she sees my example. And she knows what's going on.

What does the daughter learn is "going on"? In addition to teaching her daughter that the husband has authority over her, including the right to say what she does with her body, this example conveys the necessity to avoid open conflict. The daughter learns that open conflict brings the threat of separation and that pretending to be compliant is better than speaking her mind.

As these examples illustrate, a girl learns early to create an outer appearance of harmony that will allow the feeling of oneness, of a false intimacy, of a family unit. The threat of separation directs the woman's behavior as she follows the rules of relationship she learned from her family and the culture at large. These patterns of interaction, reproduced in generation after generation, carry the man's sense of entitlement in intimate relationships and the woman's difficulty in acknowledging, voicing, acting on, and taking responsibility for her own needs.

Jean Baker Miller links the covert resolution of conflict with inequality. Noting that "growth requires engagement with difference," she paints the complications resulting when partners attempt intimacy without overt conflict:

> Within a framework of inequality the existence of conflict is denied and the means to engage openly in conflict are excluded. Further, inequality itself creates additional factors that skew any interaction and prevent open engagement around real differences. Instead, inequality generates hidden conflict around elements that the inequality itself has set in motion. In sum, both sides are diverted from open conflict around real differences, by which they could grow, and are channeled into hidden conflict around falsifications. For this hidden conflict, there are no acceptable social forms or guides because this conflict supposedly doesn't exist. (Miller, 1976, p. 13)

Depressed women's anger and covert rebellion also appear in imaginary scenes in which they speak their minds and confront their partners. These mind-rehearsals siphon off some of the anger, just enough to let the woman stay in what feels like an intolerable situation. Susan, angry with her husband, fantasizes about escape:

Divorce is always on my mind, always on my mind. It's my outlet that I think of and that I fantasize about whenever he puts me down or hurts me in front of the girls or cuts me off with a sarcastic comment or treats me as though I'm under him. My way of getting back at him is that I fantasize about someday divorcing him and "showing him." This is my only way. I can't physically get back at him because I'm weaker than him and I just don't have it in me to be sharp-tongued and be yelling. My only outlet is to just bite my tongue, not say anything, and fantasize about getting a divorce. It is the thing that I'm holding inside me, that I'm saving up for when I finally get enough courage to let him get what he deserves—that's when I'm going to get a divorce from him. Sometimes I think, "I can't wait, I can't wait another day to get it." Sometimes I think, I plan, a year from now, or six months, or right after the holidays, that's when I'll do it.

But Susan is aware of the sharp discrepancy between her everyday life and the world of her thoughts. The vengeance rehearsed in her mind contrasts clearly, and painfully, with her outwardly compliant behavior. In the gap between what she does and what she thinks, her valuation of herself plummets.

I think there's a weakness in me. Because I want to believe he's going to be different. We've got children. And so I feel like I want to keep it together and I want to believe him when he says he's sorry, so I'm always making sure that everything is smooth and agreeing with him. But sometimes I wonder, it's like I'm prostituting myself to this high income level that I have being married.

Although the aim of anger, when aroused by threats to an intimate tie, is to preserve relationship, anger weakens the bond if conflicts are never resolved but instead continually feed a reservoir of rage. Since inequality stifles a woman's direct communication, she often first tries to accomplish change by an inner revolt against the outer structures that feel so confining. Angry mind-rehearsals like Susan's may serve to dissolve the relational tie enough to prepare her to leave it. Interestingly, Freud observed that depressed people

> make the greatest nuisance of themselves, and always seem as though they felt slighted and had been treated with great injustice. All this is possible only because the reactions expressed in their behavior still proceed from a mental constellation of revolt, which has then, by a certain process, passed over into the crushed state of melancholia. (1917, p. 248)

The origins of the revolt Freud observes exist in the structures of the relationship, not, as he argues, in a depressed person's intrapsychic structure. The "mental constellation of revolt" is an inner attitude of refusal to give any more, arising from anger and resentment about issues in the relationship. This covert rebellion is expressed as indirect anger in all aspects of the relationship, such as by withholding sex and emotional warmth.

Psychoanalytic tradition considers depressive symptoms themselves to be a form of hostility. Freud explains that, through symptoms, depressed persons succeed "in taking revenge on the original object and in tormenting their loved one through their illness, having resorted to it in order to avoid the need to express their hostility to him openly" (1917, p. 251). This revenge through symptoms has been assumed by the psychoanalytic tradition to be associated with reduced hostility during the acute depressive episode. But research clearly points to *increased* hostility during depression, often deflected from the problematic relationship with the husband or partner to the children. Depressed mothers' interactions with their children are characterized by friction and lack of warmth, a hostile style of interaction, and lack of responsiveness to the children's expressed needs for affection.[9]

> Question arises as to why children are the objects of the most hostility, even greater than that found towards the spouse.

Clinical data suggested that the spouse in a small number of cases was providing emotional support; therefore the patient did not feel hostile toward him. More often, the patient was hostile and tempered direct expression toward the spouse out of fear of the consequences. She was less fearful of the immediate consequences with the children, and they became the misdirected targets of her unexpressed rage towards her spouse. (Weissman and Paykel, 1974, p. 147)

Perceiving that others will not give to her when she feels strongly in need of affection and support, the depressed woman becomes more angry with her partner, blames herself, and withdraws further into hopelessness and self-condemnation for her anger.

Depressed women alert us to their experience of self-loss within unsatisfactory relationships. Seeking love and closeness, a woman attempts to create intimacy by altering herself to meet what she perceives to be the needs of the man she loves. But the act of altering herself—of putting herself "as a person out of the picture"—results not in the emotional and spiritual rewards of authentic intimacy, but in a diminished self.

IMAGES OF SELF IN
INTIMATE RELATIONSHIP

. 3 .

I thought maybe I could help him, and I know that's
probably a common thought, that by being a good, understanding, loving wife that maybe I could help him.

Depressed women talk about "helping" their partners, about
specific "ways to help," about "pleasing" their men, and
about "oneness." As we listen to this language, it becomes apparent that we are learning about specific behaviors that are
designed to secure intimate relationship. At one level, the wom-
en's aims are genuinely other-directed and altruistic. But on
another level, as we attend more closely to their descriptions, we
also hear strains of a less well-articulated and less conscious
goal: to control the partner's response. Both levels seek the same
outcome: to ensure the safety and survival of a primary relationship.

The attachment behaviors by which women seek to accomplish this outcome have a distinctive aspect: they are *culturally
defined as feminine.* They are taught to girls from birth on, they
reflect women's position of social inequality, and they undermine women's self-esteem. We rarely see men engaging in the
specific behaviors to be outlined in this chapter, because men
seek to accomplish a similar outcome by different means.

Each of the behaviors—helping, pleasing, oneness, self-silencing—imply that a woman cannot show all aspects of her self, that she cannot be honest. As she tries to build a relationship with these behaviors, they combine to create something she did not intend. Together they construct an edifice of false relationship that entraps a woman in dishonesty and self-betrayal. In this chapter, I will look beneath these culturally prescribed feminine attachment behaviors to uncover their cultural foundations, and we will see their disastrous consequences for the woman's sense of self and for the relationship.

THE GAME

A number of women told me about behaving in certain ways out of a wish to help a man with a limited ability to love, or to help a man feel strong and stable. Depressed women use the metaphor of "playing games" when describing their attempts to connect with a man whom they perceive as having problems. These women enter such relationships not only with a *wish* to help their partners, but with the perception of a *way* to help that includes a false presentation of self, a self designed to "build up" the man and secure the attachment. As the pretense is enacted over time, the game goes out of control and takes over reality, destroying the woman's confidence in her own perceptions, as well as her self-esteem.

When depressed women talk of playing games, they are explaining how they play at being women, how they feel they have to act a part to be a woman as the culture defines one. The female role allows for many character parts, which shift depending on the context in which a woman plays the game. Depressed women use the following labels as they describe parts they must play: "the good wife," "the Boston matron," "the housewife," "professional, wearing blazers and going to my office," "totally confident and self-assured," "a mother who never gets angry at her children," "give all with love and patience to my husband and children," "friendly and smiling all the time," "slim, sexy, and alluring."

Not only does the game metaphor refer to a woman's need to

act a part assigned to her by the culture, it also refers to taking on a role in order to interact with a man. Used in this way, the game presents one way to solve the puzzle of how to create intimacy within inequality. The woman only *pretends* to be submissive and, in a detached manner, watches herself behaving in ways designed to secure relationship. By detaching from her outwardly conforming behavior, she expects to retain her personal authenticity.

The rules of this game, the positions of the players, guidelines that determine what players may (or must) do, what winning means, are part of a complex maze of gender interactions. The game is learned throughout childhood, often at the hem of the mother while watching her behavior with the father. Along with the game rules, the girl internalizes the complex reasons a woman plays the game.

Jan, age 24, describes the rules she followed in her marriage and how they led to her loss of self. Asked in her first interview how she would describe herself, she responds:

> Well, I would describe myself as a strong woman—I would say sympathetic and empathetic, sensitive, intelligent, talented, modest (laughs). Um . . . I would say with a quick wit, although my husband does his best to stifle that. He does not have a sense of humor when it comes to me. He takes—he's very critical of me.

She says, "Marriage has really been an exception for me, and I'm headed back to being Jan now, because I like the qualities that were Jan." Explaining how her marriage had been the exception, she describes the way she had perceived her husband's weaknesses and how she had tried to help him. She heard about this guy in college who was a legend; "he was into pottery and there were these monuments to Jim all over the place." But when she met him, she immediately saw his clay feet, his vulnerability.

> I was in the pottery room working and Jim came in, and I thought, gee, you don't look so hot to me, I was very

unimpressed. Here, you know, everybody was measured to Jim. And I thought, "Oh good, that legend's been shot to hell," so I just kind of went home. And I'd see him now and then around the university, and then we went to Guatemala, we were in the same group. And I kind of sized up the group and I thought "he looks like the most substantial of anybody around." The rest were kind of bubble-gummy and the women were looking at the men and the men were looking for women and I didn't know what I had gotten myself into. I had gone down to study the Mayan and Aztec ruins, and so had Jim. So consequently we ended up sharing plane seats, bus seats, having our meals together, hiking together, and our friendship grew. And he told me about his [mental] hospital experience . . . but our friendship kept growing. And it seemed to me to start out very healthy . . . When we got back to the States, he wined and dined me. I remember the first tiff that we got into . . . I was responsible for it and he brought me roses and I thought "Good grief, how can you go wrong, when you start the fight and he brings you roses?"

Exploring what did "go wrong," Jan goes on to describe a kind of pretense she entered into in the desire to help her husband-to-be.

Well I'm realizing now that he must have tried to start controlling me. And, not wanting to hurt him, and knowing how deeply I felt about him, I guess I . . . I was trying to help him, and he was telling me about the family he grew up in and everything which—I think it's a very strange family and I could see where he'd picked up a lot of these things, and all the things he'd gone through and he was thinking that he was a very weak person and everything. And I thought to myself, "Well, okay, Jan, let him think that he's the strong one for a while." And I—it got out of hand. I was really making myself be weak, and "okay, you make the decisions," and "anything is fine," and placating, and it got out of hand.

Empathetically perceiving this man's vulnerabilities, Jan invents a self to fulfill the role of the "weak" submissive woman, thinking that this will be helpful to him. She adopts the culture's gender rules, which prescribe that a woman respond to a man's emotional and physical needs and that she hide her own strengths. Women are taught to lie with their bodies: hair is shaved, make-up applied, physical attributes are made over to please men.[1] What prevents a woman from creating a fraudulent self, designed to please as surely as is the outer body?

The man's position in this game is much safer. He does not have to experience his vulnerability by asking to be cared for, or openly reveal his dependence on the woman to fill his needs. The man's part is to follow the cultural prescription to appear emotionally strong, and to provide for the woman's economic needs. The traditional rules for the woman's role push her to disguise her needs as she responds to what she perceives as his. In Jan's words, she was "playing games" as she adopted these rules as her own, thinking they were a temporary measure to help this man gain confidence.

But Jan's control over what was at first purposeful activity became confused by the self she created to help a man she cared for. She grew increasingly unable to distinguish between what she had invented and what she knew as real about the relationship. She tried to demonstrate her love by going along with Jim's wishes, but the effort required to make herself appear compliant invaded her earlier sense of competence and strength:

But I had a particular group of friends, and Jim kept telling me that it was unhealthy, the relationship that I had with these friends, and I should stay away from them. And I thought to myself, "Okay, I'll do this to show him how much I value his opinion," even though I didn't believe it was an unhealthy relationship at all. But again, I think I was kind of playing games and trying to see—show him, "Hey you really are stable." But things really got real screwed up.

If a woman presents an inauthentic version of herself to the person with whom she lives most intimately, she may begin to feel a loss of her own self. Since a person is brought into being, shaped, and reflected in intimate attachments, a woman's primary relationship will profoundly affect her core sense of identity. In R. D. Laing's words, *"the sense of identity requires the existence of another by whom one is known;* and a conjunction of this other person's recognition of one's self with self-recognition" (1969, p. 139).

The game of lets-pretend-that-I'm-weak-and-you're-strong calls for dishonesty in the service of relationship. It also requires self-compromise and duplicity. It led Jan to the split, characteristic of depressed women, between an outer mask of compliance and an inner reality of confusion and deepening rage. Trying to act outwardly deferential while inwardly preserving her authenticity and freedom led Jan to the place where she felt "there was always an inward struggle going on, kind of a 'Hey, let me out, Jim doesn't know who I am.'" Increasingly, Jan herself did not know which self was real, which view of the relationship, the world, reality itself, was credible.

Jan herself was drawn into the fantasy that she had created to help Jim: "It got out of hand." She began to lose touch with her own strength and integrity; she began to see herself through her partner's eyes, and to question the legitimacy of her own needs in the relationship. From the viewpoint of her authentic self, her "I," she also condemned herself for falsification, for "lack of courage" to say or live her own truth. She fell into deep confusion over her marriage.

I'm not very hopeful. And I—we're still hanging in there, I don't really know why, because I am thinking more and more, "Hey, Jan, you are young, you are only 24 years old. You deserve to be happy—there's a lot of pain in here, in this relationship, maybe you should just bail out." But there's a lot of other in there—you know, morally, religiously . . . Divorce isn't a happy ending. And there's a lot of family things in there. There isn't anybody in my family that has ever been divorced or even separated. And that's kind of a hard mold to break out of . . . My husband thinks he's fulfilling my needs. And he wanted to know why I was unhappy yesterday and it's very hard to respond. I mean, to say "I'm unhappy because you're this and you're this." Nobody wants to hear that. I don't want to hurt him. So it's—I'm feeling trapped right now. I can't really say that my needs are not being met. He was shocked, he could not believe that my needs are not being met, and then he started implying that it's because I was too needy. But all I wanted was a goodnight hug and a kiss and I don't think that's too needy for my husband. But I don't know, things are all out of focus. Maybe I *am* just too needy.

Switching back and forth between her perspective and the perspectives of others, Jan lost sight of her own viewpoint. Seeing oneself through others' eyes, be they the eyes of the family of origin, the culture, the partner, leads to doubled vision—the feeling that things are, in Jan's words, "out of focus." Not knowing which view is the right one, Jan is uncertain about asserting her own perspective, which challenges these authorities who pronounce what she should do or how she should feel. The trap, which may appear external, also exists internally, as these voices of authority reside not only in the outer world but within her own moral imperatives as well. Her husband's words—"he started implying that it's because I was too needy"—echo the voice of the culture that tells her asserting her desires is selfish and immature.

What appears in Jan's interview as the wish not to hurt others, and the willingness to accomplish such goodness by self-sacrifice, carries more complex goals than moral goodness and altruism. In Jan's willingness to silence her authentic voice as she enters heterosexual relationship, in her wish not to hurt her husband, we see both cultural norms and personal aims at work. The culture's rules about how a woman pleases a man, how to keep relationship by fulfilling others' needs, are reflected in Jan's behavior. This way of being in relationship—a way that Jan calls playing games—carries the personal goal of ensuring attachment. It is critical that we notice the tremendous amount of conscious energy and willpower Jan expends to make herself appear outwardly compliant, traditionally feminine, submissive to the wishes of her partner, in order to connect with him.

Ironically, what initially attracted Jim to her—"he told me he was looking for the strongest woman he could find"—is laid aside as she dons the behaviors she thinks will foster the relationship: "I was really making myself be weak, and 'okay, you make the decisions,' and 'anything is fine,' and placating." Recall that Jan said she acted this way because she empathetically perceived the source of her husband's feelings of weakness and wished to "let him think that he's the strong one for a while." But alongside her empathy and genuine wish to help occurs the wish to control her partner's response, to make him love her.

The tragedy of the gameplaying lies in the mistaken understanding that this deception will further intimacy. Many of the women are unaware of the controlling aspects of their helping behavior, and are confused over the anger they arouse in their partners. Focusing on their goal of securing attachment, they also often remain unaware of the significant erosions of self that are occurring until they become severely depressed.

Within intimate relationships, women are tempted to succumb to conventional definitions of feminine interpersonal "shoulds," not only because of the social context of male domination, but because they have been taught from childhood a socially sanctioned way to interact with men to show love and caring. The attachment behaviors that lead to depression—helping, pleasing, silencing one's voice, attempts at control—grow out of women's desire to create closeness and continuing attachment. As a woman and her partner interact, each bringing individual shortcomings and the variations of personal history, they create together a situation that carries the risk of her depression. Though the woman's anger is directed at her mate and at herself, the true villain may be the dilemma in which they find themselves: how to create intimacy within inequality.

ONENESS

In order to understand in more detail the link between depression and culturally prescribed feminine attachment behaviors, let us listen to women talk about the goal toward which they strive: intimacy. "Oneness" is the metaphor women most often use to represent their image of intimacy. After fourteen years of marriage, Therese says:

> When you say, "I do," you are one. Hopefully you will do things as one.

Twice divorced and now a single parent, Maya observes:

> When a woman marries, she becomes one with her husband, and I think that my thinking is literal on that. That she sort of molds and melts into him and that he just sort of takes over all the responsibilities. Somehow the woman gets lost in there and she becomes like her husband.

In Western thought, oneness stands as a universal image for intimacy. The poets write about overcoming the boundaries of separate selves when they sing the raptures of romantic love.

> because two bodies, naked and entwined,
> leap over time, they are invulnerable,
> nothing can touch them, they return to the source,
> there is no you, no I, no tomorrow,
> no yesterday, no names, the truth of two
> in a single body, a single soul,
> oh total being . . . (Octavio Paz, 1987, p. 19)

Oneness occurs in a moment of ecstasy when the confines of two bodies, two separate consciousnesses are overcome by passion. In its positive meaning, oneness can connote wholeness, integration of two separate realities into a whole that is large enough to contain them both. It speaks to an immediacy of feeling, a transcendence of boundaries, a connectedness that is a return to the "source." It is more reminiscent of the closeness between mother and infant than of adult love, except in the exquisite returns to oneness possible in sexual passion.

The Western romantic image of oneness, carried through the centuries, provides an ideal whose shining brightness leaves inequality in the shadows, unilluminated and unexamined. For women, the image contains its own contradiction and defeat. When depressed women speak of oneness in their marriages, they leave no doubt that the new unity mirrors the husband's likeness, with his personality, his preferences, and his purposes providing the image. Holding to this image and its promise for intimacy, the women describe how they eliminate their difference, how they become invisible in order to attain closeness with the partner.

Cultural images of intimacy as oneness reinforce many girls' experiences of early patterns of attachment with their parents. Mothers and fathers who demand conformity with their opinions and values as a condition of being loved lay the groundwork for their daughters' later adaptation to a partner's wishes. A clear example comes from Merton Gill and Irwin Hoffman's transcript of Patient B in a psychoanalytic session:

> In our family we weren't ever asked in anything that really mattered: "What do you think?" or "What do you want?" That I can recall. And even if we were, still my parents made it very clear that their opinions were the ones we should have and that if we didn't agree then we just were stupid and didn't know anything, and, or immature, and when we grew up we'd understand. And then the other thing is—I think is perhaps even more important—is just the way my father is when you do

agree with him, when you choose the same foods or agree on political philosophy or anything. That it's almost like you're a comrade. You—there's a closeness and he's very moved by this because, well, in a way it's giving him his confidence, I suppose, that he needs. But even, just like ordering an ice cream cone at a Howard Johnson's or something. If you chose the same flavor as he did, then there was somehow an intimacy between you and he'd get in a very good mood. And I don't know, you got his approval and, in a way his affection by choosing as he chose. And I th—, I don't know, I was thinking, too, in terms of how so often I'm ask—, I want F [husband] to make his decision first because now I think I'm doing this with F—that if we both are eating the same thing or somehow share the same opinion, there's a certain intimacy or closeness. [pause] And on the other hand, that this would lead me to assume that if you strike out on your own, have your own ideas or choose your own kinds of choices, you get disapproval. (Gill and Hoffman, 1982, pp. 35–36)

As this woman so clearly explains, conformity in attachments has been rewarded with love so that sameness itself becomes associated with "a certain intimacy or closeness." Since autonomy of thought and action has been punished, she begins to think that independence—speaking her own opinions, having her own perspective—leads to insecurity of attachment. Trying to create security and closeness in their relationships, women bridge the distance between self and other by trying to become "one" with their husbands.

To most psychologists, women's talk of oneness suggests an unhealthy wish to merge with another. Historically the attempt to solve the conundrum of intimacy within inequality by disappearing into the outline of the husband has been blamed solely on the flawed psyche of women. Overlooked are the commands of our society that dictate to women the acceptable and unacceptable ways to relate to men. The ideal of romantic love portrays a selfless transcendence and a union of mutuality. This ideal promises expansion, growth, creativity, and joy. It obscures the problem of inequality; after all, where the end is perfect unity, there can be no problem of inequality. Where all is gained, nothing can be lost, especially the self. In real life, by contrast, the social roles of wife and husband carry duties, obligations, and rules of relationship that drive the partners toward inequality. In depressed women's descriptions of oneness in marriage, they reshape the romantic image of intimacy to accord with their subordinate role in marriage: oneness means sameness.

THE WISH TO HELP

Depressed women describe entering into or remaining in their hurtful marriages because they want to "help" the man. Unspoken is their wish to secure the partner's presence by making themselves necessary to his well-being. In their words, they see a damaged child within the grown man and want to help him heal. Thinking that one teaches another how to love not through justice but through care and forgiveness, they are willing to accept some hurt (some injustice) if it will help their partners learn to love. They talk explicitly about responding to their spouses as if the men were hurt children who need comfort, patience, and time in order to be coaxed into loving.

Maya was married for six years to a man who abused her and her son. When asked why she didn't leave her husband early in the marriage, after the first sign of abuse, she responds:

> I thought maybe I could help him, and I know that's probably a common thought, that by being a good, understanding, loving wife that maybe I could help him, which was not realistic at all, at least not in that situation, maybe with other marriages it might be the case.

Maya conceived a child shortly after they were married:

Because I thought that maybe having a child of his would help straighten things out, would help him. I knew he had a lot of emotional problems, I recognized that after we were married, I thought well, maybe a child will bring us closer together and that things would smooth over, but it didn't change at all.

Susan, at 32, with two small children, had also been physically abused in her eight-year marriage:

In a lot of areas in my own marriage, I have taken the treatment I have because I realize, I try to make excuses like Harry's treating me like this because he must be a very frustrated person deep inside. Or he had—I usually blame his childhood. And I have a tendency to allow myself to be treated the way I do and I always use this excuse, "Well he had such a horrible childhood. He doesn't know how to show love and affection, so don't expect it from him." You know, this kind of thing.

It is intriguing that in many instances when someone chooses to leave a relationship we view her as healthier; we consider that separating requires more strength than does maintaining an attachment. When someone chooses to remain in a difficult relationship and try to improve it, we more readily classify her as having low self-esteem, as dependent and clinging, as having no real backbone. But to end a relationship is to end personal involvement, whereas to live within a difficult relationship, trying to improve it, is to keep actively participating. To leave is celebrated while to suffer life for others is sick or immature (Holub, 1990). It is important to recognize that the value these women place on relationship leads them to believe that staying is the right thing to do, and that it requires strength. We need to acknowledge the women's genuine attempts to love their partners into relatedness, and recognize the cultural as well as psychological impediments to realizing such a goal.

Yet this premise upon which the relationship is based, a woman's sincere belief that she can help a man limited in his ability to love, may lead to a progression of hurt in the relationship. This is because the woman does not engage directly with the man's problems to say how they affect her, but takes a stance of compliance to create the appearance of intimacy and hopes that "things will work out." She protects her partner from her own reactions to support the illusion of intimacy. In the effort to attain closeness, she creates an ever widening gap between the potential relatedness toward which she is striving and the reality of their relationship. Ironically, the basis for intimacy becomes deception—deception about her feelings, her perception of him, her own ambivalence, and her growing rage.

Depressed women obliterate their own criticisms of their husband or partner, excusing his current actions because of his past childhood problems. In these transactions, the woman can feel herself to be powerful and strong indirectly, through caring. She can act for herself—to control the relationship—but disguise it as action for the other. Like all human behaviors, "helping" the husband can be both positive and negative, depending on how truth evolves in the relationship. Truth itself must be defined within the context of each person's reality. As Adrienne Rich says:

> In speaking of lies, we come inevitably to the subject of truth. There is nothing simple or easy about this idea. There is no "the truth," "a truth"—truth is not one thing, or even a system. It is an increasing complexity. The pattern of the carpet is a surface. When we look closely, or when we become weavers, we learn of the tiny multiple threads unseen in the overall pattern, the knots on the underside of the carpet. (1979, p. 187)

Threads of authentic moral striving run through these women's wish to help their husbands; strands of ineffectual attempts to win and maintain love by self-sacrifice also wind their way through these actions. Together they weave a complex net that ensnares a woman in self-negation as she tries both to liberate her partner from his limitations and to create a secure relationship within which she will be needed and loved.

These women's actions also reveal a belief in transformative love. This belief, that one can save others through love, is a central tenet of Christianity. Transformative love implies the willingness to give one's most precious possession—a part of the self—in order to redeem others. "For God so loved the world that he gave his only begotten son . . ." For a person like Mother Teresa, personal discomfort is irrelevant when she engages in a devoted caring for those who have been abandoned by society. But transformative love and its possibilities for creative connection can become distorted in the translation from an ideal to specific human actions.[2] When acted out within relationships of inequality and physical or emotional abuse, transformative love becomes an imprisoning myth.

As these women present it, transformative love or "helping" also carries the intent to bind a man in order to make his love dependable. The need to secure attachment in such a way appears to be directly related to the woman's lack of self-esteem. Many of the depressed women I talked with grew up with low self-esteem, particularly in the area of their "attractiveness" to men. By attractiveness is not meant simply physical attractiveness, but a fundamental sense of self as worthy of love, as good enough to keep the affection of a desirable man. Because of the dynamics of her parents' relationship and through identification with her mother's low self-esteem, a girl can see herself as having to please a man in order to "keep" him. She may grow up thinking that if a man needs nothing from her, he won't stay around. Maya talks about what attracted her to her second husband:

> I found him physically attractive, and also that he paid particular attention to me, that he was interested in me, that he had a problem and I wanted to help him with it. And I can remember my mother saying, "A woman can change a man if she really tries." And just the other day I read something in one of the books I've been reading,

that you can't change the basic makeup of a person, so don't try and waste a lifetime doing it. Oh, I thought, how well I know that one.

(*What was the problem that you saw in him that you felt you could change?*) He was lonely and he had, he was an alcoholic, and I knew that they can go through treatments. Just that, that's it in a nutshell. The desire to help.

Asked what her response would have been if she had met a man who seemed "great" and "emotionally intact," Maya replies:

I couldn't have handled it, I would have been afraid.

(*Of what?*) Of him. I don't know why. Because he would seem so above and beyond me, like I couldn't relate to him, and he wouldn't need me, so what would be the point of anything?

(*What do you mean that he was real above and beyond you?*) That I was so inferior. That I wouldn't be able to relate to him. There wouldn't be any purpose for me to marry him, because he already has his needs provided within himself, and why would he want to marry me? I felt like I needed to marry someone that needed me, that I could help.

Maya goes on to make the connection between her needing to help a man and her own lack of self-esteem.

And I wonder if the root of that is my lack of self-esteem. I didn't think highly of myself, I never did growing up. I always felt I was below everyone even though I did well in school and I had friends, I never felt like I met up to them.

Extending the logic of Maya's thinking, we find a circular pattern that illustrates how she binds herself into self-defeating thought and relationship (see Figure 1).

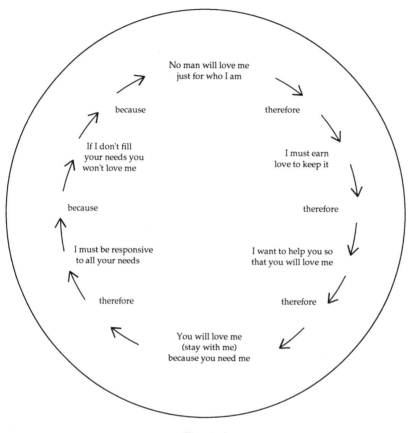

No man will love me
just for who I am

because

therefore

If I don't fill
your needs you
won't love me

I must earn
love to keep it

because

therefore

I must be responsive
to all your needs

I want to help you so
that you will love me

therefore

therefore

You will love me
(stay with me)
because you need me

Figure 1

When low self-esteem prevents a woman from believing she will be loved "for free," that is, for her own qualities and characteristics, she chooses a damaged partner she intends to help. If the husband or partner *needs* the woman to give him strength, or if she supplies some essential lack in his personality, then he is less likely to leave her. The woman believes that if she demonstrates her willingness to heal her partner through patience, love, and forbearance, he will become firmly attached to her. In this way, she maintains a sense of control over her submissiveness, and expects a reward of secure relationship for her self-sacrifice. At the same time, however, she becomes weary of the burden of having continually to "earn" love and resentful of the trap in which she feels caught.

Feeling "inferior," and devalued by the culture's estimate of her worth relative to the man's, the woman seeks to equalize the relationship by giving something the man needs. The sense of oneself as giving something that someone else needs is ego-expanding, while receiving places one in the possible position of feeling indebted, with the potential for feeling diminished (Gaylin, 1978). If a woman's self-esteem is low, she can feel herself to be unwhole, incomplete. Knowing she must search for wholeness and healing, she chooses a partner who also is incomplete, who must also search for wholeness and healing, and whom she can help. Their symmetry of incompleteness seems to hold a promise of exact fit and greater wholeness.

The cultural stereotype still decrees that men do the choosing and women are chosen. Because men have more of the power of choice, women both consciously and unconsciously try to please them in order to be chosen. Being chosen demonstrates to a woman her feminine identity and her sexual desirability. Thus a woman may concentrate her energies on understanding the man in order to have and to hold him with the power of her responsiveness to his needs.

THE WAY TO HELP

A woman's wish to help her husband overcome his problems is not in itself unhealthy or dependent. It becomes unhealthy in the *way* a woman attempts to secure relationship, by the coercion of selfless giving. Women learn this way to help their partners from their parents and from the culture at large. As women enact these prescribed feminine attachment behaviors (these ways of interacting that are supposed to secure intimacy within heterosexual relationship), they are condemned for being "dependent," though these are the very rules the culture has set for them. At the same time, if they try to break the pattern, they often encounter censure for focusing on their own needs, goals, and desires.

Many women, when entering an intimate heterosexual connection, automatically enact the rules of relationship they have learned from early experience. As Sandra, age 40 and separated from her husband, says:

> I know that the traditional sort of role that I played in my marriage was almost like an automatic pilot. My parents did it this way and it worked for them so therefore it would work for me.

The chief characteristic of the role that Sandra and others describe learning is "giving all and giving as much as was possible for me to keep the relationship together." Maintenance of the relationship appears paramount.

The role of the selfless giver contains its own blindness and leads a woman straight into what is called dependence. After Jan separated from her husband, she reflected on the relationship and mused about their "power struggles." Describing how "I was wanting to be close, and he was wanting to hold me off," she goes on to talk about the struggle they had around giving to each other:

> Well, I'm trying to define power struggle, because that's what it was. I guess, I don't know if we were both trying to give at the same time or take at the same time, or something, there is just a lot of turmoil of intention. I think it was, well, there was give and take, but it was for the wrong reasons. I think it was giving for ourselves and not for the other's benefit. In taking maybe for the other and not for ourselves. It's like we had it backwards.
>
> (*How would you take for the other's benefit?*) Maybe to hurt them, because they didn't give in the proper way or something. Or maybe I would take to please Jim because early in the marriage he would say that I would give, give, give but I wouldn't take. Okay, you want me to take, I'll take. You know, if that's what you think I should do.

These actions, "giving for ourselves" and "taking . . . for the other," backward in their intent and effect, originate in a relationship marked by problems of communication and mutuality. When neither partner provides a secure base for the other, then neither can express a desire for support directly, so they do so indirectly or in a demanding and aggressive way. The hidden aspect of the transactions Jan describes is that what the self wants is disguised as what the other wants, and yet the other is never asked if she or he wants to be given to in this way. In her focus on trying to please her husband, Jan "took over" the function of giver, leaving her partner little room to give back, yet expecting him to be appreciative of her actions.

Jan provides a clear example of the difference between role-based and relationship-based responsiveness. Are the actions for the other founded on the other's real needs and concerns, or are they based on the role of the "good wife"? Ironically, Jan never really knows what her partner wants or feels. In giving what she *thinks* he wants, she responds to another role stereotype, that of the "husband." In this situation, giving becomes blind to the real needs of the other:

> I think that we were giving what we thought each other should need, and not really looking to see.

The image of the "good wife" exists independently of what the actual person who is the woman's husband might want. When a woman steps into the role of wife, her wish to give is accompanied by the clear perception of the *way* to give. Jan puts it this way:

> Another thing finally occurred to me, that if I was as intelligent as I thought I was, then why do I keep doing these stupid things that are making me unhappy. Like insisting that my standard of a "good wife" was what my husband should want in a good wife. And that, you know, we were constantly locking horns on that. He wanted me out of the house. He didn't want a square

meal for dinner every night. To him sometimes it was okay to have sandwiches or nothing, popcorn, who knows. Where at first in our marriage it was like, oh my god, you know, if I'm going to be a good wife, I have to fix a balanced dinner, or I failed as a wife.
(*So that's what you went in feeling and trying to do?*) Oh yes. Oh yes, and these come, I know now, all from my mom. I was ironing handkerchiefs, you know, my mom. I was ironing all his clothes because that's what good wives did. They took care of their husbands. You know, every whim. They're always right there when their husbands needed anything.

Jan was responding not to Jim's stated needs, but to her own image of a "husband's" needs, learned through identification with her mother's behaviors and attitudes. The mismatch between reality and role became clear when Jim complained to her that "when I ironed his handkerchiefs, they scratched his glasses."

In defining the "good wife," Jan says, "This has always been my baseline, and that is, to please my husband . . ." She gave to her husband in ways her mother had taught her would please— balanced meals and ironed clothes. In retrospect, she found she had also given him something more critical: "I found myself depending on Jim for, well, for my self-esteem, really." She describes how this happened:

Well, I found myself not wearing things that he didn't like, or not buying things that he didn't like, like you know, "What do you think about this shirt," knowing that I liked it, and then he might say, "Well, it's okay." And then I'd find myself putting it back, because I wanted him to really like it. So I was dressing for him. All of the physical, you know, hair, makeup, whatever. Not really making a move without, without his strong approval. And I think there's a lot of discussion and approving in a relationship naturally, but this was not natural. I'm trying to think of a move that I would not—I can't think of any offhand. But it just seemed like things were revolving around him, which was very frustrating for me.

Though Jan entered relationship feeling strong and stable, she increasingly saw herself through her partner's eyes, thus giving him the power to evaluate her. In such ways, Jan moved into dependence on her partner for self-esteem. This kind of dependence does not indicate regression, helplessness, or developmental arrest. It is not a character trait but rather is specific to the situation: it comes into existence as a woman lives out the role of wife, with its imperative to please the husband. This imperative reinforces gender inequality in intimate relationship, and stops a woman from voicing her own perspective. Thus the conception of the way a woman gives to a man, lived out with the intention of helping him and securing the relationship, leads to self-alienation and to interpersonal distance.

Guided by an image of oneness and the wish to help, struggling to connect intimately within inequality, depressed women speak of common patterns within heterosexual relationships. The following string of thoughts shows the patterns of interpersonal relatedness described by depressed women:

My wish is to be good and loving in relationship

and

I want closeness, intimacy, and security with my partner

but

my understanding of closeness and goodness means that I do not initiate conflict or show anger

therefore

if I disagree with my partner I must silence myself to prevent separation and hurt to the relationship therefore

I can't be authentic to my partner

therefore

he stays with me for what I appear to be
not for what I am

and

I have lost myself in this relationship but still haven't
achieved intimacy

therefore

I feel hopeless because I can envision no way of
gaining intimacy without losing myself

and

I am angry that he does not love me for who I am. I
feel bad and hateful in this relationship and I feel
frustrated and self-alienated for not living out my
authentic self

but

my wish is to be good and loving in a secure
attachment.

THE IMPORTANCE OF PLEASING

Depressed women speak often of the importance of "pleasing"
their men. How does pleasing become so important? To understand this from the depressed women's point of view, we must
enter their narratives at the point where they begin to bring in
the language of pleasing their husbands or partners. The pre-
ludes to talk of pleasing cluster around themes of male strength
and a woman's lack of responsibility for herself within marriage.
Most of the women describe their partners as "stronger." Anna
says:

He's so strong that I think I need him more than he needs
me, maybe.
(*What do you mean when you say strong?*) He knows
which way he's going, what he wants, how he wants
things, and so on. Hmmmm, maybe he has his way
more often.

During her first marriage to a man who abused her, Maya says
she saw her husband as "strong" and "right," even though she
perceived his problems.

I never felt protective of him because maybe my thinking
was the other way around, that he was the protective
one. But I'm beginning to see that I protected him.

After fifteen years of marriage, Linda describes how her husband appeared to be the "strong one" while she was "emotional,
irrational." Yet, during a time of separation and filing for divorce, Linda reviews these images of self in relationship and
calls them into question.

I realize now that *I* was the one who made the decisions
and he followed my lead. And I'm the one who decided
to buy a car, and buy a house and a lot of the things that I
thought in a lot of marriages the man would be . . . more
involved.

These women idealize the partner as strong for a variety of
reasons. In intimate relationships, one must necessarily idealize
the person to whom one becomes subordinate. If the self is
experienced as vulnerable, the other needs to be seen as strong
to create a sense of safety. The feeling that the man is stronger
also rests on the men's tendency to disguise and hide their
needs.
    Cultural stereotypes also perpetuate the myth that the man
is strong and the woman is weak. Jessie Bernard writes of the
shock of "discovering the fallacy of the sex role stereotypes that

the wife has been socialized into accepting and around which she has built her life."

> Her husband is not the sturdy oak on whom she can depend. There are few trauma greater than the child's discovery of the fallibility of his parents; than the wife's discovery of her husband's dependencies; than the discovery of her own gut-superiority in a thousand hidden crannies of the relationship; than the realizations that in many situations his judgment is no better than hers; that he does not really know more than she; that he is not the calm, rational, nonemotional dealer in facts and relevant arguments; that he is, in brief, not at all the kind of person the male stereotype pictures him to be. Equally, if not more, serious is her recognition that she is not really the weaker vessel, that she is often called upon to be the strong one in the relationship. These trauma are all the more harrowing because they are interpreted as individual, unique, secret, not-to-be-shared with others, not even, if possible, to be admitted to oneself.   (1971, pp. 154–155)

Jean Baker Miller says that "women's major difficulty lies more in admitting the strengths they already have and in allowing themselves to use their resources" (1976, pp. 35–36). She also observes that women believe in the "magical strength" of men in order to feel a sense of support: "Many women develop a great need to believe they have a strong man to whom they can turn for security and hope in the world. And, while it may seem improbable, this belief in the man's magical strength exists side by side with an intimate knowledge of the weaknesses to which she caters" (1976, p. 34).

The hierarchical image of the husband as more important, the genuine wish to help and the culturally learned ways to help, the projection of strength onto the partner—all these images of self in intimate relationship lead to the abdication of responsibility for oneself. When asked "How do you think you will work out being responsible for yourself within a marriage?" Therese responds:

> Hmmmmm (long pause). That's a good question. You know—because—that's interesting. I see marriage as

someone else taking the responsibility for me, so that is
not an easy question. I don't see it, I just don't see it.
(*Don't see what?*) Me taking responsibility in a marriage. I don't see me getting married and taking responsibility for myself. Hmmm.

Therese's thinking about responsibility is clearly influenced by
the fact that her intimate attachment in adulthood replicates the
unequal position in relationship she occupied as a child. She
goes on to say that the reason she does not envision responsibility for herself in a marriage is that "the man is in charge."
Even though she had opinions,

the deciding factor was always John. He would weigh
pros and cons and decide. So I am not used to being
responsible for any decisions. I can make a lot of comments and suggestions.

To accept this child-like position, Therese must give up responsibility for herself.

Other depressed women voice the same ideas about responsibility because they share society's concept of marriage that puts
the husband in the position of authority (father) and the woman
in the position of subordinate (child). When asked "How do you
think you take responsibility for yourself in a marriage?" Maya
responds:

I don't know. It isn't there. You don't have responsibility
for yourself in a marriage. I must be believing that in a
marriage a man is responsible for you. Isn't that right,
isn't that where I'm going? I don't think of a woman
taking responsibility for herself in a marriage.

The similarity of Maya's and Therese's statements (as well as
those of other depressed women) indicates their origin from a
common wellspring: the culture of inequality. This vision of
responsibility demonstrates the power of the mental images that

affect the course of these women's lives and their vulnerability to depression. The belief that entry into marriage involves setting aside responsibility for oneself contributes directly to the loss of self experienced by depressed women. Also contributing to this abdication of responsibility for oneself in marriage is financial dependence, because of its influence over decisionmaking and feelings of independence.

The women's thinking about responsibility within unequal relationships can be represented schematically as follows:

My responsibility is to make my husband happy

and

his responsibility is to take care of me.

He is in charge of the shape that my life will take

therefore

I don't have responsibility for my own happiness

because

I'm responsible for his

and

I hold him responsible for mine.

Depressed women's talk of pleasing their husbands or partners rests on these assumptions about responsibility. Many of the women emphasize the importance of pleasing their husbands, as well as the entanglement of pleasing with male authority and decisionmaking. Exploring why she never told her husband of eighteen years that she did not like working in their business, and why she did not follow her own desire to go into teaching, Cathy describes a hypothetical example she has read:

where a woman had a chance for a certain type of career or something . . . But her husband also was making a career change at the time or something. And she had, I think worked and supported him while he got through college. And I think the question that was being raised was now shouldn't he help her reach her goal. Or should she just follow what he wants to do. And . . . I don't know, I think what would be ideal would be that the husband would really, really want her to reach her goal and do his best to support her. And even give up something to help her. I think it should be mutual that way. But if the husband really doesn't want to do it, then I still have to say that she should bow to his wishes. I mean, that's just my opinion.

To understand what Cathy is saying, let us follow the logic of her thought. She describes an "ideal" of equality, reciprocity, and mutuality: the husband would want her to reach her goal, would do his best, and even give up something to help her, just as she had done for him. But if the relationship is one of inequality, a power dynamic enters in. What he wants, he gets. In this situation, Cathy perceives only one choice, which is to try to influence what he wants. If the bottom line is inequality, that a woman "should bow to his wishes," then she is likely to try very hard to make his wishes coincide with hers. But she cannot do this through direct self-assertion. The bind is that to maintain the security of pleasing the partner so that he has no grounds for dissatisfaction (no reason for leaving), she must consider his wishes first, while still trying to influence them to her own benefit.

Others have seen women's indirect attempts to meet their own needs as manipulative. In its indirectness, such action appears manipulative; in its intent, the goal is to maintain relationship by removing the bases for deep disagreements. The woman's actions to meet her own needs must remain hidden, even to herself. And this indirection and "manipulation" originate in the woman's sense of powerlessness to act directly for her own interests.

Pleasing the husband, in Cathy's and other women's

thought, also helps preserve a certain kind of relationship. Saying "I would have jumped at the chance" if her own husband had encouraged her wish to do other work, Cathy explains, "if he isn't supporting it, then it seems like communication is broken, you're going different directions, and the bond is not there." Cathy would rather walk hand-in-hand with her husband down his path than strike off to pursue her own goals and, perhaps, end up isolated. She fears that self-assertion, expressed through development of her unique talents and interests, could cause a rift that might threaten relationship. In her marriage, she maintained the outward picture of a harmony of wills, while inwardly, year by year, she became more angry and bitter, feeling, in her words, "like I was dying inside." Unable to assume responsibility for herself because of the tightly interlocking network of ideas that told her to do so was selfish and would jeopardize attachment, Cathy found the alive, creative spark of self that seeks self-expression and mutuality growing increasingly hopeless about its possibilities and becoming encased by a bitter, angry self. Not knowing whom to blame, unwilling to risk losing the relationship by speaking and acting on her own needs, Cathy went along with the status quo and became deeply depressed and immobilized.

When adult attachment echoes the inequality of a parent-child relationship, a woman experiences powerless and helpless emotions that feel like the terrors of childhood, including fears of abandonment. As well as the familiar dread of being forsaken by others, a woman in this position can also feel a nameless anxiety that comes from having forsaken herself. Pleasing the important other offsets these overwhelming fears and diverts a woman from facing responsibility for the self she leaves behind as she takes her partner's path. But this situation of needing to please makes Cathy feel "emotionally dependent" in a way she does not like. Asked "What's bothersome about it?" she replies:

Well, because I guess maybe it makes you feel like you're sort of on a string or something. You—if you do something that—like I've felt that if I do something that my

husband disapproves of, then he would withdraw his
love. And so therefore, to keep his love I always thought
I had to do things the way he wanted.

Such unequal emotional arrangements lead women straight
into dependence, which these narratives show to be clearly
tied to unhealthy forms of connection encouraged by the culture. Rather than reflecting an internal, psychological weakness,
what appears as dependence is actually a set of survival strat-
egies evolved by generations of women who have lived intimately with men within relationships of inequality. The strate-
gies—helping, pleasing, compliance—that look "dependent"
are women's active attempts to achieve intimacy given the cards
dealt them from the cultural deck. A woman's healthy attachment needs (the wish to love and be loved) are deformed into a
figure that looks like dependence; rather, it is more accurate to
call it a set of attachment behaviors that have been shaped by
cultural norms and inequality.

THE CULTURAL CONTEXT

These ideas of self and of the qualities a woman "should" have in
order to be loved are culturally and historically specific. They
do not spring up anew with each individual or with each historical era. Psychologists cannot afford to be ahistorical; our ideas
contain the teachings and expectations of our mothers, grandmothers, great-grandmothers.[3]

Relationships, the locus of women's vulnerability to depression, also take place within a historical and cultural context.
Within the husband-wife relationship occurs the juncture of
public and private spheres, of inner and outer worlds. The roles
of wife and mother bring together society's expectations about
the roles and importance of women with a woman's own personal history, self-perception, and hopes. "Nothing less than the
full sweep of cultural activity is brought into consideration in the
single case of depression" (Becker, 1964, p. 11).

Each of us bears the imprint of the culture's history at the deepest levels of the psyche. For centuries, women's bodies and nature have been simultaneously defined, exalted, and devalued by a male-dominated culture. This legacy of thought, and the long history of gendered patterns of interaction, profoundly shapes women's self-perceptions. Over centuries, women have seen themselves being seen by men, and have adopted many of the same negative attitudes and perspectives toward themselves: a fear of the rounded female form, evidenced by the rise in eating disorders; a devaluation of feminine biological events such as menstruation, childbirth, and menopause; a dismissal of feminine modes of knowing as intuitive, irrational, or scattered (Belenky et al., 1986).

The historical legacy of the "good woman" lives on in the inherited collective image of the feminine to affect a contemporary woman's wish to help a man through being understanding, loving, kind, and forbearing. These depressed women's images of self in relationship and the metaphors they use to convey such images are not accidents of individual personality or pathology. Rather, they are powerfully influenced by culture, both past and current, as it intersects with women's orientation to their relationships. Oversimplifying a woman's depression by attributing it to "dependence" or "codependence," does not help her loosen the power of images of self in intimate relationship that tightly bind her.

Our maternal forebears were the designated "carriers" of civilization and morality. Women's moral superiority, their role as moral instructors to errant men, became firmly formulated in the nineteenth century (Cott, 1977). Feminine social worth resided in the contribution to men and children and hence, to society, through "goodness." Much of the literature directed to women in the nineteenth century exalted "woman's sphere" of home and family as one of peace and harmony, love and devotion, in contrast to the selfishness and immorality characterizing the "public sphere" of business, the world of men. And these ideas about public and private spheres still organize the perceptions of contemporary Americans (Caplow, 1982; Bellah et al., 1985).

The chief characteristic of the private sphere is a morality based on love, family loyalty, and unselfishness. Not only were women required to be morally superior, they achieved their superiority through fostering the morality of others. Thus it was not enough to be good in oneself; a woman had to have a positive effect on others in order to fulfill her true nature. Coventry Patmore, in *The Angel in the House,* a book of poems extremely popular in the mid-nineteenth century, conveys in her heroine, Honoria, the image of woman as angel on earth:

> No happier post than this I ask,
>   To live her laureate all my life.
> On wings of love uplifted free,
>   And by her gentleness made great,
> I'll teach how noble man should be
>   To match with such a lovely mate.
> (quoted in Gilbert and Gubar, 1979, p. 22)

As Sandra Gilbert and Susan Gubar observe, "Honoria's essential virtue . . . is that her virtue makes her *man* 'great.'"[4]

Virginia Woolf attests to the power of the continuing image of feminine goodness in silencing the authentic voices of twentieth-century women. Resurrecting the image of the "Angel in the House," Woolf describes how she had to do battle with this phantom in order to have "a mind of her own" and to be able to express what she saw as the truth "about human relations, morality, sex." Of the "Angel in the House" Woolf writes:

> It was she who used to come between me and my paper when I was writing reviews. It was she who bothered me and wasted my time and so tormented me that at last I killed her. You who come of a younger and happier generation may not have heard of her—you may not know what I mean by the Angel in the House. I will describe her as shortly as I can. She was intensely sympathetic. She was immensely charming. She was utterly unselfish. She excelled in the difficult arts of family life. She sacrificed herself daily. If there was chicken, she took the leg; if there was a draught, she sat in it—in short she was so constituted that she never had a mind or a wish of her own, but preferred to sympathize always with the minds and wishes of

others . . . I turned upon her and caught her by the throat. I did
my best to kill her. My excuse, if I were to be had up in a court
of law, would be that I acted in self-defence. Had I not killed
her she would have killed me.   (1942, pp. 236–238)

Woolf tells us that "she died hard": "It is far harder to kill a
phantom than a reality. She was always creeping back when I
thought I had dispatched her" (p. 238).

Idealized images of feminine virtues remain. The shadow
from the wings of the Angel in the House still falls across the
individual consciousness of today's woman and makes it difficult for her to be authentic in relationship. Traditional feminine virtues are stated in a language of constraint: self-denial,
self-sacrifice, self-effacement, self-restraint. Depression simi-
larly connotes a diminution in the experience of an active self
and its possibilities.

Even today, most girls are still being socialized according to a
slightly watered-down version of the nineteenth-century cult of
true womanhood. Yet the social reality within which women live
out these images of femininity is stark. The feminization of
poverty increases at alarming rates. Women work longer hours
for less pay than men, and frequently return home to a second
shift of housework and childcare (Hochschild, 1989). Inadequate
facilities for childcare put a strain on women's finances and
emotions. Many women face chronic conditions of poverty, sexual and physical violence, racism, and ageism. Particularly because they coincide with a time of women's rising expectations
about their economic possibilities, these social conditions contribute to the high incidence of depression in women (Weissman
and Klerman, 1987).

The ease with which women have *appeared* to adapt to idealized images of feminine characteristics—pleasing the man,
adapting to his needs and values—has rested on psychological theories regarding woman's nature. Early psychoanalytic
writers asserted that women are innately weak, dependent,
masochistic, passive, and limited in their capacity for independent thought. Since psychological theory, and especially devel-

opmental theory, is explicitly normative, cultural stereotypes harmful to women are furthered by authorities who describe them as healthy. Karen Horney describes the effect of these psychological theories on women's self-concept:

> It is fairly obvious that these ideologies function not only to reconcile women to their subordinate role by presenting it as an unalterable one, but also to plant the belief that it represents a fulfillment that they crave, or an ideal for which it is commendable and desirable to strive. *The influence that these ideologies exert on women is materially strengthened by the fact that women presenting the specified traits are more frequently chosen by men.* This implies that women's erotic possibilities depend on their conformity to the image of that which constitutes their "true nature." (1967, p. 231, emphasis added)

Whether or not Horney's statement that men choose women who are submissive is true, women fear that it may be.[5]

The finding that depressed women speak with a common language about how one "should" act in relationship in order to achieve intimacy implicates the culture's role in the high rates of female depression. Rather than regarding these images with an eye for how a woman's thought may be distorted or pathological, let us recognize that such images—of how to form intimate relationships, how to maintain and protect them—are vital for understanding women's depression.

MORAL THEMES IN WOMEN'S DEPRESSION

. 4 .

I feel like I did my best in all the areas I could and my marriage didn't work out. So I feel like I'm a failure.

I feel like I'm trash, I really do. I can't face my friends.

I feel like a lost cause, I'm overweight and I don't have enough patience with my family.

I'm always worrying about other people instead of myself—but sometimes when I do something for myself, I feel very guilty.

Depressed women consistently use moral language—words such as "should," "ought," "good," "bad," "selfish"—as they assess themselves and their role in causing the problems in their relationships. Self-judging declarations such as "I don't measure up," "I'm a liar, a cheat, and I'm no good," "I feel like a failure," are also pervasive in their narratives. As we seek to understand women's depression, it is important to uncover the beliefs that guide such harsh self-reproach.

Negative self-evaluation is linked to central aspects of depression. It affects self-perception, self-esteem, anger directed toward the self, and feelings of worthlessness, hopelessness, and paralysis. Among the diagnostic symptoms of major depression, DSM III (1980) lists the effects of negative self-evaluation as follows: "self-reproach, inappropriate guilt, feelings of worthlessness" (p. 214).

Both historically and currently, the fall in self-esteem, basic to depression, has been tied to harsh self-judgment. As early as 1917, Freud observed that the "most outstanding feature" of the clinical picture of melancholia was the patient's "dissatisfaction with the ego on moral grounds" (pp. 247–248). Freud also asserted a difference in superego development and activity between women and men. Yet the illness in which the "superego" is most active—depression—has not been explored in terms of gender difference, or with regard to gender-specific standards women use to evaluate themselves.

In my view, self-evaluation holds the key to understanding gender differences in the prevalence and dynamics of depression. Developmental and psychoanalytic theorists consistently portray differences in the formation and functioning of men's and women's moral concerns. Regardless of theoretical perspective, observers find a female morality attuned to relationships and affection, and a male morality based on abstract principles expressed in laws and rules. Freud, for example, wrote that women are "more often influenced in their [moral] judgments by feelings of affection or hostility" and are consequently "less ethical" than men. While most theorists, including Piaget and Kohlberg, consider with Freud that a relationally oriented morality is less mature, less "independent of its emotional origins as we require it to be in men," the feminist critique has clarified the bias of such evaluations (Freud, 1925, pp. 257–258).

Carol Gilligan (1977, 1982, 1990), tracing the characteristics of women's moral focus, finds its roots in an orientation toward relationships and interdependence. Growing out of the female relational sense of self is a distinct vision of the social world and morality. What Freud and Kohlberg describe as women's less developed ethical sense, Gilligan (1982) reinterprets as a morality attuned to the specific contexts of people's lives that follows an ethic of care with the imperative not to hurt others. Within this framework, responsibility means an extension of self to protect another from hurt, whereas for the separate self, responsibility implies a restraint of aggression. Thus, what is seen from a traditional perspective as women's lack of ego boundaries, dependence, and weak superego, Gilligan reinterprets as a valuable strength, a reflection of a developmental context that values interdependence, empathy, and emotional closeness.

In spite of these longstanding observations of differences in male and female ethical orientations, and the clear tie between self-evaluation and depression, we have not had systematic analysis of the moral themes in depressed women's narratives. Given the sex differences in rates of depressive illness, the increasing rates of depression, and the rapid changes in women's social roles outside the home, it is imperative to explore women's experience of depression through their moral language.

THE "GOOD ME"

The culture contributes powerfully to gender differences in the standards people use to judge the self. By imposing divergent expectations for girls' and boys' behavior, it creates different yardsticks that each gender uses to measure attainment of a "good me." Obviously, some of the characteristics men and women strive to attain do overlap, but many, particularly those associated with intimate behaviors, are gender-specific.

Gender is socially constructed from the moment of birth on. Caretakers attribute different characteristics and qualities to infant boys and girls, and, on the basis of those ascribed attributes, engage with them differently. The infant learns to expect different types of encounters with adult males and females. Brazelton's (1982) videotapes of interactions between three-month-old infants and their mothers and fathers show radically different patterns, with mother-infant interchanges mapped as a smooth, wave-like undulation of initiation, sensitive response, and elaboration. Fathers "jazz up" their babies, often initiating interactions by playfully poking at them. Infants react to their father's arrival with more motor excitement, and the duet moves quickly to more assertive and explosive interchanges, sometimes ending with sensory overload for the infant. Such patterns of interaction, deeply affected by gender, profoundly shape the developing child's sense of self in relationship.

Not only do interactional patterns with parents affect a gendered sense of self in relationship, but the cultural norms that govern male and female "goodness" in relationship also reinforce different behaviors and prerogatives. Boys are allowed and encouraged to express more anger, aggression, and competition; girls, even now, continue to be praised for interpersonal sensitivity, for being "nice" to others. Parents give boys and girls different toys to play with, encourage them in different pursuits, and expect them to respond differently.

Schools reinforce patterns begun at home, with most teachers unaware of their different responsiveness to gender. Teachers give boys more of both positive and negative attention than girls; girls are more likely to be the quiet and invisible classroom members. Boys receive praise for the intellectual quality of their work; girls are more likely to receive praise for the neatness of their work and its compliance with rules of form (Harvey and Stables, 1986; Sadker and Sadker, 1985, 1986). Meanwhile, the media, while powerfully transmitting cultural symbols to the growing child, clearly convey not only sex-role stereotypes but the message that masculine values and traits are more highly regarded than feminine ones. At each stage of development, females and males encounter different expectations, including social norms about what it is to be a good woman or man. All these experiences convey images about who a boy or girl is, and what he or she *should* be like in order to be recognizable in gender and acceptable to others.

The growing child shapes the self into the parents' vision, into a "good me," to gain their love and acceptance. These forms of good behavior, particularly when they fit the outlines prescribed by the wider environment of school, media, and peers, are difficult to challenge. Thus, ingrained in both women and men are gender-specific images of how to be good in relationships in order to be loved. These images guide behavior *and* self-evaluation, and are deeply entwined with understandings of how to achieve intimacy. They include an individual's experience of freedom and compliance within early relationships: how much one was loved "for free" and allowed the leeway to be oneself, and how much one had to comply with the parents' images and develop a "false self" (Winnicott, 1965) in order to be loved.

Images of the "good me," profoundly affected by gender, enter into the story of depression. From the perspective of ego psychology (Bibring, 1953), the low self-esteem and feelings of hopelessness characteristic of depression stem from an impossible gap between the self one would like to be (the ego ideal) and the self one is (the actual self). The greater the discrepancy between these two senses of self, the lower the self-esteem. Despite important theoretical differences, theorists agree that depression results from an early environment where the child learned that, in order to be loved, she or he had to repress authentic feelings and present an outwardly conforming, false self, becoming self-alienated and cut off from emotions in the process.[1]

Since the culture presents women and men with different images from which to create an idealized self, striving to attain these diverging configurations of the ideal affects them in gender-specific ways. Further, if events in the interpersonal sphere are especially critical to the definition and evaluation of women's core sense of self, then analysis of a woman's images of a "good" self in relation is essential for understanding her depression.

In this chapter, we will enter depressed women's experience through the moral language in their self-judgment. Self-reproach provides a window through which to see not only the inner landscape of female depression but also the interaction of culture, personality, and gender. We can learn about this interaction by examining which cultural standards a woman accepts and uses to judge the self, what forms of relatedness she strives to attain, motivated by what images of intimacy.

THE INNER DIALOGUE OF DEPRESSION

In the narratives of each depressed woman, a dialogue between two parts of the self becomes apparent as the woman talks about the sources of her sadness and feelings of loss. One hears this dialogue as a woman shifts her self-portrayal from the first-person to the third-person voice. The first-person voice is the self that speaks from experience, that knows from observation. This voice says, "I want, I know, I feel, I see, I think." The bases for its values and beliefs are empirical; they come from personal experience and observation. In this sense, the first-person voice is authentic; I will call it the "I," the authentic self.[2]

The other voice in the dialogue speaks with a moralistic, "objective," judgmental tone that relentlessly condemns the authentic self. It sounds like a third-person voice, not because it never uses the pronoun "I," but because it speaks *to* the "I." It says "one should, you can't, you ought, I should." It speaks to the self, and like the classical psychoanalytic concept of the superego, it has the feeling of something *over* the "I," which carries the power to judge it. Or like the object-relations notion of the false self, it conforms to outer imperatives and perceived expectations in order to gain approval and protect the true self. I will call this third-person voice the Over-Eye, because of its surveillant, vigilant, definitively moral quality.

The Over-Eye carries a decidedly patriarchal flavor, both in its collective viewpoint about what is "good" and "right" for a woman and in its willingness to condemn her feelings when they depart from expected "shoulds." The Over-Eye persistently pronounces harsh judgment on most aspects of a woman's authentic strivings, including her wish to express herself freely in relationship, her creativity, and her spirituality. Because the judgments of the Over-Eye include a cultural consensus about feminine goodness, truth, and value, they have the power to override the authentic self's viewpoint.

How a woman judges herself and makes choices for her life is critical for an understanding of female depression. The analysis of voices in the inner dialogue provides a framework for hearing how a depressed woman's understanding of herself shifts between the terms of the dominant culture and the reality of her own experience, a personal reality that she often has trouble believing and even conveying. Listening to these inner voices and the shifts in a woman's perspective on her self gives us the possibility of standing with her to comprehend her experience of depression. Attending to the two-voice dialogue also lets us hear how claiming one's authentic perspective on the self and experience, and acting on its values, coincides with a woman's movement out of depression.

In the following interview, we hear the voice of Maya, age 31, who attended college for five years and began a career in teaching. She was married for seven years to a physically abusive man, had two children, and was divorced. Two years later she married again, and then separated from her second husband when she was three months pregnant. At the first interviews, Maya's son was seven and her daughter was three. She was still severely depressed a year and three months later, when reinterviewed. At that time, she was divorced from her second husband, was on welfare, and had a third child, an eight-month-old daughter. Approximately two and one half years after the first interview, Maya had emerged from her serious depression. The excerpts come from the transcript of Maya's first interview. After Maya's own words, I paraphrase the negative judgments implicit in what she says so as to clearly convey the cultural imperatives carried by the Over-Eye.

In the columns below, Maya's two voices reflect disparate points of view from which she sees and evaluates herself and her relationships. The authentic self, based on her own experiences and feelings, is at odds with the "right" or conventional way to think about how relationships should be and what is a good woman. These two perspectives result in a central disparity between what Maya in fact sees and knows from her own experience and what she thinks she *should* think, influenced by role expectations, family history, and cultural norms for women.

Authentic "I"	*Over-Eye*
	I have an inferiority complex, I suppose. (Judgment: *You are inferior.*)
I'm going to start crying. I don't know why I do this, every time, I start crying.	
	It's the idea of having been divorced twice. It bothers me something terribly and I don't know . . . I think it's just because I was raised . . . you know, you marry and you live happily ever after. A lot of my friends have been divorced once and that seems more acceptable than the fact of making the mistake twice. I think maybe because when I was growing up I always felt divorce was wrong and I've always felt that when people got a divorce, it was the woman's fault. (Judgment: *Divorce is wrong; the divorces are your fault: you are responsible for the failures of relationship.*)
But I don't know how it could be the woman's fault. I don't know, that doesn't even make sense now that I look at it. I don't know where I came up with that.	
	But it's probably because she didn't please her husband. You know, whether it's, I have this idea . . . marriage . . . the woman is there to please her husband, just to provide for his

Authentic "I"	*Over-Eye*
	needs, physical, sexual, and whatever else, and if he's not satisfied then that would be reason enough for him not to want to be married. (Judgment: *In order to be loved, you must meet a man's needs.*)
And that's what's so difficult because I feel like I did the best in all the areas I could and it didn't work out.	
	So I feel like I'm a failure. (Judgment: *You met men's needs and the relationships still failed; something is wrong with you.*)
I don't know, I can't pinpoint what happened, because I know it wasn't all my fault. I think, "What went wrong?" I don't have any answer for it. Oh, people give me answers, "They were creeps and you shouldn't have married them." But for myself, I don't have answers.	
	That's been a real affliction on my self-esteem and it has been really difficult to build up because I think that if I can't succeed at something that simple, as an everyday thing as marriage, then how can I be successful anywhere else? (Judgment: *You don't know how to keep love while everyone else does; you will never succeed at anything.*)

Authentic "I"

Over-Eye

I want to accept a lot of the new ideas, new thoughts that I have, but something inside is afraid that they're wrong, afraid of being wrong. Unacceptable. Unacceptable to whom I don't know. That doesn't even make sense. I'm afraid of them not being accepted but there's nobody to worry about, I don't know why I'm concerned about that because that's something I'm choosing within myself and it has no reflection or bearing on anyone else. I don't know why there's such a conflict.

If you please, you're the kind of woman, the kind of wife you should be. And if you don't, then you're not. (Judgment: *You must please in order to be loved/to be good.*)

I know the latter is true, a marriage working if you each have your own degree of freedom and you come together for sharing. It's not realistic and it doesn't work out when marriage is one-sided and it's the woman having to give of herself all the time.

I didn't leave because I thought marriage was binding, for life. That boils down to the idea of divorce, I didn't believe in it. I didn't think it was right. I guess because you say a vow before God. It's just not to be broken.

Authentic "I"	*Over-Eye*
	(Judgment: *Divorce is emotionally, socially, and morally wrong; you are a failure.*)
But that's not even human, but that's it, anyway.	
	They've [marriages] made me feel like I'm unsuccessful. That I've failed. As a wife and a woman, as a person, I guess. They've made me feel like I really don't count, like I'm a no-body, that I can't achieve the goal that I've set out to. That I'm not competent. (Judgment: *If you fail at relationship, you are morally worthless and incompetent.*)
And yet, they have to be just feelings because I know that what I'm feeling I'm not seeing.	

In these arguments of voice, the Over-Eye pronounces what a woman "should" do in relationships, while the authentic self responds with what Maya knows from her first-hand experiences of relatedness. The conflict of these perspectives about attachments, morality, and responsibility creates more than just a clash of ideas. Maya's different perspectives on her relational experience lead her into confusion about what is "reality." Is it what the "I" observes and feels, or is it what she has been taught she *should* think and feel? As Maya's Over-Eye says, "If you please, you're the kind of woman, the kind of wife you should be. And if you don't, then you're not." This voice goes on to conclude that if you don't please, "you're an unsuccessful woman."

But this construction of feminine goodness was lived out in two marriages in which Maya was physically and emotionally abused, and she has come to doubt its accuracy. She says: "everything is dependent upon what a woman *should* do and if my concept isn't clear about what is reality, then that's the reason why I'm so confused." In other words, Maya's view of the relationship's reality depends on her moral construction, which is divided between what she believes is the "right" way to think, based on personal history and cultural dictates, and her personal convictions, arising as she has tried to live out these imperatives in adulthood.

This inner division makes reality-testing almost impossible, since testing reality requires a mind of one's own which can observe and choose to act on those observations. Not knowing what is real, Maya feels paralyzed about what direction to pursue. The dilemma is critical, because the outcome determines the most important issues of her emotional life: how she will relate to others to attain intimacy, and how she will relate to herself, either to understand, forgive, and change, or harshly to condemn her "failures." It also affects the broader arena of relatedness to her culture: whether she accepts prevailing views of "the way things are" about gender, about conventional morality, about self-expression. Ways of relating dictated by the Over-Eye—trying to please—have failed her in two marriages. She doesn't "have any answers" for why her attempts to make intimate connection with others have been unsuccessful. In Maya's dialogue, each feeling has its opposite, leaving her suspended about what she, in fact, does feel, and how she should judge her feelings.

What is the Over-Eye—the conventional, compliant self—saying to her? It is not a superego that is warning: "If you break this rule or that rule, you will be punished." Rather, it insists: "If you want anyone to love you, this is what you have to do." It is an Over-Eye that has a theory of how to make and maintain relationships (and of who is to blame if they fail). This theory of attachment carries not only Maya's developmental history but also the culture's injunctions to women about relatedness, both to their intimate partners and, more broadly, to the extended world of other adults and to the abstract sphere of ideas and knowledge. So standards held by the Over-Eye include both personal constructs that incorporate the moral "shoulds" and idiosyncratic values of the family, and social norms acquired from the culture. If the family standards and cultural norms reflect and magnify each other, a woman will find them difficult to challenge on the basis of her personal observations.

The threatened punishment for disobeying the requirements of the Over-Eye is loss of love within real relationships. Unlike Freud's superego, this inner authority is not roused into action by the possibility of directing aggression against a hallowed figure, or by repressed sexual wishes directed at unacceptable targets. Rather, the Over-Eye is activated in situations where a woman wants to enter into intimate relationships or wants to be included and accepted by others. This inner oppressor continually demands behavior based on the norms and authority of the culture—that is, its shoulds: how to behave in order to be loved, in order to be included within the community of peers. This voice confuses the authentic self and obscures what it knows from personal experience, discounting such experience with the weight of shoulds, collective judgments, and negative self-evaluation.

When relationships are troubled or fail, the voice of the Over-Eye becomes even louder, pointing out how a woman's own shortcomings caused the problems, and blaming her for whatever went wrong. Rather than being undermined because it did not work, the theory of how to secure love held by the Over-Eye can gain in strength at this point, since the convictions of the authentic self carry less authority than those imposed by the culture and personal history.

When we employ the two-voice analysis, it becomes clear that what women lose in depression is not the whole self but only a part of the self: the "I," the authentic, creative self. When problems or distance arise in relationship, the Over-Eye turns as a condemning accuser against the "I," the person responsible for the problems: the no-good, fraudulent, selfish woman whom nobody should love anyway. The Over-Eye, mouthing moral shoulds directed at women, continually assaults the self-esteem and legitimacy of the "I." In this way, the harsh inner authority reflects outer configurations of relationships—a woman's personal history of relationships, her current attachments, and the larger social hierarchy of gender. Since we know that the relational self is socially constructed, it is not surprising that a woman's inner world reflects power relationships based on gender.

For example, Jan, who has been married two years, turns against herself as she talks about the problems in her marriage. Despite her awareness of her husband's earlier hospitalization for an acute psychotic episode, she blames herself for the difficulties in the relationship. Presenting her "thoughts of despair" which "make things worse for me," she switches back and forth from the third-person, blaming voice of the Over-Eye to the active voice of the authentic self. Jan responds this way to the question "What has tended to make it (depression) worse for you?"

> I guess thinking thoughts of despair. Like, you know, this marriage isn't going to work out. You're doing everything you can; you're no good. Even though I can objectively say, okay, I am above average in looks, I have been very successful with my art, I used to sing, I was very successful at singing. I'm gregarious, I make friends easily. I can say all that, and still there is this, you are no good, what's the use.

In the interviews with depressed women, the silencing of the "I" corresponds to the loss of self and the despair of depression. This inner dynamic occurs within relationships marked by emotional distance and lack of communication. The ascendance of the first-person voice marks the women's recovery from depression, and corresponds with asserting one's voice within relationship, or with leaving relationships that do not allow such freedom to be authentic.

Maya traces the beginning of her movement out of severe depression by describing, in a literal sense, her recovery of voice:

> One of the first things I learned right after my divorce was that it felt good to get it out. It felt good to cry and

laugh and do all those things that I hadn't done. I remember the first time I laughed out loud and it seemed strange to me to hear my own laughter . . . and then I realized that I never laughed in my marriage. I never let anything out, but then I never felt laughter. I sounded so loud—it was really, really frightening to hear that, to hear the sound, the loudness. It really caught me by surprise because it was so loud, and I must have been so quiet all the time. I talked in a very quiet voice, more than I do now, and you could hardly—nobody heard me and I would have to repeat myself. And that was even more frustrating because I would have to repeat myself all the time.

Through voice, we locate ourselves in the world and can be heard and found. When a woman fears the consequences of voicing her own perspective—whether from an abusive husband, a business that expects her to perform just like men, a classroom that negates her orientation, a culture that has devalued her—then she becomes quiet in order not to draw negating attention.

CULTURAL IMPERATIVES IN THE INNER DIALOGUE

With Maya's and Jan's examples, I have presented the two-voice dialogue in its conventional form. The standards held by the Over-Eye are almost like cartoons of the stereotypic "good woman": please the husband; divorce is wrong. These imperatives seem extreme for women of the 1980s and 1990s. Maya had a masters degree and had taught school. She had been exposed to feminism and new images of intimacy. Yet these fell away when she met her first husband:

I just got really messed up in my thinking. I mean, I thought I was a pretty stable and strong person, and I knew what I wanted out of life, and then when I met him, all the things he started sharing with me, I started thinking, "Well, maybe what I want isn't really right," and then I really got scrambled.

How can contemporary women continue to be held by these dated imperatives? Where do the imperatives come from? What is the source of their power? As we explore their source, it is worth bearing in mind that despite having achieved new freedoms in realms historically reserved for men, women are still held to more traditional standards when they return to the roles of home and hearth. Because norms governing intimacy comingle with fears of loss of love, they are strongly resistant to change. When these ideas are reinforced by men who expect traditional behaviors from their partners, and when they are also conveyed as normal by the culture, they gain power and authority.

The standards used to judge the self can take forms other than that of the conventional good woman. Whatever the form, the outline, most probably, has been drawn by male authority. The Over-Eye's shoulds are not genuine moral strivings, such as altruism or a search for truth, but are derivatives of masculinist culture that embody ideals of "woman" and "successful adult."[3] Not only are women still expected to diminish the self in order to fit into Cinderella's small slipper, they have inherited a new set of cultural shoulds—the requirements of Superwoman. If a woman rebels against conventional femininity by trying to live out her competence and creativity, she can easily step into the demands of the normative masculine role. Superwoman is expected to succeed in the marketplace, where success requires behaviors (such as self-assertion, competition, winning) that are opposed to those expected of women in intimate relationships (interpersonal sensitivity, concern for others' needs). These opposing standards continually work to undermine a woman's sense of adequacy both within and outside of her intimate relationships.

Jennifer, a lawyer interviewed in an earlier study of attorneys' moral reasoning (Jack and Jack, 1989), describes the division of self that occurs when women are called on to meet conflicting sets of shoulds in their work and in their intimate relationships.[4]

> People are mean to you a lot. I hate it . . . A lot of times I'll have a bad day, with a number of different people calling up and yelling at me about various things. And I try to put on a persona that makes it appear to them that it's water off a duck's back. And as I grow in the profession, my skin gets thicker, and it increasingly is water off a duck's back. In terms of doing the job and surviving emotionally, it's essential. I remember, when I was first starting out after law school, it was my first phone call . . . and a secretary was really mean to me, and I got off the phone and cried because she'd been mean to me—you know, very calmly walked to the door of my office, closed the door, sat down and cried, wiped my eyes, and kept going. You can't do that every time somebody's mean to you. You know, you need to develop defenses so that those things go away. But as you do, that carries over into the part of me that's not a lawyer.

Explaining that "Being a lawyer makes you real good at things like arguing and cross-examining, which are not especially positive elements to bring into a relationship," Jennifer lays out some of the complexities involved in fulfilling the superwoman role. While she values the opposing qualities associated with being a lawyer and being a woman, the contradictions between her private and public lives work to make her feel compromised in each.

For many women, standards held by the Over-Eye include two sets that appear fundamentally opposed: those directing behavior in intimate relationships and those guiding goals and behavior in the realm of achievement. Seen in a different light, these conflicting standards are essentially the same. Both exist as male definitions of a female self. Both deny the creative possibilities of a relational self, and together, they create a con-

tradiction between adulthood, defined by the culture as achievement and independence, and femininity, defined as interpersonal sensitivity and emotional dependence. Ready-made by
patriarchy, both are available to put on as forms of existence, and
are donned either by complicity or by co-optation: "In complicity
women embody patriarchal definitions of the feminine self; in
co-optation women embody patriarchal definitions of the normative self (i.e., man's). Both produce 'male-identified' women,
but in the first instance through complementarity, in the second
through imitation" (Keller, 1986, p. 16).

Current definitions of the female self limit our conceptions of
love and creativity, and cramp the transcendent possibilities of
imagining new forms for their expression. Adrienne Rich en-
countered the tensions in male definitions of the female self
during her years of being a wife and mother. Loving and caring
for her husband and children coincided with a felt loss of her
creative poet's voice:

> The choice still seemed to be between "love"—womanly, ma-
> ternal love, altruistic love—a love defined and ruled by the
> weight of an entire culture; and egotism—a force directed by
> men into creation, achievement, ambition, often at the ex-
> pense of others, but justifiably so. For weren't they men, and
> wasn't that their destiny as womanly, selfless love was ours?
> We know now that the alternatives are false ones—that the
> word "love" is itself in need of re-vision.   (1979, pp. 46–47)

The false dichotomy held within patriarchal definitions of feminine love and masculine creativity—either sacrifice the self or
sacrifice the other—works to keep women trapped within its
confines. If the alternatives are hurting the self or hurting the
other, surely women will choose the first, in order to escape condemnation by themselves and others as monsters—cruel, cold,
calculating, unnurturing, ambitious, "animus driven" furies.
Or, women will choose not to engage in certain relationships,
fearing that the demands of love and caretaking will require the
sacrifice of an authentic, continually developing self.

Depressed women's thought reflects this either/or image of self in relationship: subordination (relationship) or authenticity (isolation). Either sacrifice the self's own needs and feelings to stay in relationship (subordinate the self) or act on one's own needs and feelings and be isolated (lose relationship). This structure of thought about the self in relation does not allow a person to integrate self and other—to hold the self's and the other's needs in view at the same time. When a woman is living out the "selfless" side of the equation, her depression appears to be the dependent type: she focuses on the important other, fears the loss of the relationship, but experiences a loss of self. When she rebels against the image of feminine goodness in order to develop herself, her depression often looks hostile, angry, and defiant. She fears a loss of self if she steps into traditional roles. Gloria Steinem used this contrast of self-development with nurturing others (leading to entrapment) when she described her choice not to get married and have a baby: "I either gave birth to someone else, or I gave birth to myself" (1988, p. 88). Within current images of intimate relationship, women find it difficult to integrate self-development with caring for others.

In the narratives of depressed women, the standards by which they judge themselves to be failures most often stem from both of these images: the conventional good woman and the achieving superwoman. The superwoman image translates the human desire for creative self-expression into career success and a mystique of "professionalism," including impossible standards of appearance (slim, fit, fashionable) and behavioral qualities (coolly competent, confident, in charge, slightly detached, going places).

The deep motivation to maintain connection but also to develop the self combines with cultural definitions of femininity and masculine autonomy to trap a woman within confining limitations. Thwarting both her relational possibilities and her creative authenticity, such definitions of masculinity and femininity are part of the cultural factors that contribute to her vulnerability to depression, the loss of self within relationship.

THE DEVELOPMENT OF THE OVER-EYE

I have argued that these standards for how to make and maintain intimacy and for how to be "good" are carried in the Over-Eye. The imperatives of the Over-Eye are not authentic moral strivings, but are aspects of roles defined by a patriarchal culture. However, the imperatives are not experienced as deriving from roles. Instead, they feel like part of the self, a voice that tells a woman to act in certain ways in order to gain approval from others, from the culture, and from herself. As well as these explicit standards, visible in a depressed woman's self-reproaches, the Over-Eye contains diffuse images of relatedness—of how one *should* be or behave in order to be loved. How do these standards and images come to be organized in the Over-Eye, how are they tied to identification with the mother, to gender, and to culture? How are they related to women's notorious "dependence" and lack of ego boundaries?

First, as the feminine relational self is a product of development, so are the moral themes that appear in the voice of the Over-Eye. From the early matrix of the mother-child relationship, the growing girl's sense of self-in-relation is profoundly influenced by identification and interaction with her mother. Ideally, when connection to the mother has been positive, women's relational capacities are characterized by empathy, sensitivity, and responsiveness. But regardless of the *quality* of that mother-daughter relationship, it is governed by different norms and interactions than those a woman encounters as she steps into heterosexual relationships.

Though Freud located superego formation in the oedipal period, later psychoanalytic theorists (Blatt, 1974; Jacobson, 1971) suggest that the core of the superego originates much earlier, and thus is subject to influences of the pre-oedipal period: a lack of differentiation between outer and inner, between self and mother, a generalized sense of relatedness and connection. These earlier aspects of the mother-child relationship are more repressed in men, who replace early dependence and attachment to the mother with an identification with maleness, based on separation.[5] In addition, a boy internalizes the moral values and cultural prerogatives which derive from that male identification. Thus the father's (not only the personal father, but the more generalized cultural Father, including God the Father) morality supplants the mother's in male development, while girls' moral values and sense of prerogative remain primarily derived from identification with the mother—or the more generalized Mother, culturally devalued and stripped of mythic power. Since women do not "distance from their origins" in the same way as men, their morality (as well as their ego capacities and orientations) arises from an earlier period and continues to bear the strong imprint of early attachment with the mother, whose image was diffuse, unstructured, and undifferentiated.

Second, daughters observe and internalize the ways their mothers interact, both with them and with others, including husbands and other men. Most daughters notice *differences* between the way a mother acts in relation to the male world—of particular men, of ideas, of professions—and the way she acts in the female world of friends, children, and women's groups. If the mother and father have an unequal relationship, the daughter begins to see that her mother usually defers to her father's needs. Through specific behaviors such as these, a mother instructs her daughter in the ways of living in the Fathers' world and gaining approval and love: males are more powerful, please them, put their needs first, adopt their values. These patterns of relating, these rules for how a woman "should" behave in relation to the male world, take on moral value and become part of the standards held by the Over-Eye. In this way, girls learn images and ways of relating to men that differ from their primary experience of intimacy with their mother but that grow out of identification with her. As this feminine identification with the mother and her values continues, the growing girl experiences how maternal authority is overruled and replaced by paternal authority, both literally and metaphorically. Female authority teaches her by feeling, word, and example how to relate to male authority.

Because many of these images and feelings about how to

relate to men come from early experiences and are tied, through identification, to the mother's actions in relationship, they are diffuse and unarticulated, and thus difficult to battle consciously and rationally. By the time a girl is old enough to recognize her mother's mode of interaction with men and say "That's not for me," it has already been internalized at a deep level and is resistant to change. Though children seem to reject disliked aspects of their parents as often as they follow them, these elements of how to be a female self in relationship run deep. By the time she consciously notices them, a girl has already imitated them long enough that they have become part of her identity, hard to break and hard to replace because of their tie with critical issues of approval, love, and feminine identity.

In adulthood, a woman is particularly vulnerable to depression if she equates caring for others with self-sacrifice. From what Gilligan (1982) has called the conventional perspective, goodness is understood as conformity to social norms and values, as fulfilling the obligations and functions of the roles one occupies: wife/mother/daughter/woman. At the conventional stage of development, the imperatives attached to the traditional female role converge with the woman's early-formed value on caring and responsibility. The cultural definition of feminine goodness as selfless giving in relationship moves in to restrict and to channel the authentic wish to love and care, and provides a stereotypic conception of the way to do it. This image of goodness as selfless love joins with the deep desire to make and maintain relationships to create a powerful obstacle to self-expression and recognition of anger. In tandem with social conditions that limit women's self-concept and expression, and with stereotypic prescriptions for female behavior, this ideal of goodness renders women particularly vulnerable to loss of self in heterosexual relationship.

Depressed women describe how they were taught throughout childhood to anticipate and react to male needs and how they, in turn, prepare their own daughters for similar interpersonal patterns. For example, Susan discusses her daughter, Jane, now 8:

A lot of times when he's [her husband] gone, we're all relaxed and happy, we're harmonious, things are so nice.
He'll drive up in the driveway and I see Jane start looking
around the house thinking, "Now what can we do to
make sure that Daddy does not get set off. Is the room
picked up, what are we going to have for dinner tonight
Mommy, is dinner ready?" I mean, I really am picking up
some things like that from her that I'm really concerned
about.

Jane has already learned to see her interpersonal context through
the father's eyes. Though she and her mother are "relaxed and
happy," Jane has learned that her father will not evaluate the
domestic scene in the same way. Though maternal authority is
present—Jane has her mother's approval, things are harmonious—the paternal world inserts a different authority. Jane has
already learned to become a housekeeper of the man's feelings,
has learned that her role is to pacify the male, to make things nice
for him, to protect him from the disruption of daily life. In her
concern that things be right for her father to avoid argument,
Jane is already enacting her mother's role and submissive position. When mother authority defers to father authority, a mother
hands her daughter over to the patriarchy without teaching her
how to resist. Such early learnings make it difficult for women, in
adulthood, to bring their own needs and feelings, their *agency*,
into heterosexual relationships.

Susan elaborates about her daughter's response:

She's already the kind of a child that wants to please.
She's like how I was when I was little, doesn't want to
rock the boat, always wants peace and so when there are
arguments, she hates arguments, she hates any raising
of voices, so when Harry says something harmful to me
or hurtful to me, she wants me to just stay quiet. She just
wants me to stay quiet. She feels that that's what I should
do. She's only seeing that when we're arguing its probably Mom's fault because she said something that really
got to Daddy and made him mad.

Beyond learning to be reactive, this daughter has clearly internalized the belief that the man's needs come first, and that the woman's needs and reality are not as important. Also, she has already learned the pattern of self-silencing to avoid the threat of disharmony.

Eleven of the twelve depressed women interviewed in the longitudinal study described their mothers as the submissive ones in clearly dominant/submissive relationships with the husbands. This pattern of personal history has also been found by others (Arieti and Bemporad, 1978; Slipp, 1976). Arieti and Bemporad report that "for most but not all mild depressives the father rather than the mother was the dominant parent"; the mother is described as "loving though weak and submissive" (1978, pp. 183–184).

Children whose parents have a dominant/submissive relationship will observe the mother's powerlessness in relation to the father. Daughters have to make sense of seeing their own mothers and most other women in unequal relationships and have to learn to value their own gender while seeing it devalued culturally and within their own families. As children, these depressed women observed inequality in their parents' relationship: inequality in the intimate bond between man and woman, where the wider social attitudes about the role and importance of women are personalized to *this* woman in relation to this man. Accordingly, these women incorporated an understanding of inequality into their views of relatedness, how one resolves conflict, what it means to give and care for another person, and one's own worth and importance. As girls, they learned to associate giving to others with *subservience* to others, so that giving and caring for others carried the implicit arrangement of putting others first and discounting the needs of the self. This early experience then joins with the cultural view of women as subordinate. The perception of such a hierarchy of needs disappears from conscious awareness—it seems simply to be part of the way things are.

Reinforcing the understanding of subservient giving, mothers frequently turn to their own daughters for nurturing, validation, and support. This forces a daughter to deny her own emotional needs as she cares for her mother. Learning to feel responsible for others' moods comes early from this mother-daughter role reversal; the girl may feel that her mother's depression or general unhappiness results from her failure to care well enough for the mother. Empathy does not always lead to empowerment; a girl's ability intuitively to know and respond to her mother's feelings makes her vulnerable to taking on those feelings.

A number of the depressed women described taking care of their mothers and, in the process, learning to ignore themselves. Linda, age 33, who has been severely battered in her five-year marriage, says,

> My father was cold emotionally and couldn't give anything to us. My mom was giving and caring for other people, but not to us children. I had to take care of my mother. She divorced my dad when I was five, and that's when I really had to start taking care of her. I would comfort her when she cried, and try to help out in any way.

Marcia Westkott describes the feminine nurturing imperative as "manifested in the role reversal between mother and daughter, in which the undernurtured mother looks to her own daughter for reinforcement, care, and validation; and in the father-daughter role reversal, in which expectations for emotional validation and sexualizing aggression—expressed in the extreme in incest—secures unconditional access to the powerless but giving daughter" (1986, p. 139).

If a girl learns that others' needs come first, then the unspoken (and perhaps unconscious) corollary is: "My needs are less important than those of others and they will never be met, or will be met reciprocally only as I care for others." This childhood learning, passed on through identification between mother and daughter, in tandem with a social structure in which women hold a lesser position, lays the basis for pervasively low self-esteem as well as for repressed anger over unmet needs. Depressed women describe a sense of self-diminution that results from seeing themselves as less important than others in their relationships. Investing a large amount of self into their intimate relationships, they feel a gradual "loss of self" as they continually compromise the expression of their feelings and needs, and as they evaluate themselves as unable to attain intimacy.

A personal history of maternal submissiveness and paternal dominance leads to an Over-Eye that has a theory of attachment based on the authority of the Father world, on what a woman must do to please men and to connect with them. Many psychoanalysts have remarked on women's tendency to adopt the values of their mates, and have interpreted this as evidence of women's weaker superegos. Edith Jacobson, for example, described "the female tendency to . . . acquire his [the partner's] superego through her love" (1976, p. 536). Presenting examples of women's weaker superegos, Jacobson described women who changed their values and standards to conform to those of their husbands or lovers. But, as we have seen, the close tie between the developing female morality and a continuing attachment to the pre-oedipal mother leads to a mingling of relational issues with moral issues. It can also make role imperatives such as "put the man first" or "go along with his wishes and interests" become indistinguishable from moral standards. Women have appeared to lack their own standards and to take on the values of their partners precisely because of the content of their own moral beliefs, which direct them to do so. Rather than revealing women's "weaker" superego, women's adoption of their mates' values shows how powerfully the imperatives of the Over-Eye are enforced. It takes tremendous activity and strength to enforce such self-denying directives. In describing women's weaker superegos, drive theorists did not observe the content of superego imperatives (Bernstein, 1983), nor the activity required to be compliant to the feminine role, part of which is to acquiesce to the standards and values of her mate.

Maya makes very clear how such a theory of attachment held

by the Over-Eye led her to compliance with her husband's values and attitudes. The foundation for the abdication of her own values was laid early in childhood:

> I have a sister who is two years younger. We're really close. There's a lot of love in my family, we did a lot of activities and lots of vacations together, and it was stressed to both my sister and I that to maintain a family, unity in the family was really important and that the other people needed to be considered, even above ourselves.

Throughout her childhood, the picture of relatedness presented to Maya by her parents was distorted by her mother's need to avoid conflict, even the appearance of conflict, in her marriage. Recounting how when she was growing up, she "saw a mom and dad very happily married, never any arguments and they never fought," Maya remembers her mother saying many times about her marriage, "We don't argue and we never have." Maya learned that disagreements were somehow forbidden and dangerous to relationships. To agree with her mother's statements, she had to deny her own perceptions of differences, disagreements, or "cold wars" between her parents. This early training in seeing the world through others' eyes, in accepting ideas which fit the stereotypes of the way things "should" be in relationship, taught Maya to mistrust her own perceptions of emotional reality. Maya describes the impact of her learning about disagreements:

> If I had known, if I had seen them argue or get upset with one another—I mean really upset, then I would have been able to stand up for more in my marriages. I would have known it would have been okay to have a disagreement or to argue at some point. But I always heard them say it was going smoothly, perhaps that's a real rose-colored view of life. I find it hard to believe now that I didn't see that that wasn't real. Then I don't think that

my first marriage would have lasted very long. It would have changed my entire future if I had stood up for what I really felt I believed in.

As a child, Maya deeply internalized what she learned from her mother about how to relate to a husband. These images formed part of her feminine identity—how to be a woman in relationship to a man.

Most of my feelings about what a woman is are tied directly into a man. A woman isn't anything by herself. That's interesting. So the only comparison I can draw is a woman is what she is to her husband—kind and gentle and sweet and understanding, and a good listener and a companion. I guess it is idealistic because I know that no woman is like that in all its entirety. So I suppose it's an idealistic view, it isn't a reality.

After marriage, these childhood learnings about avoiding disagreements and putting others first to ensure harmony were reinforced by Maya's husband, who expected deference to his needs and wishes. When asked, "Did you believe all women were like that?" Maya replies:

Yes, being submissive. Yes, I thought all women were like that. I never thought couples ever fought with each other or disagreed. That was my view of marriage, and then when I got married I found that in order to maintain that I had to be quiet and not say anything to avoid arguments. And that's when I started stepping back into that real submissive role and losing, and not being able to speak out.

This silencing of herself within her marriages, denying her own perceptions,

led me to a place of being a nobody. As far as a person, I lost my identity, and my will and my desire even to live.

It just didn't matter one way or the other, I didn't care. I didn't care what we did or what we didn't do. I didn't have any strong feelings one way or the other, I really didn't have feelings anymore. I just became numb to it.

Maya's cognitive schemas representing critical aspects of her identity—woman, self-in-relation, goodness—led her to inhibit herself to the point of psychic numbing. The idea that she should be one with her husband meant that she should not disagree with him: difference highlights the fact that there are two separate people in the relationship. According to her either/or vision of self in intimate relationships, she had only two choices: subordination or isolation. Maya said she "felt that if I stood up and argued a point, they would leave me, and then where would I be?" The requirement not to disagree led her "to a place of being a nobody," a feeling of disappearing into invisibility. In this hollow of self-negation and silence, Maya lost her desire to live.

In addition, Maya's husband brought the authority of the church into the marriage to reinforce his dominance:

It is that thought that my husband started our marriage off with, he played on that because he flipped open the Bible on our honeymoon, and I was getting tired and I didn't want to do something he wanted, and he flipped it open and he said, "It says right here that a woman is to be submissive to her husband. If you don't believe that, then you're not a Christian woman and you are not a good wife. I want you to sit here and read it while I go out." He left and so I read it. And, I said, "Yeah it does say that. Well, maybe my thinking is wrong, maybe I'm supposed to do that." And that's just what I did.

Against the agreement among such authorities as her early childhood teachings, the Bible, and her new husband, Maya judged her own thinking and finds it "wrong." Wishing to create an intimate and lasting relationship, Maya consciously and actively gave up her own viewpoint.

Though Maya knew about the mutuality of intimacy from her experiences with her mother and other significant childhood relationships, she was unable to connect with the important men in her life in the same way. Following her primary female model, she began to imitate her mother's subservient position in her own marriage. She willingly took on stereotypic feminine behaviors in an attempt to secure intimacy within inequality. The groundwork for this willingness had been laid in her childhood. Her mother had instructed her in the ways of pleasing the Fathers: a woman molds herself to fit her husband; put others first, above oneself. Out of identification with her mother's mode of relating to men, and out of fear of loss of love, Maya enacted the injunctions of the Over-Eye when she stepped into marriage. The psychological tension of conforming outwardly while critiquing inwardly contained the seeds of self-alienation and conflict.

Rather than showing a lack of ego boundaries or of her own standards, Maya's example shows the activity required to fulfill the imperatives of her Over-Eye. Such directives erode an active self within relationship, and allow a woman to see herself through the eyes of the culture—as weak, dependent, passive. Linda describes the effect on her sense of self this way:

It's like water running over a rock in a river. You can't see the rock change shape, but you know it does. The little remarks, the small put-downs, my fear of standing up for myself because I could lose the relationship—these eroded my sense of self and took away any self-esteem I had.

A woman's beliefs about marriage also strongly affect her willingness to tolerate a situation that is damaging to her. Kim, age 40, married seventeen years, describes a situation in which role imperatives have become indistinguishable from moral standards.

I was brought up with the traditional sorts of values that say that once in a marriage, you stay with it for whatever it brings. And seriously, in the sense of the vow "in sickness or in health," "'til death do us part," and coming to terms with the promise that I made to do that, I saw that as part of my identity of success, of giving all and giving as much as was possible for me to keep the relationship together.

These social beliefs, that marriage is forever and that the woman is responsible for the maintenance of relationship, become translated into moral values, while their achievement feels like part of the goal of feminine adulthood.

Why are these beliefs so resistant to change? Why can't a woman simply see that they are destructive to her and embrace new, less restrictive ones? In addition to their being internalized through identification with the mother, the difficulty arises, as well, from the qualities of moral thought. One characteristic of moral thought is that it cannot be reality-tested in the same way as can objective facts and stereotypes. This indelible quality is rooted in the way moral imperatives impress themselves upon a child's mind, and in their powerful unconscious tie with loyalty to the parents and with images of how to remain safe in relationship. Moral values, attitudes, and judgments are presented to a child as if they are truths beyond question. They are often delivered with more emotion than are simple statements of fact, adding to their power for a young child. Given her level of cognitive and moral development, a child is unable to distinguish "objective truth" from her parents' opinions. Nor does she have any grounds on which to disagree with statements of moral judgment. The child can differ with her mother's statement "These peas taste good" on the basis of her own sensory, personal judgment, and can form her own idiosyncratic taste preferences different from those of her parents. But the statement "You are bad for not liking those peas" cannot be evaluated by a young child on the basis of experience; rather, it carries implicit moral imperatives, "Thou shalt (like those peas)" and/or "Thou shalt not differ from your mother's opinion." A child has no basis for judging the validity of such moral statements with their accompanying imperatives, but has to accept the parents' statement of them in "fact" form as true (Hartmann, 1960). Through this process of internalizing injunctions, including those of the female role, cultural standards become part of the personality, experienced as a part of one's self.

The child not only incorporates statements of moral value and their imperatives in early childhood, but also observes as fact, as "the way things are," the rules that govern her parents' relationship. These "givens" of relationship carry with them moral judgments and values which the child learns along with her ideas of male and female behavior in a marital or intimate relationship. For example, when one parent is not living up to the role expectations of the other, the child will probably hear emotionally laden value statements around the themes of "You should be a better father/mother/husband/provider."

The morality of relatedness the girl internalizes has a critical integrative function in her life. Most important, it integrates the role accorded to women by society with her internal valuing of that role. Thus, the link between the female social role and women's vulnerability to depression lies in a set of moral imperatives that dictate how a woman *should* care for another—that is, how she should relate interpersonally, particularly to the male world. Learned first from the maternal world, care is highly valued as the medium that creates and cements connections to others. Yet, in relation to the male world, care becomes narrowed to a compliant relatedness that excludes significant aspects of the self, and caring becomes a well-marked path leading not to relation and expansion but to loss of self and depression.

The imperatives of feminine goodness, internalized in the Over-Eye, operate as a demanding taskmaster and an inner judge and jury. They require a posture in relationship that is doomed to failure, as well as self-perfection that is impossible to attain—perfect looks, perfect qualities, perfect behavior.[6] Because the dictates of the Over-Eye promise to secure intimacy, a woman can rationalize them as legitimate, positive ways of being in relationship with a man and can overlook fundamental inequities in relationships between the sexes. In this way, the demands of the Over-Eye operate to keep a woman "in her place" both within heterosexual relationship and within the wider society.

In its defensive function, the morality of the "good woman" protects against anxiety: it guides a woman's actions to keep her "safe" from abandonment. Following the dictates of the Over-Eye protects against fear of loss of love, and against the fear that others in the wider social environment will judge her negatively. Thus, deviation from the standards of the Over-Eye feels so frightening to a woman because external and internal imperatives recite in unison the possible consequences—loss of relationship.

The imperatives of the Over-Eye regarding women's goodness in relationships are strengthened by the social reality of women's subordination—the experience of being a target of male violence (including sexual abuse), and the difficulties of financial dependence and poverty. In the world of achievement, conformity to male patterns—dedication to career that excludes a focus on children, norms of competition, detachment, self-promotion—are enforced by clear sanctions if one does not follow the established path.

MEASURING BELIEFS ABOUT INTIMACY

Depressed women's images of self, role, and morality create a characteristic model of goodness which directs their behavior in relationships. These underlying beliefs about how to connect intimately with others lead a woman to subordinate her own needs to those of her partner and to believe that acting to get her own needs met is selfish and/or will disrupt relationship. These beliefs about how to make and maintain intimacy lead women to socially supported self-negating behaviors and feelings that erode both their relationships and their sense of self. These core images of relatedness, when activated, are *prior to* and *create* in women what Aaron Beck (1970) describes as the characteristic pattern of thoughts central to depression—a negative view of self, the past, and the future.

The importance of cognitive schemas (patterns of thought by

which a person organizes and interprets experience) to clinical depression has been clearly demonstrated by Beck's extensive work. Assuming that cognitive, neurochemical, and affective systems are interrelated, Beck argues that "certain cognitive patterns (schemas) become activated and prepotent in depression and structure the kinds of interpretations [of experience] that are made by the patient. These negative interpretations, consequently, cast their shadow on the patient's mood and motivation" (1984, p. 1113).

The findings of the exploratory, long-term study of depressed women described in this book provide support for the hypothesis that a certain pattern of beliefs about how women "should" act in relationships in order to secure intimacy is associated with female depression.[7] To allow for more systematic study of how this pattern of beliefs correlates with depression in women, I constructed the Silencing the Self Scale or SSS (see Appendix B). Sentences in the scale present the specific images of the self in intimate heterosexual relationships that I heard most often in the narratives of depressed women. Respondents agree or disagree on a five-point scale with thirty-one sentences that carry underlying moral standards. For example, Item 3, "Caring means putting the other person's needs in front of my own," includes an imperative of the traditional female role, a belief about how one should behave in intimate relationships, and a standard used to judge the self. The scale has acceptable psychometric properties, reliability, and predictive validity (reported in Jack and Dill, in press).

In order to allow for continuing research concerning the standards depressed individuals use to judge the self, Item 31 of the SSS asks the person to agree or disagree with the statement "I never seem to measure up to the standards I set for myself." For those who answer that they agree or strongly agree, the questionnaire then instructs, "Please list up to three of the standards you feel you don't measure up to." Space is provided for people to write answers in their own words. Examples of standards depressed women use to judge the self have been collected from three diverse populations—63 college women (and a comparison male sample of 38), 140 residents of battered women's shelters, and approximately 175 new mothers who used cocaine during pregnancy. At the same time, the Beck Depression Inventory (Beck et al., 1961), was used to measure the level of depression.[8]

The standards people feel they don't live up to (as reflected by their responses, formulated in their own words) reveal the imperatives of the culture. Women and men list different standards, but the imperatives sound remarkably the same when they come from women, even women in very different stages of life, socioeconomic groups, and types of relationships.

Residents of battered women's shelters endorse the conventional "good woman" standards at a significantly higher level than the college student women. Battered women's agreement with these imperatives seems poignant when we consider that such moral beliefs constitute one of the factors that lead women to stay in hurtful relationships. Part of the trap of such beliefs stems from the interlocking, multifaceted nature of the imperatives: they include a *vision* of self in relationship, they guide *behavior* within it, they direct self-blaming *judgment* toward the self, they incite *anger* but demand its repression, and they directly affect *self-esteem.*

For example, if a woman believes that "Considering my needs to be as important as those of the people I love is selfish" (Item 4), then that standard directs her vision of the hierarchy of needs within relationship; it directs behavior by dictating how she should choose when her needs conflict with those of others she loves; it provides a standard for harsh self-judgment if she veers from its command. Further, it arouses anger as, following its dictates, she places her needs second to those of others; yet it also commands the repression of anger by purporting a moral basis for the suppression of her own needs. It reinforces a woman's low self-esteem by affirming that she is not as worthy or important as others, and, finally, it legitimizes the historical and still prevalent view of woman's nature as essentially self-sacrificing and maternal.

Thus, in the group of battered women, when a husband uses

force and/or emotional cruelty, women blame themselves for not loving enough, or in the right ways. Anger becomes a club that is used against the self, and further entraps a woman in a damaging relationship and in debilitating depression. For example, Subject #7007, age 51, with eighteen years of education, has two teenage children at home and is raising two preschool grandsons. This woman has extremely high scores on both the depression measure and the Silencing the Self Scale.[9] She lists incidents of all three types of abuse: psychological (including threats, humiliation, and isolation), physical (beating, slap, punch), and sexual. Yet, in response to Item 31 (which asks respondents to list, in their own words, standards they fail to meet), this woman states standards of perfection that keep her attention focused on her own failure rather than on an accurate perception of what is happening in the relationship:

> I can never get everything done; I can't seem to keep the peace between family members so that all are happy; I consistently fail to achieve my own goals: weight loss, appearance, business activities, recreation desires, needs, etc.

Likewise scoring high on both measures,[10] Subject #1002, age 26, with two children, writes:

> I'm not able to keep up with two kids, a house, and a husband with special problems, and daily tasks as well as I feel I should be able to. I'm not able to deal with my husband's disability in the sense of helping him deal with it, and I don't make myself look my best.

On the abuse history form, this woman listed incidents of psychological and sexual abuse in her current, nine-year marriage.

Finally, evidence of the hopelessness of depression appears in women who have given up on themselves. Subject #6040, age 26, with thirteen years of education and one child: "I've quit setting standards because I feel like nothing." Subject #6028, age

38, with twelve years of education and two children: "No self-confidence, can't keep a job, I feel like a lost cause."

Fifty-four percent (75 of 140) of the battered women's sample agreed with Item 31, "I never seem to measure up to the standards I set for myself," and listed their own standards. The following categories encompass the range of standards they listed: wife/partner, personal appearance/weight, mother/homemaker, employment/finances, personal characteristics, self-esteem/self-assertion, and education. For example, eleven women listed standards that fit the category wife/partner, such as "perfect wife," "loving him, making him happy," "being a good wife," "being a better wife," "making my relationship work," "trying to please my husband," "being married three times."[11] Fifteen women listed failure to live up to standards for personal appearance, such as "poor looking," "I don't feel pretty enough," "be slim, healthy, and 'put together,' " "not able to be beautiful and slim," "don't have slim figure, shiny hair, manicured nails," "overweight," "fat and ugly," "gained weight, eat whatever." Under employment/finances, twenty-eight women listed standards for financial independence and meeting career goals such as "can't earn acceptable salary," "want to be financially stable," "choosing what I want as a career," "don't think I could ever support myself and my children," "can't get better-paying job," "can't make my check last," "I don't make enough money," and more of very similar statements.

The superwoman image appears when women endorse conventional standards for the "good woman" and then also list demands for filling career or work goals.[12] Subject #8009: "I should be able to work an eight-hour job and still be a great Mom." Subject #9002: "Have trouble keeping a job and dealing with family problems/housework/being wife and mother. Not enough energy."

Among cocaine-abusing mothers, a group who are currently under intense public scrutiny and condemnation, the standards sound similar to those battered women use. Most of the standards center on parenting, relationships with partner or husband, personal appearance, drug use, and on improving the self through education and employment. For example, Subject #4853: "I set too high of daily goals, I don't commend myself for what I do accomplish, I set others' goals and let myself down when they don't meet my expectation." Subject #4236: "I try to do things just so and it always fails." Subject #3110: "Being consistent as a mother; giving friendship to others, doing the things that I want to in life." Subject #2738: "Being more under-standing of my older children; being the best mom and wife I can; opinion of myself is low and has been for a long time; fat, ugly, etc. But not having the willpower to do anything about it!" Subject #4142: "Should look better, should be able to do more, want to give more of myself." Subject #2901: "To always be there for my son and husband; to work and take care of my son (giving 100% to everything all the time)." Subject #4120: "Not able to keep up my house and other family needs as well as would like to; lost a lot of energy that I would like to use being a more assertive wife and companion to my husband; wish I could have patience with *all* my children." Subject #3498: "Consistency—in housework, childraising; also there are things I want to do like artwork. I'll get started but usually don't finish. I'm discouraged before I get started."

These standards, sounding so similar across different groups of women, channel massive amounts of feminine energy and desire toward illusory goals. They divert women from seeing and accurately naming the impediments to their development and lead them to stay in negating relationships by making them believe the fault lies within themselves. Striving for perfection by trying to fulfill such standards is a quest doomed to failure and frustration. These standards also divert women from reach-ing the goals of their search: intimate connection and authentic self-development. Women strive for connection, but the *forms* of connection lead to self-defeat and low self-esteem. These forms are supplied by the culture and appear to promise love; yet enacting them leads to the loss of an active, authentic self.

The moral themes in depressed women's narratives reveal internal impediments that prevent women from claiming the authority of their first-person, authentic voices. It is difficult for women to know and to speak what they feel, think, and perceive when to do so challenges a tradition of male authority and female silence. Yearning for connection, a woman adopts the forms of relating she learned from her mother, from her father, and from culture, and ends up self-alienated and paralyzed. Mother authority, with its mythic, powerful connection to creation and life, teaches the daughter to defer to Father authority, with its emphasis on rules, hierarchy, and obedience. In so doing, the maternal world hopes to prepare daughters to live safely and to find love in the paternal world. If a woman tries to defy such authorities, lodged in the Over-Eye, she is assaulted from within by harsh self-condemnation, while she faces the external possibility of rejection or physical assault from males simply because she is female. These inner and outer restraints operate as invisible bonds, restricting a woman's freedom to be an active, responsible self within relationship. As women with the potential for raising daughters and sons, we must ask ourselves and our partners, "Into whose hands are we to deliver our children, who are we training them to obey, and for whose benefit?" (Rich, 1979, p. 218). Mothers fear their daughters will meet with rejection, isolation, and danger if they stray too far outside social norms that govern gender interactions. Trying to save their daughters from a certain kind of pain and loss, mothers unknowingly teach them a way of relating to the male world that leads to a different form of loss.

SILENCING
THE SELF

. 5 .

We're doing everything he wants to do and I'm not
getting nothing done that I want to do, but I won't open
my mouth and say something. I'm keeping it in my mind
and drilling, and letting it drill on my brain, you know.

Depression disturbs a person's most fundamental experience
of self. Not only does it negatively affect thought, feeling,
appetite, and sleep; depression robs one of a sense of meaning
and purpose. In a major depression, a veil of numbness settles
over the self to form an invisible shroud that separates one from
others. Ashamed of the authentic self and condemning its past
actions and future prospects, depressed women withdraw from
social contact. They speak of having "given up"; either they have
no energy or they feel a despairing anxiety that drives an aimless
restlessness.

In depression, the active, creative, spontaneous self is effec-
tively silenced. We have already heard snatches of how women
silence themselves in the previous chapter, while listening to the
inner dialogue of depression. Everyone has inner conversations
of one sort or another, and almost everyone hears a moral voice
chastising, praising, or cajoling certain thoughts, actions, or
feelings. What distinguishes the inner dialogues of depressed

women is not only an incessantly judgmental tone but also the ease and power with which the Over-Eye silences a woman's self-expression, vitality, and perspectives—her very self.

In this chapter, I explore in more detail how self-silencing relates to moral themes, to identification with the mother, and to the anger and hopelessness of depression. The invisibility of actions required to silence oneself helps explain why women's outward compliance and seeming passivity have been systematically misinterpreted as dependency and masochism. Depressed women's statements such as "I have learned 'don't rock the boat' with my partner" and "I won't cause waves, I won't say anything" show their conscious awareness of making themselves "look" passive for an intended effect: to keep outer harmony, to preserve relationship. These efforts to keep harmony make the women appear outwardly weak-willed and dependent; yet inwardly, a different dynamic unfolds. Listening closely, we notice the tremendous cognitive activity required to maintain this outward presentation of self. We can begin to hear, in George Eliot's phrase, the "roar which lies on the other side of silence" in depression, a roar full of anger and despair which a woman feels she must control because of its destructive possibilities.[1]

THE ACTIVITY REQUIRED TO BE PASSIVE

Self-silencing appears in women's narratives when they try to change their thoughts and when they tell themselves how they "ought" to feel. For example, Cathy voices some forbidden feelings in the interview and then reveals how she controls her thinking:

> Like for a while, I was just down on all men, they're all no good. And sometimes I still catch myself thinking that, you know, generalizing and saying to myself that, well, you know, a wife gives of herself a lot more than a man. And that's probably not true, but I catch myself reliving old hurts. And the more I think about them, the

worse they get. So I just force myself to quit thinking
about them. Because I know it's not going to do me any
good, let alone anybody else.

Considering the consequences of taking her feelings seriously, Cathy evaluates their impact on others along with or
ahead of their impact on herself. She concludes that since no
"good" will result from either feeling or communicating the
thoughts that cause her pain, the solution is to prohibit them,
since "the more I think about them, the worse they get." Forcing
herself to stop thinking is the method she uses over and over to
accomplish the major self-inhibition required to remain adjusted
to the marriage.[2]

In rendering themselves "passive" in this way, women are
not complying blindly or inconsistently. In fact, we see specific acts of perception and discrimination occur as women
decide what thoughts they need to censor. Desiring to keep
relationship, they take the cognitive actions required to adapt
themselves to existing structures. Rather than outwardly challenge the forms of their relationships, they take this inward
action against themselves. Cathy, for example, perceives exactly what thoughts are dangerous and need to be eliminated.
She inhibits a type of reflection—"I catch myself reliving old
hurts"—through which she could examine the situations that
have caused the hurts, her own part in creating them, and how
she could change the status quo. This is a type of reflection that,
though painful, could lead her to a different perspective on her
interactions and the meaning she makes of them. She subverts
the whole process by literally stopping herself.

The acts of self-perception through which women curb their
wills and stop their feelings most often occur from a third-person
perspective. This Over-Eye viewpoint most often aligns with the
dominant competitive, materialistic values of the culture, increasing its authority. Evaluating the self from this vantage point
challenges the women's private opinions, based on different
values. Susan, deeply dissatisfied with her seven-year marriage,
says of her negative feelings toward her husband:

I bury them. I've always buried them. You know, because I guess I look at my life from what, how other
people see it. I look at my life from how my neighbors
see me. From how—I think to myself, boy, they must be
so envious of me. I mean, I've got so much financial
freedom, I get to travel with Harry, I get to, you know, if I
want to go visit my mother, I have the means to buy a
plane ticket.

How can you be unhappy is what I guess I keep telling
my—have told myself, and I have buried my frustrations
and my angers and my other things, because I have felt
that Harry gives me so much in that area that that should
be enough to carry over and fulfill all my needs.

The burial of her authentic self is accomplished by acts of self-
perception through the Over-Eye, with its collective vision: "I
look at my life from how my neighbors see me." Its third-person
voice says she has no right to negative emotions or problems
because of her privileged socioeconomic status. Through such
inner division, Susan relates to herself as an object, directing
hostility against herself for unacceptable feelings and thoughts.

Yet moments later in her narrative, Susan's "I" or authentic
voice argues with the Over-Eye's third-person perspective, presenting an alternate scheme of values:

I didn't grow up that way, I've never valued material
possessions. I've never tried to pretend that they make
me happy, although since I've been married, and like I
just described to you, because my needs were not being
met, I have accepted that as a replacement. I hurt right
now, I ache for closeness. I really ache for closeness with
people that think, that have similar thoughts like I do. I
feel like a lot of my friends, while they're as loyal as loyal
can be, and they really care for me, I don't really feel like
I can truly be myself. I'm just beginning to realize I've got
these needs and no amount of money or material comfort is going to soothe that. It's still going to be there.

In these opposing voices, Susan struggles to define her wants when they vary from what the Over-Eye says she "should" want: those things valued by her husband—money, material possessions, social status, leisure. As the Over-Eye dismisses her feelings, it tells Susan to comply with the scheme of things, to take what she is offered. This perspective carries such authority for Susan for two reasons: it tells her what will make the marriage continue to work, and it aligns with the culture's materialistic values about what should be most important to her. To argue against these values both jeopardizes the relationship and goes against the culture itself. Regarding herself from the Over-Eye's perspective, Susan distances herself from her own feelings, judges them in cultural terms, and can experience them as unacceptable, wrong. She can come to judge her healthy wish for intimacy as weakness, as a sign of immaturity.

What is this penchant for seeing and evaluating oneself from the third-person perspective when one is in moral conflict? George Herbert Mead, writing about the social nature of the self, describes the internalized presence of the "generalized other" as the form by which "the community exercises control over the conduct of its individual members; for it is in this form that the social processes or community enters as a determining factor into the individual's thinking" (1956, pp. 219–220). The generalized other represents the way a person takes the community's perspective on the self, and stands for a kind of "corporate individual, a plural noun, a composite photograph" which a self composes of the other members of society (Pfuetze, 1961, p. 84). In Mead's terms, "the attitude of the generalized other is the attitude of the whole community," a sort of consensus of values that comes out of a "system of common or social meanings" (1956, pp. 218, 220). Only by taking the position of the generalized other can one understand or evaluate personal conduct in social—that is, moral—terms.

The problem for women enters precisely here. Taking the perspective of the generalized other divides a woman's experience of self in two along lines specific to her gender. One part of the psychic whole identifies with patriarchal values and looks on herself from that internalized male gaze.[3] This is part of what I have called the Over-Eye, which critically regards the woman's feminine, authentic self as an object and discounts its values and worth. The generalized other, representing dominant community values, stands over her with the threat of censure if she dares to challenge what her partner, the church, the institution, or the patriarchy thinks is "right." The threat of censure empowers the self-censor, who, gazing through the lens of the generalized other, perceives what may disrupt relationships and silences it. Because the collective "other" has the power to enforce its dominant vision, a woman finds it difficult to defy the authority and judgments of the Over-Eye and easily slips into seeing herself from its perspective. The internalized male gaze, like a cataract over clear vision, occludes a woman's ability to see for herself and silences her willingness to speak from her own perspective.

Examples of silencing the self run throughout depressed women's narratives, most often in relationship to a male partner. A man can come to embody collective social judgments to a woman, either because he manifests them in his behavior and demands, or because she projects them onto him. Rita, age 19, was referred from the community mental health clinic for depression. She had also been a multiple substance abuser for two years. Rita describes how her partner looks at her, a look that channels the judgments of the culture through one pair of eyes.

Bill had the terrible habit of giving me this horrible look that I, which was to me a Mr. Yuk look, when I would— let's say if I was just basically talking about something that was unpleasant or being selfish, or eating too much, he'd just give me this horrible look. I don't know if it was really conscious to him that he was doing it, but it showed me that I was being very unpleasant in his eyes. And because I wanted to impress him, because I wanted him to like me so bad, well because I wanted our relationship to work, it really bothered me. I don't know how to explain it but it really got to me because it wasn't just every once in a while. A lot of the time it was all the time, like, "Yuk, what am I doing with this lady? Get her away from me," this type of a thing. So I got drunk and obnoxious, you know.

It was, I think it was just really hard for him to be around me because I was a very unpleasant person to be around, I was unladylike. I think when I was more heavier he was probably made a lot of fun of by his friends, you know, about my weight and being porky and this and that, because a lot of his friends are, you know, skinny and good-looking guys and they all got beautiful girlfriends and here Bill had this porky fat girl. But I can put my makeup on and have my hair fixed all perfect and be in good clothes and look in a mirror and see that I'm not this big fat ugly cow that guys used to bark and laugh at.

Reining in her unruly, unacceptable self to conform with the judgments contained in "the look," Rita loses weight. Though she used to be "mouthy," "blowing off my cork," and "loud," Rita says that Bill's "Mr. Yuk" look has toned her down, and now she catches herself *before* she says anything.

We're doing everything he wants to do and I'm not getting nothing done that I want to do, but I won't open my mouth and say something. I'm keeping it in my mind and drilling, and letting it drill on my brain, you know.

This powerful, headstrong young woman enters heterosexual intimacy through female rituals expected by the culture—self-silencing, dieting—and enacts them to capture male approval. Instead, these behaviors result in a kind of cultural lobotomy; she (like other women) cuts off part of her physical and emotional self in order to come into conformity with prescriptions about what women "should" be, prescriptions present in the internalized and external male gaze. Women undertake this exacting conformity because they believe it will help them reach their deeper goals: relationship with a particular man and acceptance by the wider (male) world.

We see in Rita's comments the results of internalizing the culture's sexualization and devaluation of women. Marcia West-kott, describing the "onlooker phenomenon," points out that "Critical observation of herself and others may be the way a woman looks at herself being looked at. She becomes the omnis-cient observer of her own sexualization, the voyeur of the voy-eurs of her unintentionally exhibited body. As a spectator she rises above the trivialization that she cannot otherwise avoid" (1986, p. 190).

Identifying with the male gaze is a gender-specific form of what psychoanalytic writers have called "identification with the aggressor," and this phenomenon explains the fundamental ag-gression against the self—the acts of self-alteration and hostile self-judgment—described by depressed women. Further, iden-tifying with the aggressor in the form of directing the hostile, negating male gaze toward oneself allows a defense against the devaluation a woman undergoes as object of the gaze. It gives her an illusory feeling of control, for while she exists as the object of a critical, devaluing look she is simultaneously the powerful spectator, observing and judging herself. She feels in control when she, as object, gains the approval (by losing the weight, wearing the right clothes, acting loving and patient), and when she, as observer, feels satisfied that commands are being fol-lowed.

But the fundamental self-alienation underlying this illusory control contributes to a woman's depression. Westkott describes the alienation that pervades a woman's experience:

> Her alienation from masculine civilization is defined by her visualized presence in it, by being taken as a fetish by others and therefore by herself. The alienation is also defined by her marginality, by the lack of power, influence, or will that is accorded her. She is detached even when she is engaged, because she is the other, the outsider, the intruder. She is of necessity an onlooker even as a participant. Together her expe-rience of standing out and being disregarded, her obtrusive

objectness and her trivialization, form an experience of alienation that informs perceptions and judgments.   (1986, p. 193)

This self-alienation, which runs through depressed wom-
en's narratives, reinforces their willingness to silence themselves. Listen to how Cindy, age 26, referred with the diagnosis
of recurrent major depression with psychotic episodes, hears
herself through the ears of the culture, and how its imagined
judgments cause her to lower her voice:

I don't have a very high image of myself. I—I'm fat. It
seems like the only time I'll put makeup on is when I'm
going out. There's lots of times Matt comes home from
work and I'm just myself with my glasses on and no
makeup and I—I have a loud voice and it really . . . I
think sometimes that if I could hear myself, if I could
kind of be me out of my body and outside, that I could
hear myself right through the walls and what all the
other neighbors would be hearing, you know. So I try to
tone it down.

As Mary Belenky and her colleagues observe, "The continued injunction against articulating needs, feelings and experiences must constrain the development of hearts and minds,
because it is through speaking and listening that we develop our
capacities to talk and to think things through" (Belenky et al.,
1986, p. 167). The requirement that women literally soften their
voices, the negative way they judge themselves as they look at
themselves being looked at by particular men and by the culture—these factors significantly influence their susceptibility to
self-alienation and to depression.

Therese, for example, speaking of her decision to stop saying anything to her husband, describes how he would not listen
to her opinions regarding decisions about the farm they ran
together. While at first she offered ideas and suggestions, his
refusal to listen created frustration and anger, which led to
disagreements and her fear that such differences would dis-

solve the relationship. Trying to maintain a marriage by self-censoring, instead she finds that silence becomes her intimate partner, a silence that forms a wall between her and her husband.

> Finally I got to the point where I thought my opinion was worth nothing . . . and I thought, when this thing or that thing happened, I thought I won't cause waves, I won't say anything. We'd come in to breakfast in the morning and eat in complete silence . . . at night, we'd watch TV in silence . . . there was nothing to talk about. I knew how withdrawn I was and it amazed me that he never felt that. He never sensed that come between us, that wall of noncommunication.

Forcing themselves to stop thinking, judging their own thoughts, and silencing their voices and opinions are methods by which women keep themselves from expressing anger and resentment. Therese's icy silence is not only a form of withdrawal, it also stands as a statement about the condition of her inner world. The Over-Eye, with prohibitions about how one "should" think and feel, casts a chill over the inner world and freezes its vitality. The women silence themselves, not because they are dependent and passive, but because they value relationship. The bitter irony is that in the hope of saving relationship and furthering intimacy, the women eliminate any possibility of real mutuality, intimacy's prerequisite, which requires two selves interacting in dialogue. Paradoxically, methods employed to reduce anger lead instead to its continual arousal, while the Over-Eye sits in judgment and demands its repression.

Depressed women talk about three kinds of fears that lead them to "bite their tongues" and to conceal themselves behind the safety of silence. The apprehensions differ only in degree, and one anxiety feeds the others, since often all are present. The first feels like a threat of annihilation, a threat that a woman or her children may not survive if she reveals herself—her feelings, opinions, or will—to her partner. This fear arises most strongly when the woman's economic security depends on the relationship, or when her partner is abusive. For example, if a woman's circumstances—such as three children, a high school education, and a husband who controls the money—allow few options, then she may see silencing herself as the least of three evils, far preferable to the other options depressed women perceive: suicide or divorce. If she thinks that divorce will lead to poverty and fewer opportunities for the children, then she may consider self-silencing a positive moral choice as well as a strategy for making the best of a bad bargain.

On a psychological dimension, this fear of annihilation threatens what feels like the core of self. Particularly when a woman has molded herself to fit her partner's values and preferences, she fears that the loss of relationship means a loss of self (Miller, 1976). She does not recognize that it is within unsatisfactory forms of relationship that the self has already undergone its most serious erosion.

Second, some women, particularly those who were abused as children, hide their authentic selves out of the conviction that they are unlovable. These women enter adult intimate relationships already encumbered with the belief that they are worthless and "horrible." Through brutal childhood experiences of being devalued and silenced, they have learned to conceal their feelings and needs in order to protect themselves. They expect condemnation, reprisal, and loss if they reveal their inner core, so they veil themselves behind the safety of silence.

Third, women silence themselves out of a fear that their feelings and perceptions are somehow wrong and, if revealed, will give others reasons to reject them. Depressed women articulate a fear of isolation or reprisal if they express themselves truthfully in relationship. The reprisals they envision range from physical abuse to ridicule or "put-downs." As we have seen, some depressed women enter heterosexual relationships with a positive sense of self, but then begin to follow "game" rules for building up a man at the expense of the self. This leads eventually to lowered self-esteem, to feelings of self-betrayal, and to deep anger. If a woman's authentic self has been devalued in her relationships, in childhood learning, and in impoverished stereotypes of femininity, the authentic self becomes silent to protect the integrity of its own vision.

The origins of these fears are ubiquitous. As female, one inherits an ancestral, collective feeling of vulnerability that is linked with centuries of economic dependence and physical violence against women. Social practices create pressures toward self-censorship; for example, women are not allowed the opportunity to speak as often as males in families, social groups, and educational institutions (Belenky et al., 1986). Additional fears that lead women to inhibit their voices are learned from specific experiences within their own families of origin.

A woman's actions against her best interests in relationship make her look outwardly "passive" or "masochistic." But behavior that masquerades as passivity often stems from masked terror in the face of what is felt as a paralyzing threat. The rabbit frozen in the headlights, the barely breathing fawn melting into the tall grass—we do not call these animals passive, though their behavior could be interpreted as a refusal to act to avoid danger. A woman who believes she cannot make it on her own does not challenge the status quo of her unsatisfactory relationship. She does not say: "This is how I feel, and these things have to change or I will leave." She does not test whether her partner is willing :o change. Instead, she hides her feelings behind false compliance.

Believing that she is more able to control her own emotions than change her partner, the woman hugs her resentment tightly within her. She lets it out in little intense spurts, as if from an overfilled balloon, angry outbursts that leave her feeling ineffectual and childish—deflated, flat, dispersed. The outbursts change nothing, and are often seen by herself and her partner as evidence that she is "immature," "stressed," or "neurotic." The emotional outbursts increase feelings of guilt and diminish self-worth as they provide ammunition for self-criticism.[4]

ANGER

The fears that lead a woman to hide her authentic self both arouse anger and, at the same time, require its repression.[5] A woman quiets her anger not only because she thinks it will cause reprisals or drive away the love and closeness she seeks, but because anger potentially brings a clarity of vision and a requirement to act that threaten the established order of her life.

To take one's feelings seriously, to acknowledge and consider them, pulls one beyond the confines of ordinary thought. Authentic feeling enlarges the scope of moral reflection by calling into question dominant authority. Such authority not only defines right and wrong, but also decrees social propriety in interpersonal interactions, such as when and why a woman should submit to "the way things are." Authentic feeling can also require action by making a person too aware, too unhappy to remain within the status quo. Or feelings may unalterably change one's perception—of a person, a situation, or the self—and compel one to act. Alice Walker, in *The Color Purple*, portrays the character Celie as initially accepting male authority because of the brutal circumstances of her life. After awakening to her emotions through a relationship with another woman, Celie begins to see from a new perspective, and discovers her husband's fallibility: "I notice his chin weak." This change in perception, made possible by a new relationship premised on respect, love, and interest, frees Celie to challenge the violent authorities that have surrounded her since childhood.

Because feelings carry this unsettling potential and often stray outside of accepted social norms, we all censor them to some degree. Depressed women's self-silencing appears to be a more extreme form of ordinary self-censoring. Behind the silence of depression, a woman vigilantly weeds out the expression of emotions and thoughts that threaten relationship. Or, in the case of women who choose isolation to protect themselves from the vulnerability of relationships, the activity of self-silencing is directed against inner longings of need or "dependence." In less extreme form, as in chronic but milder depressions, self-silencing is a way of coping with the status quo by hiding the self, putting authenticity safely behind an accepted facade to keep it alive, protected, unjudged. In the extreme, in major depressions, including those with psychotic episodes, depressed women treat feelings as dangerous, foreign, other, and not only harshly condemn them but try to shut them out. These women put the authentic self into solitary confinement, forbidding it to think, feel, or communicate with others. Successful silencing of the authentic self leads to an inner sense of defeat, the feeling of giving up and living in despairing resignation. If the part of the self that is banished to solitary confinement sees no possibility of escape without disaster and becomes resigned to its fate, the whispers of the authentic self that send disquieting messages to awareness become less and less audible. They may eventually seek communication through physical symptoms, or through voices that clinicians label auditory hallucinations.

The link between self-silencing and anger is clear in Susan's description of her interactions with her husband:

> And so when he speaks to me in a harsh tone, or criticizes me for something that I have done wrong or haven't done or whatever, I've tended to think to myself, "Now you're supposed to be submissive, so just ignore him." Just, just, you know, don't confront the issue sort of thing. And so inside I've been building up a lot of resentment and a lot of anger.

Aware of power differences, Susan consciously chooses to maintain the relationship on inauthentic terms. She implicitly "flatters" male authority and power in the belief that her acquiescence will further relationship more than her direct confrontation with the inequity. But her self-abnegating behavior carries unexpected consequences: it reinforces hierarchy in the relationship and also leads to "building up a lot of resentment and a lot of anger."

Susan becomes antagonistic to what she perceives as an external power over her, yet she does not recognize her assistance in strengthening its presence in the relationship.

Resentment also results from the setting aside of her own needs and wishes and from the lack of mutuality in her relationship. In an effort to conform to the cultural prohibition of female anger, the depressed women I interviewed deflect their anger from their spouses toward themselves. The women believe that if they love "well enough," that is, selflessly enough, they will be loved in return. Blaming the self rather than looking at the relationship reinforces power imbalances, and, perceiving herself as inferior to her partner, a woman tries even harder to please in order to avoid conflict and to prevent separation.[6]

The resentment eventually erupts in angry outbursts, followed by periods of self-blame and guilt. The outbursts "prove" to the woman her underlying selfishness, destructiveness, and worthlessness, and heighten her fears of loss. She redoubles her vigilance in silencing herself, and her efforts to give, to please. The cycle begins again. Cathy describes her interactions with her husband:

> I know that part of the problem was the lack of communication where I did not express my real feelings. I was just wanting to do certain things and not wanting to do what he wanted me to do, but not telling him why I did not want to . . . I think I was generally pretty submissive, but then I would feel resentments inside and leave them inside until all of a sudden it got to me and I would be very aggressive.

All of the depressed women in the longitudinal study described this pattern of not communicating their real feelings. They experience a divided self of outer, false compliance and inner rage, growing resentment, and explosions of anger and hostility toward the partner or children.

The inner division is manifested in divided behavior. Women describe alternating between being overly nice and being cold, angry, and withholding. Aware of the reservoir of rage, they compensate by attempts to live out the behaviors of the "good woman," following the commands of the Over-Eye. But attempts to gain intimacy by such inauthentic means do not work, and this increases the depth of rage. The shame of letting anger out in destructive, repetitive ways that do not change the relationship, and the recognition that in most transactions with her partner she is inauthentic, lead a woman to self-blame and confusion.

Let us listen closely to Cathy to understand more fully the links between self-silencing, anger, self-loss, and depression. Cathy describes how, in the wish to create a stable marriage, she adopted a socially sanctioned structure of relatedness that demands her self-repression:

> We were married when I was 18 and he was 20, and I wanted to prove that our marriage was going to work, you know, and so I read everything I could about marriage and what a wife should be and—so my idea of a good wife was one that would build her husband up and, you know, be real careful of his ego and take care of his physical needs around the house. I think I always tried to put his wishes ahead of mine, but then I would resent it underneath.

While choosing to build up the partner or, at times, to put his wishes first is a healthy part of the give and take of relationship, depressed women describe a caring imperative that requires adopting the other's perspective permanently rather than temporarily. In order to maintain such a self-negating arrangement, Cathy must force herself to stop thinking about the things that bother her, including the fundamental inequity in her marriage.

Saying that "he would take a lot for granted and then I would, like I said, I would resent it, but not say anything," Cathy traces the turning points in her eighteen-year marriage by recounting issues around which she focused her rancor. The first time she "noticed" her bitter feelings was during the process of choosing how to spend vacations, when she realized that "he always got his way." We hear that the times Cathy feels most aggrieved are when she abdicates her own *self,* rather than when her husband takes action against her.

> And then, probably the next turning point was about two years after we had bought the business. And I remember him asking me, after we had been in business for a year, before we bought it, if this was what I wanted, if we should stay with it, if we should go ahead and buy it. And I wasn't real honest about how I felt. I just told him, "If that's what you want, you know, then it's okay."
> (*Do you know what was operating at the time, what was going on that you weren't really honest about your own feelings with him?*) I was pretty sure it was what he wanted. And another thing—before we had gone into the business, he wasn't happy in a farming partnership. He wasn't happy there and I knew he wasn't. And the reason was because we were not getting our bills paid and he felt like a failure . . . But the business is just not my type of work. You know, I just—I'm sure I was cut out to be more like a school teacher. And I wasn't good at selling, I was not real good at meeting people a lot, and I just didn't like it. Besides just being away from the kids a lot too. But I knew that, I knew that he liked it, I knew that it gave him a feeling of success, built him up, and I knew that was what he needed. And so, I guess I just didn't—I didn't feel my reasons were as important as his or something.

Cathy excludes herself from being part of decisionmaking, but then resents her husband, for whom she has abdicated her point of view. He asked for her opinion and she does not know how he would have reacted to an honest response. She helps create the structure of self-negating relationship that goes directly against her own interests, desires, and development. Listing the reasons for such fundamental betrayal of self, Cathy reiterates themes that run through other women's narratives: "it was what he wanted," it "built him up," "he liked it," "it gave him a feeling of success," and the bottom line, "I didn't feel my reasons were as important as his or something." Making herself, in Virginia Woolf's words, "the mirror to magnify man," Cathy never let her husband know that she had a mind of her own, with interests and talents that pushed for expression. She *appears* to have a soluble self that dissolves into the outlines of her husband (Keller, 1986), but we see the conscious acts of will required to keep herself permeable, to squelch her authenticity and her potential powers. She *appears* to lack firm ego boundaries, but she consciously erases lines of self-definition to obey the moral imperatives that promise her safety and security in relationship. Cathy knows that she has a part in creating the confines of her unhappiness. Such knowledge of her own self-abdication contributes to her confusion over who to blame, and to a deepening inability to act on her own desires and needs.

This type of self-desertion, abandoning one's own growth in favor of another's, leads not only to a feeling of being psychologically stunted but also to a profound sense of inauthenticity and guilt. Cathy recognizes that in her marriage "there were so many years of not growing, you know, not progressing." She elaborates:

Well, so many years of being so busy that we didn't have time for anything. You know, no relationships really with anybody. And didn't have time for each other, didn't have time for the kids and didn't have time for friends and so—I don't know, I just, I feel like—maybe there's a lot of growing up to do that I haven't done.

When her husband turned to an affair in the eighteenth year of marriage, Cathy felt he was justified and blamed herself. Saying "I had resented him so badly up until that point, and I was seeing all the negative things. I couldn't see anything positive," Cathy holds herself responsible for his actions. She feels a pervasive sense of dishonesty toward her husband, not because of untruths told, but because of truths not told. The feeling that

her inauthenticity and rage make her responsible for what happened keeps Cathy from taking control, from recognizing her
choices, and from taking action. Her overwhelming sense of
living a lie, her awareness of the discrepancy between the outer
self (a surface interpersonal style of being nice and helpful) and
the inner self (which feels controlling, betrayed, and destructive), keeps Cathy's blame and criticism focused on herself.
Thoughts such as "I wonder if all of these marriage problems
didn't happen to make me reevaluate myself and what he
needed and whether I was giving him what he needed or
whether I was, you know, worrying more about what I needed"
direct her attention to her own lapses and keep her from accurately recognizing the relationship's problems or planning for
her future. Listening to the voice of the Over-Eye, the part of the
self that moralistically mouths cultural demands placed on
women, she misnames her anger as selfishness, and condemns
the part of herself that could bring clarity and change.

Yet at the same time, Cathy also feels intense hostility toward the person to whom she gave the power to create her
security. Her male partner comes to embody the cultural demands that have been placed on women over the ages. While
she blames herself for causing problems in the relationship, she
also holds him responsible for her own actions and regards him
as the cause of her deep, confused unhappiness.

Placing responsibility for her self-betrayal on a partner, who
may or may not be abusive, overbearing, and demanding, af-
fords the woman some form of self-value. Seeing herself as a
victim of unalterable circumstances makes sense of what has
happened to her life while it preserves a few shreds of her self-
esteem. Blaming the partner and feeling victimized go hand in
hand. Not only do such psychological defenses explain her negative feelings, but they provide easy answers that continue to
mask complex questions. Challenging the structure of the relationship or leaving it would require taking responsibility for a self
who is not only little understood but deeply feared. A woman
may move into known depression rather than grapple with an
unknown self that will, perhaps, destroy life as she understands

it. She may feel depression is a necessary price to pay for the survival of a relationship she values (Krebs-McMullen, 1989).

When her husband continued the affair, Cathy made plans to divorce him and moved out with her children. It was at this critical point, with nothing left to lose, that she began to communicate honestly and directly. In her words, "I don't know exactly what changed my thoughts. But I started seeing him as a person who had feelings, and did care about somebody, and we started talking, you know, like we hadn't talked for years." Cathy's new freedom to express herself came when the Over-Eye lost its leverage of intimidation as the relationship dissolved with, she thought, no possibility of continuing. She was able to say to her husband that the marriage could not be restored without fundamental changes in their work, in their relationship to children and community, and in their own patterns of decisionmaking and interaction.

For Cathy, as for other depressed women, loss appears paradoxical. Dread of a loss of relationship led Cathy to silence herself and experience a loss of self; actual loss of relationship (or the brink of its loss) freed her to be herself within it because she had nothing left to lose. Shrinking from the risk of external loss by inventing a self designed to please creates a false safety and a pervasive anxiety from wondering when the axe of separation will drop.

In her second interview, two years after the affair, Cathy had moved back with her husband and was free of chronic depression. She described her marriage as "much better" because "he listens a lot more to what I need, whereas before I felt that he thought what I wanted was unimportant." We do not know, but it may be that her husband listened "a lot more to what [she] need[s]" because, for the first time, she clearly communicated those needs. Her husband was willing to make the changes she required. She reduced her hours at their business, "giving me time to pursue my own interests." Yet in a poignant passage at the end of the interview, Cathy wonders how her lack of confidence in her own voice has shaped her life as well as her decision to marry:

I was just thinking about an experience I had in high school. When I was a kid, lots of times I was very confident. I guess I was confident about my abilities and not very confident about my social life, you know, relating with other kids and everything. And, you know, being so confident in that one area, I may have looked down on other kids or something, I just really don't know.

But I can remember one time, I had to get up in front of a class and read a job study that I had written. And I got about halfway through it or more when I got really, really nervous. And my voice started to shake and I felt awful. You know, and I finally asked the teacher to finish reading it. I said I didn't feel well and just sat down. But that really shook my confidence, more than anything had before.

And so after that, I was unsure of whether I wanted to go on to university or nurses' training or any of those things, because I was just afraid that, you know, that I, I was just so unsure of myself, I just didn't know if I could be in those situations. And I'm just wondering if that had never happened, if I ever would have married Bud in the first place, you know, if it wasn't for security.

Cathy can only look at these fundamental issues now, two years after the separation, when she begins to examine her own part in structuring a life that has inhibited and confined her. Marriage provided a refuge from her fears and insecurities about entering the wider world, yet on some level Cathy blamed her husband for her unwillingness to take risks. For years, the inauthentic basis of her decision to marry created an uneasy sense of self-betrayal and amorphous guilt. When it came to asserting herself within the relationship, this primal feeling of inauthenticity undermined her feeling of having firm ground on which to stand, and eroded her integrity. Capitulation to personal insecurities and fears went hand in hand with an increasing bitterness over her inability to grow, or to control the structure of her life. She confined her own unlived creative potential within the narrow space of her marriage, and thwarted its expression in her adult life. Feeling like a fraud in her relationship, knowing that she had abandoned a part of herself when she married and feeling abandoned by her husband through his affair, she moved into depression, and saw herself in the culture's eyes as a bitter, empty, middle-aged woman who never dared.

LEARNING SELF-SILENCING

Eleven of the twelve women in the longitudinal study describe how their identification with their mothers' values, position, and feelings in relationship keep them from expressing their own wishes and desires to their partners. Assuming previous explanations of identification processes described by object relations theorists such as D. W. Winnicott (1965) and W. R. D. Fairbairn (1952), and by John Bowlby's (1969, 1973, 1980) attachment theory, I will draw from depressed women's statements to trace how the mother prepares her daughter to silence herself and to relate to men in a compliant manner.

The patriarchal culture exerts an influence on the mother-daughter relationship in numerous ways. Rather than detail all the effects, I refer the reader to the careful analyses presented by Marcia Westkott (1986) and Nancy Chodorow (1978, 1989). My focus will be on specific aspects of the mother-daughter relationship associated with depression, especially on how mothers teach their daughters to silence and diminish themselves as a way to attain and maintain a type of intimacy within inequality.[7] In focusing on the mother, I do not intend to overlook the culture. While it is an accident of birth to have a particular mother who demands compliance in return for love, society creates the mother's expectations about how the mother should relate to men and what qualities her daughter should have (Westkott, 1986).

Depressed women spontaneously and repeatedly call on their mothers' teachings and values while trying to understand their own actions within relationship. Women describe their mothers as either deprecating themselves, or being disparaged by their husbands, or both. Women who identify with such a mother internalize her self-demeaning, self-critical comments, and identify as female with her low self-esteem. Their recollections detail how their mothers prepare the groundwork for the daughters' tendency to experience themselves critically through the eyes of the "generalized other." Maya describes her mother:

> There was a fear of being in a crowd, fear of what people were thinking about her because she's tall.
> (*She would say that to you?*) Oh, she'd say that. People would look at her and she would always comment, "Well, they look like they—" what was it? She would always put the thoughts into their heads that she thought they were saying, and it was always degrading to her. And that's, then I sort of grew up that way too, putting thoughts into my head of what other people were saying. And so I became very self-conscious when I went into high school. I mean, people would invite me to things, parties and that, and I would think of excuses not to go because I felt so lowly of myself.

As a girl, Maya learned that outside sources strongly influenced her mother's discomfort with herself. Observing how her mother, with whom she identifies, looks to others to see (or impute) what they think of her, Maya adopts the same critical, onlooker attitude toward herself. At the same time, Maya's ego ideal of the feminine comes from her mother, and in that ideal the way to be loving and loved in relationships includes a restricted and diminished self-image.

Detailing how closeness to the mother can bring a mixture of love and bondage, Anita reiterates a common theme among women's descriptions of their mothers:

> I was and would become an extension of my mother. I tried to anticipate her needs, I felt sad when she was hurting, and I sided with her against my father in their arguments. I became her confidante, mentor, and hus-

band emotionally that she wished she had in my father. I totally assimilated that woman into my womanness . . .

I can recount numerous times being asked what I wanted and then, when I would respond, they [her parents] would say, "Oh, Anita, you don't really want that to eat, drink, wear, play with, etc." After hearing it enough I clearly got the message that I didn't know what I wanted and that my function was to know what everyone else wanted. I had relinquished my voice and assimilated the voice of my mother.

Without a voice I could not ask, which also eliminated the desire to want. Besides, my mother was the only one who knew what I wanted, and she wasn't there for me emotionally.[8]

The satisfaction and security in this relationship are mixed with a requirement that Anita take care of her mother, a requirement that not only reinforces a girl's own sense of inner worthlessness but also teaches caretaking as part of a female identity. The close bonding between mother and daughter turns to bondage when a girl feels responsible for her mother's identity and safety. She must repress her anger and her difference from her mother, not only because she might lose her mother's affection but also because she perceives her power to threaten her mother's core self. To assimilate the mother's dominating emotional presence, which named, defined, and negated Anita's desires, Anita had to relinquish her voice, that is, to silence herself.[9]

Susan, likewise, demonstrates how a mother's teachings have the power to affect her daughter's future relationships. Answering the question "What brought you into therapy?" Susan points to her marriage:

The reason why I came is because I was feeling really frustrated. I guess that would be the best word I have to explain how I felt. Not really feeling very worthwhile. Feeling really—no self-worth, and very frustrated with my marriage, I suppose, is another thing I could really—

although I don't want to blame my marriage for everything. But I was very unhappy in my relationship with
my husband.

She goes on to narrate that when she attempts to communicate a
need or communicate

> my frustration that a need or needs are not being met, he
> gets so angry at me and will get in a rage and yell, start
> yelling at me, and so I tend to maybe think, yeah, maybe
> I am being too naggy . . . And so I'm allowing his
> blaming me, I'm accepting the blame I guess, and I'm
> thinking, yeah, maybe it is my fault.

Susan describes how her mother's example provides the
model for her tendency to blame herself:

> She was that way. She was such a martyr type, I mean,
> really bad. Just always pardoning herself, "Excuse me,
> excuse me," to my father all the time. I mean, she was
> always making herself such a subservient person to him.
> "Oh Robert, dear, what can I do to make you more
> comfortable?" All he had to do was grunt or groan, and
> she would be at his mercy. "What did I do wrong, dear?
> Is there something I did? What is it?" You know, she was
> that way.
>   She's always been one that blamed herself, and always
> put herself in a very subservient position to others, and
> always was a giver, giver, giver type person. And my
> father was very much, I suppose, like my husband in the
> fact that he blamed her for things. He was always scold-
> ing her and blaming her for things.

Susan's father "emotionally abused" her and her mother. Because her mother did not leave the marriage, Susan saw the
abuse throughout childhood and adolescence. Witnessing the

situation of her mother's giving within such a context affected
Susan's understanding of strength and weakness:

> And so, at the same time I was mad at her for her
> subservience in her relationship with my father, I also
> emulated and respected the fact that she was such a
> loving, giving person. She was a person who had, in a
> way, great strength inside, a peace inside herself; and
> yet, now that I look back on it, she may have been very
> weak too, in some areas. And that's why she did just—I
> think she has a lot of fears, maybe of loneliness and
> being without my dad—she would never consider sepa-
> rating or leaving him.

Susan was left with a basic confusion about whether her
mother was strong or weak in her capacity to give so much. She
learned that to be safe in relationship—to avoid the threat of
separation—one should not speak one's opinion or confront the
partner. Also, Susan saw both sides of her mother's caring: its
strength, active love and support for others; and its weakness,
the incapacity to set limits on others, coinciding with a fear of
loss.

Susan did not intend to repeat her mother's subservient and
distant relationship with her husband. She sought to avoid such
a pattern of relationship by choosing a man who was not like her
father.

> I even consciously tried to tell myself, "Now, you know,
> you do not want to marry a man like your dad, who was
> so bossy and so critical and always putting the blame on
> other people and everything." And I really consciously
> told myself, "Harry, my husband, is just not like that at
> all, he's so much different from my dad!"

But this choice, in itself, was not enough: "Once we were married the same pattern evolved. I have tried being the quiet,

loving one that just takes this kind of treatment and doesn't say anything back, and feeling really resentful about it." Even though Susan consciously tried to break the pattern of inequality and emotional distance, it emerged over time as she interacted with her husband. The grooves of the pattern are etched deep within the Over-Eye as the mother teaches the daughter how to attain closeness and goodness in intimate relationship.

From her relationship with her mother, Susan gained an image of the closeness she expected to have with her husband.

> I was always so close to my mother. I was the caboose in the family, so I was raised like an only child. And my mother and I were so close, maybe almost too close, maybe not healthy—maybe it wasn't so healthy. Because we talked and we shared and we discussed . . . And I've always had a close friend, you know, I always *had* a close friend. Until I was married. You know, and then I guess I expected that my close friend would be my husband, and it never was . . . we don't talk on any intimate levels.

Susan's comment that she was "so close, almost too close" to her mother grows out of the frustration of intimacy she now experiences in her marriage. She is saying, in effect, "If I had not had that closeness with my mother, maybe I would not need closeness now with my husband, and without my need for closeness, this marriage would be less troublesome." The intimacy she shared with her mother fostered expectations that she would repeat such a connection with a man. But as she lives out the behaviors she learned would lead to closeness, she finds that her husband gradually changes shape to assume a critical, distant form like that of her blaming father. Finding her husband emotionally unavailable, Susan tries to recreate a feeling of intimacy by staying close to her internalized mother: by recreating her mother's relational position, by feeling her mother's feelings in response to a man. Yet the type of relationship this creates with her husband is precisely what Susan tried to avoid by choosing a man different from her dad.

As an adult, Susan is "mixed up" about what goodness is because the model she was taught by her mother allows no way to include her needs and wants within a relationship. Instead she must "be for the other guy."

> She [her mother] never, never dared rock the boat or express needs or say, "I want this." You never say, "I want," you always find out what the other person wants and—you don't desert somebody because they have a weakness or a sickness. There again, you be the servant or the keeper or the brother or we must be serving of one another. That was the constant thought that came through everything she taught. Always serve and be for the other guy. Never, ever dare think about yourself.

Being taught to respond to external expectations and to ignore the self's needs and feelings emerges as a crucial issue in the psychological development of each of these depressed women. It leads a woman to believe that silencing her own needs and feelings is morally right. Susan learned that pleasing others, giving to others, was more important, more *good*, than listening to herself. She learned that thinking about herself, or asking to have her needs met, was "selfish" and, by implication, bad. If a girl learns that her needs are less important than those of her mate, that she has no "right" to her needs, then she has learned the basis of low self-esteem.

For Susan, the morality of goodness as self-sacrifice she learned from her mother led directly to emotional and physical hurt. In addition to the "battered woman syndrome" (Walker, 1979), a general pattern of reaction to physical and psychological abuse inflicted on a woman by her spouse, these childhood learnings about goodness—that "you don't desert somebody just because they have a weakness or a sickness"—bind a woman to a hurtful spouse with the wish to "help" him. Also, Susan had a model whom she admired and loved who had "stuck it out in a bad marriage." Explaining why she did not call the police when her husband became physically violent, Susan refers back to her mother's example:

I'm sure a lot of it is that same old thing I was brought up with . . . it was what I saw, my model at home for eighteen years was a woman who was getting walked on. A doormat, living with a man who was constantly putting her down, belittling her, making fun of her, hurting her in front of other people, and she took it and took it and took it, and she was the "good" person—and so there I go.

Susan saw her mother not voicing her feelings in order to stay in relationship. The equation became: silence yourself to stay in relationship and be good, or speak your feelings, hurt someone, and lose the relationship. The identification with a submissive, loving mother, the wish to be good, the uncertainty of her "right" to her own needs and integrity, financial dependence, and fear are some of the factors that led Susan to remain in an unsatisfactory marriage and to become clinically depressed.

Susan feels betrayed by her mother's teachings because what she once believed to be her mother's strength she now considers a weakness. This leads to confusion about what constitutes strength and weakness within herself.

I really think that I'm a really wishy-wash for needing closeness, and for needing to share and for needing intimacy, because I live with a person who is so much the opposite and I see the comparison with the way I am and the way he is. I can't help but look at myself and think, "My god, I'm a real wishy-washy weak person for needing the kinds of intimacy and closeness that I do." I should be harder, I should be, I think maybe I should be more like he is.

Susan's marriage becomes an arena where the "strong" are defined as those who are not vulnerable, who do not focus on relationship, communication, or intimacy. She spontaneously ties these thoughts back to her mother, and how she was treated in relationship:

My father would get very belligerent. Never physically, but he would get extremely belligerent and extremely insulting and whatever to my mother. Her friends, everything about her, and she would just sit there and take it. That's what I was brought up to see as being good, and being good is what we all want to be, right? Well, I don't believe in that anymore. Just like I don't believe in fairy tales. I don't believe that being good means you allow yourself to be walked on and manipulated, put down, victimized. That is not being good. I feel it's being weak, and I see that I am weak in some areas like that.

In this passage, Susan equates goodness with "taking it" and "taking it" with weakness. The magic of childhood fairy tales turns into a harsh adult reality: "goodness" leads to being weak, vulnerable, and hurt, whereas callous, dominating behavior leads to power and invulnerability to pain. Susan attempts to separate her own definition of goodness from that of her mother, but she has not yet found a replacement. To act in her own self-interest is to be like her father and her husband, both of whom hurt people with their "selfish" actions. Yet she observes that being good leads to hurt to the self.

If women cannot exercise power without (in their minds) causing hurt, they may choose to silence themselves for what feel like moral reasons. Susan is confused about how she can be good without becoming a victim, and how she can act in her own best interests without being "bad," that is, causing hurt to others. These childhood learnings lead to women's common difficulty in defining the difference between healthy self-assertion and aggression that hurts others. These childhood learnings are also a large part of the reason women stay in nonintimate, self-negating relationships and do not perceive other choices that may be open to them.

Susan tries to adapt to collective values and adopt a lifestyle that "isn't really me." Like other depressed women, she becomes separated from herself through trying to conform to outer demands, be they from the partner, the career, the church, whatever. This must be the ultimate silencing: to take the culture's perspective, or the partner's perspective, on the self and condemn a human need for intimacy and mutuality. Instead of seeing her depression as a signal that something needs to change, Susan has learned to view it as pathological, as confirmation of the fact that she is a "victim" and a "weakling baby." Rather, her depression demands that she listen to what she knows from her unique experience of living, from her own feelings, and from her body.

SILENCING CREATIVITY

Women not only silence their voices in relation to the male partner; they also silence their creativity, and the thwarting of creativity reinforces feelings of worthlessness. Tillie Olsen describes the times of despair and darkness during which a writer's voice ceases:

> These are not natural silences, that necessary time for renewal, lying fallow, gestation, in the natural cycle of creation. The silences I speak of here are unnatural; the unnatural thwarting of what struggles to come into being, but cannot. In the old, the obvious parallels: when the seed strikes stone; the soil will not sustain; the spring is false; the time is drought or blight or infestation; the frost comes premature.   (1978, p. xi)

To stifle one's creativity is profoundly destructive. Historically, women have been limited in the arenas within which they could express their talents, and have had to channel them into home and family. Many daughters and granddaughters have felt the impact of an imprisoned maternal imagination that restlessly sought expression. Identifying with their own mother's willingness to turn away from the self-definition and risk involved in creativity, depressed women talk about how they left behind a spontaneous imaginative freedom when they stepped into marriage or into male-dominated professions. They specifically identify with their own mothers when they talk about being unable to make time to engage in their own interests and pursuits. Equally restrictive is women's internalization of the culture's perspective on their own talents and abilities.

Laura, age 30, describes her reasons for coming in to a mental health clinic for depression:

I was just having trouble, a lot of trouble, relating to David, the man I am living with. But mostly it was because I'm real interested in learning woodworking and I'm having a really hard time handling my insecure feelings about that. I think the hardest thing for me has been trying to find something to do I feel really good about, some way I can support myself . . .

She gives the history of her experience:

I was woodworking for a while and I got kind of scared off by it. School was kind of hard and it didn't work out for me because I felt like—I just really felt the difference between me and the men I was working with, kind of a little kidding about me when I was going through and it was hard for me to struggle through kind of not just being affected by little comments and little joking or whatever. And then I had a job, I did some kitchens for somebody, and he was just really hard to deal with and I got really scared off, you know. And not really knowing how to be that assertive and problems with other people, not being able to say, you know, I'm doing a good enough job and you need to back off.

Violating sex-role norms by entering this field, Laura receives from the men "little kidding" and "little comments" and "little joking." The sexualization and devaluation present in these actions are masked behind disclaimers of joking and humor. But, as Westkott (1986) observes, this kind of "joking objectification of another" allows men both to assert their power and sexuality and to deny any serious intent.

As Laura explores her doubts, we see that the outer "teasing" by the men echoes and reinforces inner self-negation.

But I think that, you know, if I ever got in touch with feeling okay about what I was doing I think I have a lot of potential, you know. I think I am, I have the ability to do it [woodworking]. But I'm, I'm too much afraid of something, of making mistakes, or something. The first thing I think of is ridicule, you know, of something that wasn't acceptable, that wasn't as good as it should be. Yeah, when I think of that it makes me feel real bad . . . I don't know how to work through this feeling of I'm not quite good enough or something. I mean, somewhere along the line I have got to drop that or I'm going to be fighting that the rest of my life.

Laura makes the link between feeling not good enough and her childhood:

That's interesting because I just thought about my father and just thought, well, it's the feeling of not being good enough, like you didn't do a good job. And my father was really terrible, anything I did, you know, anything, I never, never could get that final "That was a really good job," or he wouldn't say anything to me.

Although Laura talks about the personal father, his judgments about her efforts are echoed by the male collective, particularly within a male-dominated field. Laura was abandoned to her father's judgments by her mother, who did not teach her how to stand up for herself. Laura says:

My mother never got angry—well, I guess she did. But she always acted hurt, you know. So my father pretty much suppressed in her any emotions he doesn't like, so I never really had any kind of a model for how to get angry. Oh she usually—god, I just remembered feeling really guilty whenever she got, whenever she got upset with me she would say, "It's so hard when you do that," and so, it's in the back of my mind.

Laura goes on to explore her feelings of not being good enough and her lack of confidence, and we begin to hear the inner dialogue of depression, articulated with clarity and force:

You know, I think I have a voice that says "You aren't good enough." You know, I think that's where it all stems from, there's this voice that says, it's like a reinforcing thing of—it's like I blunder and this voice says "See!" It's real deep.

(*Can we explore together what you mean by good enough? I mean what does the word "good" mean in that context?*) Boy, I don't know, you know, boy, I think, it's silly but it's not silly at all but it feels like it goes back to my father. I've felt this a lot. Just the way he was gave me the feeling that I was never adequate or that I would never do anything particularly important, so I'm continually feeling that. It's definitely achievements, achievements are, you know, where it's so hard. It's not like gaining a skill, it's like you'll never learn the skill, the voice is saying, "The way you are, you'll never even learn it. You're dumb," or you know, something, "You don't deserve it," or something like that. It's so vague, it's kind of like, just like I just hear this thing of "You're not good enough."

(*So you don't deserve to achieve something?*) Right, right. I don't know if it's I'm not smart enough, because I, although that seems like it's a part of it, but there's also the thing that says, "You're not confident enough," that says that is what is really going to trip me up, it's my lack of confidence. It's all, you know, it's like I hear this voice which I feel has to do with my father, and then I hear this voice that has to do with me, and the voice says, "You're not confident enough," and it's me that's saying it, and the other voice is my father saying "You're not good enough."

Laura tells us that she feels inhibited by her father in a fundamental way. It feels like a given to her, a "vague," global judgment of "You're not good enough." In its immutability, its givenness, it seems inherent in her feminine gender: *there is nothing she can do about it*. This negative paternal evaluation stops her dead in her tracks and leaves her no hope of challenging it by her efforts. This "scar of inferiority" (Freud, 1925), a pervasive feeling of not measuring up or of a fundamental lack, is what psychoanalysts call penis envy. But we see clearly how social and cultural patterns create such a psychic response in women. Further, the paternal voice that says "You're not good enough" stems from an internalization of the critical male gaze through which a woman sees herself.

But Laura tells us about another voice, "and it's me that's saying it," which says "You're not confident enough." The "voice that has to do with me" tells her what she needs if she is to stand up to patriarchal devaluation: confidence, the confidence to value her feminine self independent of the judgments of the male world. Yet what she needs was lacking in her development. Laura identified with a mother who negated herself and who was socially devalued. Her mother was unable to offer either a model or the support for Laura to come into relation with the male world as an equal. As she explores what could make her feel "good enough," Laura tells us how her internalized mother continues to inhibit her ability to relate to others from a position of authenticity and confidence:

My mother taught me to be very polite and, let's see, you just can't say anything, can't say anything that's going to hurt somebody. You know, you shouldn't hurt anybody, that's how it works. You should not hurt anyone. That was like a real big sin to my mother. And that makes it harder for me to get what I want, in relationships and in my goals. You know, it just doesn't allow me to be straightforward. In some ways I am, I am like, I can be kind of a martyr at times and my mother's really a martyr.

(*How do you see her being a martyr?*) Oh, she won't, she

can't deal directly with things. She'll say, "Oh, you hurt me," and she'll walk away and make you feel guilty about anything that's going on, whether you did anything or not. She's real manipulative, unintentionally, totally, I think, but she really is.

Having learned that to hurt another was in her mother's eyes "a big sin," Laura still consciously tries to avoid hurting others, though she recognizes that this requirement "makes it harder to get what I want in my relationships and in my goals." It also maintains an invisible tie of identification, serving as a pledge of loyalty that she will never really grow up and separate from her mother's values (see Lerner, 1987). Her mother said, in effect, "Don't hurt *me* by asserting yourself." Her mother punished Laura for childish willfulness or misbehavior by acting hurt; refusing to hurt others, Laura remains her mother's good daughter. Inhibiting her will, her power and strength, has kept her a daughter of the patriarchy as well, searching for an illusory goodness, maintaining a false, depotentiated innocence. To speak one's authentic feelings may hurt others; to claim qualities of the feminine beyond the maternal or the maiden, qualities such as "the embodied, playful, passionately erotic feminine; the powerful, independent, self-willed feminine; and the ambitious, regal, many-sided feminine" (Perera, 1985, p. 147) will certainly disturb others.

Laura not only silenced her voice in relationship but also inhibited her creative, daring self that wanted to move beyond the acceptable confines of gender roles. Two years after this interview, she had left her relationship, moved to another city, and started a program leading to an R.N. degree. She felt less depressed, but was regretful over what she considered her "failure" at a career in woodworking.

Self-silencing does not occur only in relation to an external other. It also happens when a woman turns against herself, and with the force of paternal authority thwarts her own creativity, will, and imagination. In her lack of confidence, Laura reveals an anxiety arising from her keen sense of discrepancy between what she envisions for herself and what a cultural, paternal authority envisions for her. This fundamental anxiety of self, arising from a culture that has taught her to inhibit action so as not to hurt others, is profoundly debilitating. It keeps a woman from realizing her own potential. It stops her from taking the risks of creativity, and it pushes her to the security of following the cultural path of co-optation or complicity. It debilitates her because it curbs self-expression and then negatively affects self-esteem in a deepening vortex. In hindsight, Laura sees that she did not risk what she was capable of, and feels a sense of self-compromise that leads to further feelings of failure.

Diana's narratives echo themes present in Laura's and clarify how the tie of identification to a devalued, self-negating mother adds to a woman's vulnerability to depression. At the time of the interview quoted below, Diana, age 30, had been married for three years, had a two-year-old son, and was pregnant. Interviewed in her last trimester of pregnancy, she appeared very depressed. Exploring her feeling of being unable to do anything for herself, and why she feels selfish if she does, Diana begins to talk about her relationships with her parents:

> I've always been able to communicate with my mother better than my dad. Part of my self-criticism, I know—my father is extremely artistic. I got none of those abilities. So I think I've always been real critical of myself from the standpoint of not having talent.
>
> I've always worked very hard for my father's approval—and I think I got it. Maybe I didn't. He's not real complimentary, he's not that kind of man. Neither is my husband. So maybe I, you know, maybe I didn't get reinforcement that I needed or something. Even though I tried, if I'd just done it a little bit different it would have been better. And I guess maybe I'm always thinking I should find the better way. And I'm, maybe that is something that I grew up with, thinking that nothing I did was good enough.

The common refrain of not being "good enough" surfaces as the women regard themselves from the father's—that is, the Fathers'—perspective. Like Laura's, Diana's feeling of not being good enough is pervasive, unassailable, and appears attached to her female gender.

Turning to Diana's mother, we hear the themes of closeness that set up expectations for later relationships:

> My mom was always there. And I counted on that, and my mother was the mother that everybody else went to with their problems . . . We have an extremely good relationship. Very open. And sometimes I wonder if we're too close. You know, if that's possible.

Like Susan, Diana wonders whether she is "too close" to her mother, hinting at invisible bonds that tie her to her mother's narrowly circumscribed behaviors in relationship. She goes on to explore why she never is able to do things for herself without feeling "selfish" and "guilty":

> I guess there are reasons, too, why I can't perhaps do as many things for myself right now as I'd like to. One of those things is financially . . . In fact, just the other day, I'd been involved with the March of Dimes fashion show. And all the chairmen were getting together, and Bruce had a softball meeting. And we only have one car right now. And I stayed home. And it wasn't strictly that I couldn't, I could have figured something out. But, you know, I just felt it was real important for him to do his thing. And it wasn't as important for me to go. Although I would have liked to.
>
> That was one—although it was, it was not at all a pressure from him to give up what I wanted to do, I did it to myself. He would have said fine, he could get someone to pick him up and I could take the car. But if I had done that, I'm sure I would have felt badly about that. I would have felt that it was selfish. Even though Bruce

didn't do it to me, he encouraged me to go, he said he'd make arrangements for our son, or take him with him or something, but if I had done that, I'm sure I would have felt badly about it.

There've got to be times for all of us that we put ourselves first. And I don't probably as often as I should. My mother was much more that way than I. Because of my dad. She just didn't, my sister and I were her whole life, because my dad was doing his thing. And so in just the last couple of years, she's become a little bit independent and doing some things on her own.

And I think maybe that's where I come from, where my feelings come from to a degree, is that if Mom ever did anything for herself, or wasn't home, or didn't have dinner ready, then she wasn't being fair. You know, one of those types of situations.

(*Did you feel that as a child?*) No, my dad made her feel that way. And although my husband doesn't feel that way, and doesn't react to me in that way, I oftentimes, I think he should. And so even though he doesn't I still have the same guilt, I guess.

Consider the logic of Diana's narrative: I had a desire (I wanted to go to the March of Dimes meeting), but my husband's desires are more important than mine. He encouraged me to go but "I would have felt it was selfish," I shouldn't put myself first. (She uses exclusionary thinking—"there've got to be times for all of us that we put ourselves first"—when what the situation asks is simply that she *include* herself.) Then the leap in thought to the mother occurs through identification: "My mother was much more that way than I." But not in all ways; only in terms of asserting herself with Diana's father: "Because of my dad."

As an adult woman, Diana maintains the empathic connection, the "closeness" to her mother through experiencing the same feelings in relation to her husband as she thinks her mother did in relation to her father. Even though her husband encourages her to go out, Diana restricts herself through identification with what her mother *would have felt* in such a situation. She vicariously continues to experience, through identification with the mother, her father's criticism: "If Mom ever did anything for herself, or wasn't home, or didn't have dinner ready, then she wasn't being fair."

For Diana, pregnant with a second child and at home full time with a first child, these deep inhibitions lead to feelings "like things are just erupting and I'm just going to blow from the skin out. But I can't really pinpoint the reason for it. It just seems to happen." The depression that appeared during Diana's sixth month of pregnancy and continued until a year after her daughter's birth was caused by numerous factors, underlaid by the powerful restrictions of identification with her mother's position in relationship.

Pregnancy and childbirth powerfully reconfirm a woman's similarity to her mother. As her body changes, as she remembers being cared for, as she ministers to her infant in a cycle of maternal caretaking, a woman experiences herself as daughter and mother at the same time. Diana's interviews are filled with accounts of her attempts to define her own interests, battle her weight down, and feel "more confident and better about myself." Finally feeling better after her son's birth because of losing weight and joining outside activities, but now pregnant again, she feels she has to stuff herself back into the mold of how to be a wife and mother set by her own mother. Since Diana's mother was the sort who "was always there," who conveyed to her daughter the idea that a good mother fills the needs of her children with no inner conflict or frustration, for Diana to assert her own selfhood requires breaking her identification with her mother's ways of relating—both to husband and to children.

In tracing the influence of the mother as it appears in depressed women's narratives, it is useful to recall a central tenet in recent theory about the psychology of women. Valuing relationship, a woman seeks to avoid the pain of disconnection and separation. If a woman seeks to break with her mother's ways in relationship, she must psychologically distinguish herself from her mother by gaining more self-esteem and by feeling that she "deserves" more than her mother did. Doing so can feel like psychological betrayal or abandonment of a mother she loves. Because mother and self can become so entwined in women's development, differentiating from the mother can also feel like pulling away from part of the self. Particularly when a woman is without other positive, compelling models of how to be a female self in relationship, this separation from early identifications can be frightening.

But more is involved. If a woman separates from her internalized mother, she may feel isolated. Many women dread being alone because, in aloneness, a woman has to face her own isolation from herself and the fact that she has deserted her own development somewhere along the way. She keeps closeness with her mother to avoid that isolation, in which she can feel the *absence* of relationship with anyone. The realization that she has struggled to prevent something that has already happened—the loss of relationship, including with her own self—leads to an overwhelming sense of hopelessness and grief. This loss and this grief lie at the heart of depression.

THE DIVIDED SELF

The active silencing of the self leads to the inner split of depression, the condition of self-alienation and hopelessness.[10] Living out the imperatives of the Over-Eye, the woman begins to experience two opposing selves: an outwardly conforming, compliant self, and an inner, secret self who is enraged and resentful. Trying to live up to external standards, a woman creates a "dark double,"[11] an accompanying shadow self that undermines her attempts to be a loveable woman. The inner division was evident as each depressed woman described her life and her conflicts. The outwardly conforming self accepts the social norms for female goodness or for worldly success and tries to comply with them; the "I," the authentic self, observes that her own desires and needs remain unmet and that her attempts at intimacy remain frustrated. The authentic self grows increasingly angry; the Over-Eye gains ammunition to use against the self and grows increasingly harsh, blaming, and condemning.

The interviews of depressed women echo with a voice that is yearning to be heard, recognized, and loved for the self one "really" is. Yet this authentic voice carries anger from the frustration of its needs for self-expression, recognition, and mutuality. What is paralyzing and leads to a sense of hopelessness is the belief that if one were heard, one would not be understood and accepted but would be judged negatively and abandoned. Thus, the authentic self goes into hiding and feels angry, resentful, hopeless. The Over-Eye takes this authentic self as its object and evaluates it as morally lacking.

This inner division, created by silencing the self in relationship, is a core dynamic of female depression. Suspended in thought about how to judge, how to act, and what is real, the women experience a fundamental disconnection with themselves. They also experience a lack of intimacy and engagement in their core relationships.

The language of depressed women reflects the experience of inner division and appears in repeated references to a "real self" that is not allowed expression, in the language of "burying," and "hiding" the real self, and in contrasts between experiences of self: "I realize that maybe I'm trying to lead a style—or be something that isn't really me. But when I think about it and the needs that I really have and the way I really am, then I hurt and I get lonesome and depressed."

Between competing views (the authentic "I" and the Over-Eye) of what is real and how to evaluate the self and experience, depressed women describe themselves as

suspended   *(Maya)*

a split personality   *(Therese)*

I feel like I'm sounding like I have two sides here, and maybe I do.   *(Betty)*

I'm beginning to wonder if I'm in conflict with myself. Maybe I shouldn't be living this kind of a lifestyle at all, being the kind of person I am, that maybe this is not in agreement with the kind of person I really am. *(Susan)*

I act like I'm easy-going and things are fine on the outside, but maybe I'm not so easy-going and inside I'm angry. *(Anna)*

Therese's narrative instructs us about the relationship of self-silencing to the experience of inner division.[12] Her interview is filled with the language of the "real self" that she dares not reveal for fear of rejection.[13] Therese, recently separated from her husband, describes the impact of her marriage on her sense of self:

I can remember when I was in high school, I had a girl-friend who had two older brothers and she was speaking of her younger brother having an inferiority complex. At the time, I was not that way, and I remember thinking, "Wow, why would anybody have an inferiority complex. You're your own person, go in and cash in on being your own person."

Well, it wasn't until after I got married abruptly, married right out of high school, I lost absolutely all sense of who I was, why I was, where I was going. Anything. I lost absolutely all sense of myself. Any value that I may have ever put in myself. I didn't know at the time. I felt like I was an extension of John and that was it. And things have not gotten any better at all.

Recognizing that she had allowed her husband to "run my life," Therese also looks back to try to understand why she had been unable to "be myself" either with John or with his family.

I rated his family on a higher plateau than my family, although I felt much better with my family than his.

I was very uptight, very nervous, very high-strung. I
would withdraw so that I wouldn't let my real self out
because I thought they would snub me or laugh at me or
something.

Therese describes her attempts to live out an invented "acceptable" self, one she fabricated because of her own deep fears
that her authentic self would be rejected by her husband and his
family. "I feared they would not accept me with my crudeness,
my rough edges." Trying to present an outwardly acceptable
facade, living out someone who "wasn't me," meant that "my
marriage kept me from becoming or from showing who I was."
Socially approved conduct becomes translated into *right* conduct, which acquires a moral tone by virtue of its power to
include or exclude a woman from the community into which she
marries.

While Therese lived out a false, conforming self, she also
developed a "secret self," which had its own history within the
relationship. She blames her husband for her self-suppression
and hates him for it, outwardly "catering" to him while inwardly
fomenting an attitude of rebellion. This secret self contained a
well of resentment, rage, frustration, and despair. This was a
side of her self her husband did not know:

I catered to him as far as I could and then I started
building up a very big rebellious wall waiting, some day,
some day, some day I'm going to tell him how I feel. I
never did because I never felt I could.

Examining why she gave him the power to define what was
acceptable, she describes her sense of inferiority relative to men,
and how it divides her experience of self into two. She ties this
back to her own experience of her father. Listen to Therese's
words:

I feel more and more just like I'm a real split personality.
I'm a real loving person, I love to give love and I love to
be loved. I want to give so badly but I'm afraid to. I am so

afraid of rejection for some reason, I'm so afraid of rejection. I am my own worst enemy. I feel like I'm falling so short. I'm feeling like everything I say is like, I'm never good enough. I really feel that way, but I don't think people see me that way.

So why do I feel this way? I don't feel this way with women. I'm much more inferior feeling to men. I can hardly speak to a man. I had no relationship with my father, I think that's probably why. He wanted nothing to do with us kids and he had nothing to do with us. So I'm very fearful of a relationship, or to just talk to a man, it's hard.

In this clear logic of feeling, Therese traces the origins of her negative vision of self to her father, by whom she felt devalued in a comprehensive way. Like Laura and Diana, she feels "I'm never good enough," a diffuse self-judgment not present in her relationship with women. This inferior feeling, situated in relationship to men—"I can hardly speak to a man"—again appears to reside in her gender rather than in any specific qualities or actions. This feeling exists inwardly even when she knows it is not present externally: "I really feel that way, but I don't think people see me that way." The sense of herself as the devalued object of a patriarchal gaze, internalized in the Over-Eye and experienced as a part of the self, creates the experience of inner division. It leaves her feeling like a "split personality," with one part of the self "falling so short" and another part who "doesn't feel this way."

Therese also reveals how she experiences her father vicariously through identification with her mother's responses to him. Exploring her fear of revealing herself in relationship, she remembers her parents' interactions:

It might stem back to the fact that the man is the rule of the roost. I even saw it at my own home where we did not have finances so mother would do without this and mother would do without that and she would—I never, in my seventeen years at home, never saw my folks fight. I never heard a bad word. I never knew any cuss words, I never saw liquor . . .

From both our homes, the woman was subdued, the woman did not—well, Mother did speak her piece, but it never got anywhere. She'd run off crying into the bed-room. Our dining room set absolutely fell apart before our eyes. Our dinner ended up on the dining room floor because the dining room set was so bad. My father was a carpenter and there were a lot of wood boxes and that was what we sat on. The dining room table just went "poof." Mother begged and pleaded for a new dining room table and "We don't have the money." She'd run off into the bedroom crying because we didn't have a place to set the evening meal.

And Dad was such an authority. What he said was it. If we had a bad evening, the kids were bad or something, we got along well with Mother, but if Dad spoke the world stood still, nobody moved.

Father authority ruled Therese's family. Godlike, the father had the power to make the world stand still; in the human realm, he decided how money was to be spent and disciplined with an iron hand. A girl who grew into a young woman in this home, identifying with her mother, would learn that being in relation-ship with a man meant being subordinate, not having one's voice acknowledged, and not fighting back. Therese saw that her mother placed more importance on maintaining the mar-riage than on enacting a self within it, so the unconscious equa-tion became: silence yourself and stay in relationship, or speak your feelings and lose the relationship. By accepting her parents' relationship as the way things are, she internalized her father's negating view of her mother, and of herself.

At first, Therese recounts, her marriage was not so bad. She and her husband moved away to a large city and seemed to break from past patterns, including the wife's financial depen-dence.

When I was in Chicago, I had a job, there were people that counted on me. I knew I was good at what I did and I moved up real fast and I got my raises real quickly. We were both really happy in the city, we had a lot of fun together and we both had our own jobs. We really got along well then.

Then, through a series of decisions, Therese and her husband returned to their small community, bought a farm, and worked together. Her world suddenly shrank. She had no outside job, no sources of self-esteem beyond the farm. Her friendships narrowed to those her husband chose: "We got back into the same circle of John's friends and family and their little kiddies and we all went to church on Sunday and we're all one big happy family." Her husband disapproved of the friends she made and substituted others:

Well, I started putting out my feelers for who is around that *I* can relate to. So I met a couple of girls in town that had horses. The three of us would take the horses out and go riding. Bingo! John's nose was out of joint. This one girl swore, she would say all those four-letter words. Are you kidding? What kind of woman is this? This isn't a lady. She's a trouble causer. Well, I was a little aghast, but he wanted me to have his friends, and they did not fit into the category of my friends.

The inevitable irritations and disagreements of married life had no chance to be resolved equitably because of Therese's fear that speaking her feelings would jeopardize the marriage. The hierarchy that had existed in her parents' marriage resurfaced strongly in her own when Therese was unable to stand up for herself in relationship, just as her mother had been unable before her.

I could never assert myself. I could never say, "I'm not going to milk all them cows! I'm going to stay in the house." Or, you know, "I'm not going to drive tractor all day silo filling and beat my butt around the house trying to get lunch fixed and then be out on the tractor driving again right after lunch and then be in the barn," you know. I never did, I just felt this is the way it is. I mean there's two of us trying to make a go of this farm, but I just, I never did stand up . . .

I never could get out of that role. I guess I more or less let John take that role and I did what I felt was the woman's duty and the wife's duty until I felt, I just couldn't make it any more, doing it his way.

Therese felt she had no control over the changed circumstances of her life because she could not say anything. She grew increasingly isolated and angry at her husband.

When we came up here, why, of course, I couldn't work [off the farm]. I was required to be there sharing the workload, and that started making me despise him first, for killing that part of my life that I enjoyed doing, my own thing to do.

Though she blames her husband, Therese relates to him more as a personification of male authority in her world than as a unique person. What, at first, she overvalued—"I idolized him and I was going to do everything to measure up to the standards that were in his family"—could not be realized, either by Therese or by her too-human husband. Through disappointment, the idealization flipped to its opposite, devaluation, as she projected her rage over not "becoming who I am or want to be" onto him:

I just got to hate him. Everything that was there that was love and respect left. Every time I'd see him I'd just, be just like a cat with her fur up. I just hated him for putting me there, for putting me in that sort of a situation that he knew I was trying to get away from.

She projected responsibility for her thwarted creativity, her unlived self, onto her husband and blamed him for its loss.

Internal constraints are clearly operating here, since a man
cannot be fully in charge without a woman's acquiescence.
Therese fails to recognize her own complicity in reinforcing the
hierarchy by silencing herself. But the basis of her complicity is
complex. In part, the appeasement for abandoning her self is a
cultural promise that a man can do a better job of running her life
than she. Also operating are moral imperatives voiced by the
Over-Eye, which require her to "put the man first," "go along
with his wishes and values," under a threat of loss of love.
Identification with her mother's selflessness and powerlessness
in relationship and the belief that her mother went along with
her father's dominance because she had no other options also
push Therese to silence herself. As Carolyn Heilbrun (1988)
observes, the temptation of a conventional woman's life is a plot
well known, a path well marked, while other territories of self-
development within marriage are unknown and unnarrated.

Finally, Therese capitulated to harmful structures of relatedness out of the hope of love, the hope of a future created with
this man. Through her hopes, identifications, and fears run
threads of love, human needs, satisfactions, and self-deception.
Given these entanglements, how can she separate what is projection from what is reality, the truth from the lies, the harm
from the value? Part of Therese's tragedy is that she never voiced
her feelings, and never found out whether she interacted with a
projection or with a man who was truly domineering and rigid,
incapable of change. "I never did tell him what was happening
to me. He tells me I should have, and now I know I should
have." Because she can only imagine how her husband would
have responded to such interactions, Therese's task of sorting
out self-responsibility is all the more difficult.

Therese's reluctance to assert herself was increased by her
belonging to a conservative Christian church, which explicitly
taught that a woman should be submissive to her husband. This
message lent authority to the Over-Eye's condemnations of her
inner promptings for self-expression and freedom as selfish and

wrong. Seeing no choices, Therese "didn't feel like I wanted to live anymore. I knew I was so miserable in the life I had, and I just—I knew that divorce was an absolute sin." She saved a number of Valium tablets prescribed by her family doctor and began planning suicide. When she was at the point of "giving up," when "all I could think of was suicide, suicide," Therese's husband hired an extra hand to work on the farm. Gradually, she began to share her desperate feelings with this young man.

> I confided in him wholeheartedly. I told him I had thought about just checking out of the whole situation, the whole world, I figured that was my only way out. He knew I was dead serious about what I was talking about doing. He felt extremely sympathetic towards me and he'd really try to help me. He says, "Hey, that isn't the only way out. You can move out and get a job and try it on your own."

Over the period of a year, the relationship developed and she began to *feel:* "We had so much fun, we'd laugh at the same things, we'd enjoy the same music."

Finding support, Therese emerged from behind her mask of compliance to express her sexuality and to release her pent-up resentment and rage. She did not mind shattering the marriage that mirrored what she was "supposed to be." Erupting from behind her willed angel image came the "selfish," active woman who moved out one afternoon with the 25-year-old hired man. She, like Baubo, a mythic figure of uninhibited sexuality, seemed momentarily not to care about others' opinions. Nor Hall (1980) describes Baubo as a "sacred imp of feminine licentiousness who is ever ready to oppose 'straight-lipped' prudery. As the impulse of unrestrained life she may be constellated by restraint, over-seriousness, emotional control, or depression" (1980, pp. 46–47). Inhibited by her "religious" husband, who made her feel "so obstructed," Therese never did "instigate lovemaking" in her marriage. Describing the sexual relationship with her husband, Therese says, "There was nothing there. He didn't even have the imagination." But with this new relationship, she found delight and freedom in sexual intimacy: "We made love down and dirty."

To Therese, this young man seemed a personification of her own unlived creative potential and vitality, her desire for change. Metaphorically, sexual union represents a yearning for integration with a part of the self that is shut off and repressed. In acting out her longings and rage before she had acknowledged or voiced them, Therese chose an unconscious path, a path that frequently leads to disaster. As she said of her relationship with her husband, "Living with him, I was not what I wanted to be, and when I started to rebel, I was still not what I wanted to be." So long split off from her authentic self, confined by stories that present limited possibilities for self-realization, Therese attempts to find herself through actions that never do reflect that real self.

Without passing judgment on the path Therese took, let us join her in examining its effects on her sense of inner division and her depression. Such an affair can be the first step over a precipice of unknowing destruction, or a movement toward self-knowledge through expressing repressed parts of the self *with* someone who validates them. In her interviews two years later, Therese is deeply confused, depressed, and self-condemning. She abhors her actions, which, she thinks, prove that she is a monster. The affair lasted a year, she ends up divorced, her ex-husband calls her a "snake in the grass," she feels disgraced in the small town. From the Christian therapist Therese and her husband went to for help in saving their marriage, she felt "a real slap in the face." "To us he presented that I had hurt John enough. He said, 'Give this man his freedom, and let him find someone that will really love him.' "

With overwhelming outer judgment against her behavior, Therese retreats from challenging the authority of tradition, the church, counselors, and joins her voice with their chorus in moral condemnation.

I feel like I'm trash, I really do. I can't face my friends. I feel morally shitty, yes, because I know what marriage is supposed to mean. It was supposed to be forever and ever and I intended it to be forever and ever and it didn't become forever and ever. So, yeah, if there were anything in the world I could do, it would be to retrace my steps. Even though it was a lousy marriage, I mean an absolutely lousy marriage. We had no relationship. There was no giving and taking.

Abandoning herself as unworthy of moral concern, Therese sees a future that remains morally hopeless.

After divorce, there's really nothing. As far as the wedding goes, anything, there's nothing left after you get divorced. God's left you out in the cold, you've left yourself out in the cold.

By now, we recognize these strong judgments as coming from the Over-Eye, which accepts collective views about women's goodness and condemns the authentic self. Tightening the circle of her despair comes this voice that tells her she could have kept the relationship if only she had maintained a tighter guard:

There's a couple of ways that I will always think I did wrong . . . I just flew off the handle. I just absolutely flew off the handle. I did not want the marriage any longer, I didn't want him any longer, I couldn't stand him any longer, and that was it.

Therese flew off the handle that kept the authentic self locked away in solitary confinement. Without the restrictive jailer on duty, her repressed, unexpressed self emerged, a woman who pulled off her angel mask and began drinking, loving, laughing, and flouting the norms of goodness. Unable to live out the conventional narrative of the happily married or that of the resigned, unhappily married, Therese became, in her words, "my own maker of rules."

A critical factor in Therese's self-condemnation was not only, in Heilbrun's words, "the gender arrangements, the appropriate behavior, that had confined [her] in stories that had always been assumed to be intelligent and fair"; she was also powerfully affected by "the absence of any narrative" that could take her past her "moment of revelation" and support her "bid for freedom from the assigned script" (Heilbrun, 1988, p. 42). Therese remained caught in the conventional script in which she had to be either a good woman or a bad woman—an adulteress. As she attempted to break free and satisfy her longing to be authentic within relationship, she interpreted her actions in restricting, demeaning terms supplied to her by part of the culture that wished to control her. She had no bonding with other women, no positive connection with the murmurings of the authentic self, no way to understand or interpret them other than the traditional, well-known stories. With Therese, as with other depressed women, Heilbrun's statement rings achingly true: "Not only had these women no stories other than their refusal of the plot in which most women lived, and no women with whom to talk of what they had themselves learned, but they would have been hard put to answer the inevitable question asked of unhappy women: What do you want?" (1988, p. 43).

But Therese's problem extends beyond a lack of language or images to power: power to determine what meanings are dominant, what choices a woman has, how much she needs to go along with things in order to survive. The culture that fears women's agency and freedom has an investment in splitting women into two, in encouraging their aggression against themselves. Such inner division creates a conviction that a woman's problems are internal and idiosyncratic, and turns her energies to self-battle, diverting her from recognizing larger destructive social patterns and from waging more constructive battles.

To claim the strength of wholeness, to integrate repressed parts of the self, allows for commitment and change within relationships. As a metaphor of the psychological task of modern woman, Sylvia Perera describes the ancient Sumerian myth of the descent of Inanna, Queen of the Heavens, to meet Ereshkikal, the Queen of the underworld and of death. The unknown "dark goddess's" unacknowledged forces are "felt as depression and an abysmal agony of helplessness and futility, as unacceptable desire and transformative-destructive energy, unacceptable autonomy (the need for separateness and self-assertion) split off, turned in, and devouring the individual's sense of willed potency and value" (1985, p. 152). Without integrating these aspects, a woman remains a good daughter of the patriarchy—innocent, agreeable, avoiding confrontation with her own power to hurt and to destroy. When a woman consciously identifies with the culture's ideal of feminine "goodness" as self-abnegating support of others, she "keeps [her] strength, which she needs to foster her individual integrity, in the underworld" (ibid., p. 178).

The intensity and range of Therese's feelings came as a surprise, even to her. Observing that her attempts to find closeness and change her marital situation were destructive to her husband and to her self and brought moral condemnation from the church, Therese thinks her own vision of relationships (as well as her self) must be selfish and immoral. Since the only ways Therese was able to assert herself in her marriage were ways she now judges as self-destructive—plans for suicide, an affair, divorce—she continues to be afraid of her self-assertion. She sees no way to care for herself, to act on her own needs and feelings, without being destructive, and no way to care for a man without losing her self. She remains deeply divided and confused over the legitimacy of her feelings, including her wishes for emotional and sexual expression.

Knowing that she never spoke her feelings in relationship, aware of her self-abdication, Therese now concludes that instead of acting out her anger and resentment through an affair, "I shouldn't have left, I should have said, 'This is how I feel, and I'm not going to that barn again even if you set fire to my feet.' Well, he wouldn't have, but I didn't know that."

Therese's narrative shows the importance of the social context as well as the need for inner knowledge. Without an ear cocked and receptive to her "real self," without a positive inner dialogue that affirms and honors the values and vision of that self, a woman can act without real knowledge of her needs and how to meet them. Therese continues to be plagued by doubts about having brought a precipitous end to the marriage because she never tested whether her husband was capable of changing. Not having tried out being honest in the marriage, she is left wondering how her husband would have responded to her authentic self. Further, if by acting on her felt needs a woman violates social norms, she needs to anticipate outer criticism and develop sources of support to deal with it. Therese incurs the censure of the community and mistakenly interprets this censure to mean that concealment of her authentic self in the future is absolutely necessary.

Therese's narrative also reveals the power of externalized judgments to swing self-assessment to the negative pole when it hangs suspended, caught between the conventional view and a self-forged construction of goodness. Because traditional teachings about women's role require self-sacrifice and submissiveness, a woman must defend herself against a morality that supports the very destruction of her authenticity through rendering her selfless, a selflessness that is labeled "good" and "normal" for women. She can defend herself only through self-knowledge and self-respect, and even that, unfortunately, is not enough.

Popular wisdom teaches that we must love ourselves first, and that we are weak and powerless if we need validation from others, but relational theory holds otherwise. As selves who do not exist in isolation, who are not autonomously functioning, island-like units of self-contained confidence and esteem, we need both a positive relationship with the self *and* love, acceptance, and validation from others. In fact, as research demonstrates, these two aspects—the quality of relationships and the nature of self-regard—go hand in hand.[14] A person does not spontaneously learn to love the self in a vacuum and then go on to have loving relationships. Rather, loving relationships accompany transformations within the inner world, and those transformations foster loving relationships. The puzzle is, within a culture that teaches women to silence themselves as a way to be safe and achieve relatedness, how can a woman learn to take the risk of exposing her authentic self to create mutuality and dialogue within relationship?

THE SELF IN DIALOGUE: MOVEMENT OUT OF DEPRESSION

. 6 .

I'm on a search trip for what a woman is really like.

The high rates of depression in women can be seen as an almost inevitable response to living in a culture that deeply fears and devalues the feminine.[1] In the void of models presenting a female self who is active and authentic in relationships, women internalize prevailing cultural images of femininity, love, and achievement and become "easy targets for depression, a depression bound by patriarchy and robbed of its organic, mythic nature and consequently, its healing properties" (Holub, 1989, p. 6). With no celebration of the feminine mysteries—the blossoming of the female body, menarche, childbirth, menopause—and with few images of feminine strength, women's rite of passage to reclaim and create a self may necessarily include moving through despair about a self set aside in the quest for acceptance and love.

Nor Hall calls on myth to explain the "descent to the underworld" that characterizes woman's search for a lost self.

> Rites of seasonal and human passage are gone—the Mother-Daughter rites lasted for 2,000 years . . . We are left without meaningful rules of ritual conduct—but the mystery remains . . . the descent to the underworld, the barren period of waiting, and the long sorrowful procession . . . imitating the

Mother's [Demeter's] search—these stages of the rite no longer have visible structures, symbols, or spaces to manifest in, but rather have themselves turned inward so that the initiation is an active entry into the dark terrain of an unknown self where we still search for the lost daughter, the feminine source of life . . .

The unconscious self has an autonomous way of making itself known; if people do not gather anymore on a sacred road to search for their lost souls, the gathering together and the search will be translated into the movement and language of our interiors. Rites of passage have turned inward where they can be lived out as stages of psychic transformation.   (1980, pp. 84–85)

Staying in the language of metaphor to search for the "lost daughter," let us consider the fairy tale Rumpelstiltskin as symbolic of women's depression within patriarchy.[2] The story tells of a miller's daughter whose father delivers her to the male-ruled world with promises of her ability to please. "I have a daughter who can spin gold out of straw," says her father to the king. Entering the kingdom by virtue of her ability to give to a man what he most deeply desires—the treasure of her sexuality—the "beautiful daughter" of the tale is welcomed, but only if she is able to fulfill expectations. The king says to the miller, "That is an art in which I am much interested. If your daughter is as skillful as you say she is, bring her to my castle tomorrow, and I will put her to the test."

Following the conventional narrative of a woman's life, the daughter moves directly from her father's realm to that of the king, not arguing with the tasks or qualities assigned to her by paternal authorities. The drama that unfolds might have followed another plot had she not remained silently compliant but stood up to false expectations and said, in effect, "I choose to come into relation to the male world in my own way rather than by gratifying the wishes of the 'king.'" With only the conventional story of marriage as a model, with neither mother nor other women present throughout the story to provide guidance for alternative possibilities, the miller's daughter follows the assigned script. She has little choice: how can she possibly respond to the king's demands in ways she has never imagined nor seen lived?[3]

Represented to the king by her own father as a daughter with magical powers to please, but as someone she is not, she must comply with the image or be killed. "If between tonight and tomorrow at dawn you have not spun this straw into gold, you must die," says the king. The miller's daughter steps straight into dilemmas about relationships that confront girls at adolescence—Will she enact a pretense in order to gain male favor, safety, and security? Dare she be herself? She believes, from what she has been told, that she must fabricate the expected lie or face an overwhelming threat. At this point, she becomes depressed, hopeless about the impossible transformation she must accomplish to be acceptable to the king. As she weeps alone behind the locked door, Rumpelstiltskin (that male-identified part of the female self that knows what the male world wants and how to give it) springs into life. Explaining the reason for her tears, the miller's daughter tells him, "Alas, I've got to spin gold out of straw, and don't know how to do it."

Rumpelstiltskin is activated in her psyche by the perceived necessity to please the king—that is, the desirable man, success, achievement, whatever commands in the male realm she must fulfill to gain favor and prevent punishment. But Rumpelstiltskin demands gifts from the miller's daughter before he will help her spin the deception. At first they do not seem like much—a ring, a necklace—a small sacrifice of truth here, a slight forgoing of her interests and creativity there. These gifts of self seem to promote her own good, but they further a pretense that begins to oppose her authenticity. Rumpelstiltskin's activity enables the miller's daughter to present to the king a self who does the impossible, but she knows herself to be much less (or something other) than she appears. She strives to be someone she is not in order to gain favor and ensure survival. No wonder that women who feel they have gained the approval of the king through other than their authentic selves feel like impostors and frauds.[4]

As the fairy tale progresses, the demands of the inner tyrant

(Rumpelstiltskin) and the outer tyrant (the king) become almost indistinguishable. Instead of being appeased by her impossible feat, the king places the miller's daughter in a larger room with a greater amount of straw on the second night and orders her "to spin it also in one night, if she value[s] her life." Rumpelstiltskin reappears, to demand his gift as well. On the third night, when the miller's daughter (unnamed throughout the tale) is locked into a still larger room with even more straw, the king says, "This must you spin tonight into gold, but if you succeed, you shall become my Queen." Rumpelstiltskin again comes to ask what she will offer to have him spin the illusion. As women often do when pressed to the limit, the miller's daughter says, "I have nothing more to give." Rumpelstiltskin demands, "Promise me your first child if you become Queen." The story goes on: " 'Who knows what may happen?' thought the miller's daughter, but she did not see any other way of getting out of the difficulty."

Imagining no other options that would ensure her survival, she acts against her best interests and promises to give up the symbol of her future wholeness and creativity, the nascent self. Rumpelstiltskin once more spins straw into gold. The king comes in the morning and finds "everything as he had wished." Having fulfilled his desires, the miller's daughter becomes queen.

Caught up in enacting the role of queen—wife, professional, sex symbol, whatever—the miller's daughter forgets her promise to Rumpelstiltskin. Then comes the infant, whose birth signifies, as in dreams and myths, the existence of a fragile new self, an emergent consciousness that needs care and nurturance.

After the child is born, Rumpelstiltskin reappears, bent on robbing the woman of this dawning self. "The Queen was terrified, and offered the little man all the wealth of the kingdom if he would let her keep the child. But the little man said, 'No, I would rather have some living thing than all the treasures of the world.' " The tale continues: "Then the Queen began to moan and weep to such an extent that the little man felt sorry for her. 'I will give you three days,' said he, 'and if within that time you discover my name you shall keep the child.' "

In the tale of the patriarchal daughter, Rumpelstiltskin steps into consciousness to press his demands at two key points in her life. First, he appears as this young woman moves into heterosexual relationship. Each time she sits alone in the strained, ragged center of her despair, trapped by expectations to enact a pretense, she experiences depression, hopelessness, and fear. These are the times the authoritative, male-identified aspect of self interrupts to take over, willing to perform the activity required to yield the expected transformation. Occurring privately behind locked doors, the self-alteration required to give the king what he expects remains invisible to others, a secret known only to the miller's daughter. But the self-change exacts a price.

Rumpelstiltskin comes at a second point in the young woman's development. At this symbolic time, the birth of her "beautiful child," he demands of her, "Now, give me what you promised." This moment can be interpreted on two levels. First, if the birth of the child is taken literally, a woman encounters the commands of the authorities telling her what she must do to be a perfect mother in their eyes. Rumpelstiltskin quickly appears as the inner tyrant, ready to rob her of her own perspective and thus of her direct experience, feelings, and values. Second the male-identified aspect of self becomes conscious and demanding at points when a woman tries to nurture a new self, a new consciousness or creativity. Rumpelstiltskin comes, telling her she must give it over to him—it is *his* property to do with as he will.

To accomplish the difficult task of naming Rumpelstiltskin, the queen enlists the help of messengers, those aspects of self not immobilized by the threat of loss. She first searches culture for the identity of her oppressor. She calls "to mind all the names that she [has] ever heard, and [sends] a messenger all over the country to inquire far and wide what other names there were." Through this exhaustive search, she learns about the cultural roots of inner prescriptions and demands. But this is not enough. As the queen calls Rumpelstiltskin all the names she knows, at every one, the little man says, "No. No. That's not my name." Then the queen steps outside of ordinary frameworks to search for new ways of knowing and naming. In the story, this happens when the queen "suggest[s] to the little man all the most unusual and strange names": "Perhaps your name is Cow-ribs, or Spindleshanks, or Spiderlegs?" But this quest to confront her personal tyrant by likening him to strange figures also fails. Finally, on the third day, the queen's messenger comes across Rumpelstiltskin's identity "round the corner of a wood on a lofty mountain, where the fox says good night to the hare." Here, within the forest, that place of healing where things take root and grow, the name is discovered. In the midst of a symbolic reconciliation of opposites, where the fox and the hare live in harmony—a place where pain and death can lead to rebirth and healing—the inner tyrant is recognized and no longer poses a threat.

The fairy tale teaches that the way out of a depression bounded by patriarchy is not through continuing to enact the expected pretense or through allowing the male-identified as-pect of self to take over. The miller's daughter (now queen) frees herself from Rumpelstiltskin's despotism by her own power to correctly name and confront that which has the ability to rob her of her very self. Enlisting the aid of all her resources, she must search to discover the identity of the inner voice that urges her to fulfill collective prescriptions and demands. She must seek the origins of that voice from her own background and from culture. But the fairy tale indicates that the only way to heal the deep inner split and the loss threatened to this woman is to go into that part of the psyche symbolized by nature—the seat of spon-taneous feeling, the place where the timeless feminine mysteries of birth, death, and rebirth occur. And, moving into a search within her inner nature, apart from civilization's shoulds, she gains a perspective that allows her to overhear the voice that divides her against herself.

> Today I bake; tomorrow I brew my beer;
> The next day I will bring the Queen's child here.
> Ah! lucky 'tis that not a soul doth know
> That Rumpelstiltskin is my name. Ho! Ho!

Armed with this revelation of the harmful voice's identity, a woman then can redirect Rumpelstiltskin's destructiveness back onto himself so that, in a rage, he "[tears] himself asunder in the middle." The message is that by correctly perceiving, naming, and confronting, women can use anger to disarm the inner tyrant and free the authentic self. In this optimistic ending, the daughter, now queen, gains the freedom to nurture her emergent self within the kingdom. She can now accomplish the tasks of female development within a male-dominated world.

Women often describe themselves in the mythic position of having to spin straw into gold by morning. Gaile, age 35, trying to meet competing expectations experienced from home and from work, explains:

> The demands are impossible. The phone rings all day long and I'm busy all day long and I don't have a minute to even think about what to do about the next project. The week will start out and the first thing I'll do Monday night is I'll take a bunch of work home with me. And I'll work, work, work Monday night. And then I'll be nuts working all day Tuesday and then I'll take work home with me again. And in addition to that, you have a brief due and the clients are cranky and, you know, you snap at the secretary or the, the partner or something. And it's really stressful to have a client that you feel is either not listening to you or listens to you and then goes out and does the wrong thing anyway and you're constantly having to resolve those problems.
>
> And the other stress is time. Time is the biggest stress. There's never enough time to get everything done. Where do I find time to be with my son and husband? I'm so busy all the time that my personal relationships have suffered a lot. I'm almost uneasy if I don't take a briefcase full of work home with me. Even if I don't look at it. It's there. And I'm comforted by the fact that I have brought my work home with me and I have until morning to do it.

Like the miller's daughter who has "until morning," Gaile lives with requirements to meet inhuman outer demands for success in the kingdom.[5] In acquiescing to an expectation that she should be able to accomplish anything asked of her, Gaile must deny her realistic limits, a denial that already exacts a price.

Depressed women also speak of a perceived necessity to transform the self to be suitable for marriage to a desired man. Rita, age 19, says,

> Bill does not like fat women so therefore I lost weight, because I heard about it twenty-four hours a day and I couldn't stand it. And, you know, he has told me about one thousand times, but it was his way of helping me get it off, you know, so I don't feel like I'm being used, but he just cares about me, not for my looks or anything like that.

In a kind of doublespeak, Rita both asserts her perceptions and negates them in one breath, transforming (as does the miller's daughter) the straw of reality into the gloss of an acceptable lie: "I (don't) feel like I'm being used . . . he just cares about (me, not for) my looks." Rita sees what her partner cares about but denies that knowledge and works to shape herself to his image. If Rita and other women could observe from a different perspective, from a "corner of the wood on a lofty mountain, where the fox says good night to the hare," the deeply destructive nature of their actions against themselves, as well as the origins of those actions, might become clear.

When we consider women's depression from a relational perspective, the metaphor for movement out of despair becomes dialogue. Dialogue is a form of relation, not just of speech (Buber, 1970). It provides a way to come into new forms of relation with others, with the self, and with the world beyond the self. Women, as equals, have been excluded from the cultural dialogue; they have been the subjects of someone else's story. Women also have been the objects of male violence, a circumstance that further removes them from dialogue.

We have seen how depressed women describe loss, not of the other, but of self, and how they equate this "loss of self" with the silencing of their voices in intimate relationships. Intimacy does not occur through pleasing the "king." Rather, intimacy can only occur through a dialogue between other and self within which the "I" is present.

If a woman is ashamed of her "I"—if she sees it as worthless, incompetent, fat, unlovable—then she attempts to keep it hidden. If dialogue does not include the authentic self, then the "I" is excluded from relationship. It feels hopeless and helpless about making a close connection with another person. Depression seems inevitable when a woman abandons hope of authentic connection, or when she can imagine only two possibilities for her future: subordination or isolation, holding a form of loss on either side.

Listening to the moral themes in depressed women's narratives, we discover how and why a woman feels ashamed of the authentic self. This inner dialogue reveals not only hidden aspects of women's psychology but also the culture's direct contribution to the high rates of depression in women. Compliant relatedness, compulsive caretaking, and silencing the self—all these behaviors become channels through which to reach the desired other. The modes of making contact carry social approval and appear to offer safety and security of attachment. Instead they lead to depression. Sisyphus-like, depressed women speak of "trying so hard" to make their relationships work. But they are pushing the boulder up the wrong hill, trying to please others to ensure relationship when, instead, they should be "trying so hard" to include themselves—their feelings, initiative, values, perspectives—in intimate relationships.

Two forms of silence appear in women's portrayals of their depression. One holds despair and isolation; the other contains possibilities for movement and change. If the authentic self is locked in solitary confinement, forbidden to communicate with others, then the authentic self's silence indicates absence of relation. Such a silent, stuck depression is characterized by an angry reproachfulness toward the partner, who does not know what the anger is about, and a condemning harshness toward the self. The silence of this type of depression holds despair, resignation, and hopelessness. It seems characteristic of chronic depressions, though, in more extreme form, it also characterizes major depression.

If silence indicates a withdrawal from the authoritative voices of others and from the critical gaze of the Over-Eye in order *to be with* the "I," then that silence holds the possibility of healing. Such a withdrawal can offer a safe, incubating "egg place" (Hall, 1980) of creative darkness, waiting, and transformation, where new understandings and new strength are found. Depression becomes a descent to the repressed side of self, to the underside of the "good woman," to reclaim the parts of self that have been set aside for so long that a woman is mourning their loss. Here a woman must do inner work, work whose reference is always relationships—with the unknown side of self, with inner urgings and tasks, with the real other.

The healing possibilities arise out of a dialogue of inner questioning and attentiveness to the authentic self (rather than condemning and critical judgments directed at the "I"). Such new dialogues yield statements like the following one from Susan, who actively questions the structure of her relating and the images that have guided her choices. Susan labels the images that keep her from enacting what she needs "plastic reasons,"

> because they're superficial in the sense that they're social or not having a lot to do with my own personal needs for fulfillment and gratification and esteem and worth. I'm putting those things aside for a facade in the social realm of my life. That's what I think I'm doing.

Maya, talking about trying to leave false, restrictive images of the feminine self in relationship, says, "I'm on a search trip for what a woman is really like."

The movement into depression can become a venture into self-knowing to understand the roots of inner division and self-alienation, to name the Over-Eye and substitute one vision of goodness, authority, and relatedness for another. As a healing "rite of passage" to claim one's self and bring it into the kingdom, depression requires moving through the confusion of developmental transition. This is a time of uncertainty, when the frameworks a woman has used to interpret her experience and make meaning of her life clash with new, emerging perspectives. As these women indicate, the images of self in relationship that have guided their lives are called into question through painful experiences such as battering, separations, drug use, and depression. These experiences prove to a woman that her inherited assumptions about how to gain intimacy do not bring the desired results, but hold despair and self-loss.

A depressed woman needs courage to leave ideas and pain that have become familiar and leap, like a spider held only with an invisible silken thread, into the unknown where she must spin her own meanings. Adrift without anchors for self-understanding, without firm beliefs about role, relationships, and morality, she must trust her capacity to build her own web of meaning and connection strong enough to hold herself and, perhaps, her children. As Laura says:

> I have fears that I'm going to get up to the end and this something's going to say, "You're not going to do it" because, you know, those things of how once you break away your foundation of what you've always criticized yourself for, what's there after that? What do you do then? I guess it's the feeling that I'm used to thinking of myself as not being good enough.

Echoing the transitional theme of moving into the uncomfortable unknown, Maya says:

> The other night I laid in bed and I thought, "I wonder who I am and what I am." And I tried to formulate

something and I didn't come up with anything concrete. I'm not what I was in the past and I'm not what I'm to be, I'm just kind of in between.

Maya elaborates on the difficulty she has in thinking in new ways:

It's a real conflict. Because I'll find myself thinking, oh, maybe something I was told in the past and what I believe in now, and there's always such a big difference, a gap, a change in my thinking and it is sometimes frightening.

(*How is it frightening?*) Because I feel like I'm pulling away from something that has been with me for so long.

Unable to articulate precisely what she is "pulling away from" and unable to envision what she is moving to in the future, Maya feels "suspended." The uncertainty becomes more difficult because of low self-esteem, a global feeling of not being "good enough," which is tied to the devaluation of her gender. Carol Gilligan describes this transition as the shift from a conventional understanding of care "where right is defined by others and responsibility rests with them" (1982, p. 123) to a postconventional construction of care, where earlier beliefs about goodness are rejected "as immoral in their power to hurt" (p. 90). The shift is facilitated by a change in focus from being good to being honest, to finding out how the self and others "really" feel, and by entering into dialogue from this new position.

Likewise, this transition described by depressed women appears to be what Marcia Westkott calls a "transformation of the dependent responsibility associated with female altruism" (1986, p. 203). Elaborating on this transformation, Westkott specifies what is being left, and what is being gained:

Instead of retreating into a protected sphere, caring for others through a fearful need for them, or recoiling from their authority, the female hero believes that she herself is worthy of care and that the world is her domain. She practices an empowered caring that risks conflict to change the world so that women and the socially necessary need to care for one another are no longer devalued.   (ibid.)

Both Gilligan and Westkott detail the difficulty of this transition from powerless giving to empowered relating. The passage holds a loss of old ways of seeing and interacting and, for many women, includes the mourning of a self and of relationships that have been lost and must be reclaimed or, perhaps, recreated.

At the time when a woman feels her world has crashed around her, when her self-esteem is lowest, she must create new ways of knowing and interacting with others. Within a vacuum of self-doubt, she has to trust her own perceptions and realize she is responsible for the shape her life will take. She must become the actor and author of her own story, not the subject of someone else's plot. The crumbling of old structures in the transition of depression also brings a fearful uncertainty about how to relate to achieve intimacy if former patterns are laid aside. The women in this study do not want to give up connections with men. They seek new forms of relatedness but, not finding them available in the culture, have to create their own vision of those connections. As Heilbrun says, the culture "has failed to evolve a narrative of marriage that will make possible their development, as individuals and as a couple" (1988, p. 27).

In this period of crisis, a woman can face the uncertainty as a creative disintegration that brings new possibilities. But women also retreat to the security of familiar pain, of trying to fulfill the traditional role with all their energies. While promising safety, such retreat also deflects a woman from engagement with the larger questions of meaning-making and life's purpose that she may not be ready to entertain. It took the miller's daughter the magical three times before she faced her depression in a different way. Betty, for example, unwilling at one point to question the whole structure of her life, threw herself into "Just being Mrs. Perfect, I guess. Just being everything Bill wanted me to be, I guess, which is a tall order." As with many of the women, she entered severe depression when she realized that these efforts did not create intimacy, yet she had no vision of an alternative. When her husband had an affair, she felt abandoned, unloveable, and "like a failure."

> I felt like my worth was dependent on being a good wife and mother. When that was falling apart, I didn't feel like I was worth anything. I didn't want to live.

At this time of greatest vulnerability, a woman must create new ways of valuing herself, new ways of perceiving, and new ways of interacting. As Mary Belenky and her colleagues describe this task, "To learn to speak in a unique and authentic voice, women must 'jump outside' the frames and systems authorities provide and create their own frame" (1986, p. 134).

How does this occur? What allows a person to see through collective standards that may be false to life and emotion? The narratives of women who move out of depression alert us to several important aspects. First, the women begin to gain a perspective that leads them to question the status quo. The questioning occurs in moral language; it is the *moral authority* of dominant systems of meaning that begins to crumble. This allows a woman to evaluate herself by different standards and to move away from those which are opposed to her adult development and to her authentic relatedness. Since depression involves an alteration of one's view of self, and since self-evaluation fundamentally affects the view of self, changes in perspective that confer meaning and value become critical for movement out of depression.

The studies I draw on in this book indicate that depressed women organize their interpretations of interpersonal events and feelings according to a *moral order of meaning*. As a woman spontaneously narrates the history of her depression, she conveys the meanings she attaches to events and their effect on her self-regard. To repeat, these meanings are explicitly moral. Because women are more interpersonally oriented than men, events in the domain of relationships are most relevant to their definition and evaluation of self. If we accept the relational theorists' premise that making and maintaining relationships are primary motivations throughout life, then analysis of cognitive schemas about the self-in-relation becomes vital to the understanding and treatment of depression. The cognitive schemas most potent for a woman's depression are *beliefs about the self in intimate relationships*, specifically her understanding about what it means to be "good enough" to be loved. Thus, the moral meanings she gives to events, primarily interpersonal events, profoundly affect her self-esteem.

Changes in the moral standards a woman uses to negatively judge the self come about as her personal experiences accumulate and begin to challenge cultural shoulds. A woman begins to notice that the frameworks she uses to interpret her experiences no longer make sense of them. Too many of her perceptions spill out of the cognitive frameworks used to confer meaning and regroup outside to challenge their adequacy. Piaget described the process of changing frameworks as resulting from dynamic interactions between experience and reflection on that experience. In "accommodation," the conceptual schemas one uses to interpret experience are created and modified by one's actual experiences; in "assimilation," experiences are fitted into one's already existing conceptual schemas. In depression, the cognitive frameworks most important to the relational self—those that guide how one has relationships, how one protects them, how one is good within them—have been challenged by events and are in transition. A woman can no longer assimilate experience to existing frameworks, and must change those most vital to her sense of self. As she begins to see and interpret experience differently, she begins to question prevailing cultural values, which include moral prescriptions for women's behavior.

Listen to the following women:

It sounds kind of funny to say divorce isn't right, but then to say it's right for me though. I've reached the point where—*I saw* a lot of frustration on his part; *I saw* frustration in my children and me, that things weren't getting any better, in fact they were getting worse.   *(Betty, second interview, explaining her decision to file for divorce)*

I was able to start seeing more and more of what was going on and *I saw* that a lot of their [the church's and her husband's] interpretations were not true. They couldn't be true because they were hurting people.   *(Maya, third interview, explaining what allowed to question her husband's and the church's authority, thus freeing her to leave the marriage)*

We stayed with my folks for several months before we moved in here. And *I saw* that Mom creates a lot of her own problems. And I think *that was the first time that I'd ever really seen that, or been able to admit it.* I'm not sure which is the case. And there are times when she's not willing to take a chance that he [Dad] might do something differently. He's always done it this way in the past, therefore he's—you know . . . And so *now I can kind of see it more,* you know, just *see their situation more clearly* and realize that my mom isn't always happy, but part of it is her own fault. Then *I saw* you can't blame somebody else for your unhappiness. And, instead of thinking my husband is right, or I have to do things a certain way for him, *I need to see what I feel first.*   *(Diana, second interview)*

I asked to see a copy of the [prenuptial] agreement I had signed. I was absolutely stunned by it. I got very angry because I realized that my rights had been totally neglected, and it was an anger over the strictly tangible black-and-whiteness of the relationship. It sort of began to override in importance all the emotional stuff suddenly, and I began to realize that I had been really taken and in essence, to me, our marriage had been a big sham and it was all on his terms. It was unfair and immoral of him to trick me into signing it when I was trusting and naive.   *(Susan, last interview, explaining the basis for her decision to divorce her husband)*

These women tell us that what frees them to leave damaging relationships or to change within them is their new-found ability *to see for themselves* and to question the interpretations that had formerly guided their perceptions and actions. This language of vision, of seeing differently, comes in as women describe the process of moving out of depression. As the Over-Eye's gaze and moral authority are challenged by the perspective of the "I," a woman begins to "see [the] situation more clearly" and to notice that she needs "to see what I feel first." This new, personally constructed vision replaces the moral meanings and shoulds present in the Over-Eye that had clouded vision and silenced the "I." Seeing themselves and their situations in new ways allows women to reclaim their voices—their feelings, their perspectives, and their activity—within relationship.

These cognitive shifts that allow such changes in perception, particularly in moral meanings, appear to *precede* changes in depressive symptoms. Cognitive schemas about the self in intimate relationships both guide behavior and confer moral meaning. They determine a woman's self-assessment about her past, present, and future and, thereby, lie at the heart of depression. These schemas arise out of a culture that has institutionalized inequality between the sexes, particularly in marriage. Traditional norms dictate women's secondary status and, when internalized through identification with the mother, lead to the dynamic of silencing the self with its accompanying anger and inner division.[6] Once these schemas are challenged, behaviors and symptoms can change.

Women also point to the importance of female friendships for movement out of depression. They detail an important aspect of the support offered by female friends: the freedom to risk being themselves and to test out new images of self in relationship. Laura, actively working on "trying not to feel responsible for everybody; I don't want to see them hurt," describes how her friend, Marion, is helping her learn to bring her voice into their relationship:

> Marion's real good for me. We had an argument not very long ago. I was having my hair cut and I have had some

bad experiences with her having my hair cut, and I did not want her to be around. And so she came in . . . and I went "Oh no," so she took a brush and says, "Well, do you mind if I brush it," and I thought I really don't want to hurt her, and she got really angry at me and said, "You never say what you think, you never!" And she just went on and on, and then so I said, "Okay, I don't want you in here at all." So that was, you know, well, I'm trying to get better at that. Marion is a good help with that.

For Laura, unused to disagreeing with people she cares about, this opportunity to practice with a friend offers a first step toward bringing her authentic self, whom she describes as "not good enough," out of isolation and into dialogue.

For Maya, too, the support of her friends was critical:

It just gave me the desire to keep on going. To really try and handle the situation that I was faced with rather than just giving up and going, just going into a real depression. And I know that that's probably what would have happened. I would have been really depressed, just let myself go, and would have gone into a type of isolation I think.

Some women have been so damaged by sexual abuse in childhood that they fear revealing their inner selves to anyone. Anna, who was unable to move out of depression during the period of the study, describes her inability to risk exposure of this hidden, devalued self within any relationship:

My friends ask me, "Anna, what are you feeling? What are you *really* feeling?" and I can't tell them. I don't know why, I just can't say it to anyone.

Her friends acknowledge the presence of Anna's silent double by addressing her twice, asking what she *really* feels. Anna's hidden self not only has to be given permission to speak but needs coaxing to come out of hiding, which she rarely does. Isolated at an early age by the incest that started when she was 8 years old, she was never able to speak of her feelings until age 52, when she shared the incest trauma with therapists during her first hospitalization for a major depression with psychotic aspects. By then, Anna had built impenetrable stone walls of protection around that fearful, "worthless" self, the place where she harbored a core sense of inner badness. As is characteristic of incest victims, she altered her self-concept to account for the devaluing, sexualizing treatment she received from her grandfather. In order to continue to believe that an abusive relative is good, a child blames herself and begins to think: I must be a bad person who deserves to be treated this way. Such alteration of her self-concept allows her to hold on to a sense of hope about her self and her future as she strives to be good and come into better forms of relationship. Anna is willing to change herself in any way necessary to remain in relationships; but she believes she must never reveal her core self (which she sees as worthless and bad) or else she will be rejected (Herman, 1989).

Anna finds it too painful, too difficult to communicate from that core aspect of self, except through occasional psychotic symptoms. In those times, clinic case records report, Anna was "worried about other people looking at her and others saying she was not good enough or was a bad person. [She was] also concerned about the idea that her house was bugged and that others were listening to her." In her narrative, Anna portrays the deep inner division she feels between an angry, shamed, and isolated authentic self and an outwardly compliant "good" self who tries to connect with others by hiding her real feelings.

> Here I think I am trying to be an honest person, but maybe I'm not an honest person. Maybe this is what I was telling myself because when the kids were with us on the boat, and we got up, I don't know what it was, maybe it was when the dog was barking, and I started to cry and I said, "I'm a liar, a cheat, and I'm no good." But

maybe that's what I was saying to myself, that I was putting up with the dog when I really don't want a dog. I don't know. I don't know. I've never explained to them what I meant and they haven't asked. I guess I just have to tune into my own feelings more. But for so long I haven't . . . hmm, maybe I've never, ever.

The shamed, angry self that Anna tries to exclude from relationship breaks through the veneer of virtue she presents to others, making her feel fundamentally divided. Banished to the background, this dispossessed self works to undermine the reality of the good, loving woman she has worked so hard to construct as an adult.

The centrality of moral themes to women's depression makes it critically important to engage with them in therapy. Moral beliefs, attached as they are to gender and identity, resist change for many reasons: their unconscious tie with parental approval and disapproval, their link in thought with being "good enough" to be loved and thus able to bring one's whole self into relation, their tie with cultural imperatives for women's goodness, and the expectations of male partners and the wider social world that female behavior conform to these imperatives. Images of how to be in relationship that require compliance, yielding, and/or hiding the self are reinforced by the culture's portrayal of women who want "too much" for themselves as certain to lose their relationships.

Many therapists veer away from exploring fundamental assumptions about "goodness" or moral behavior out of concern that such examination may encourage a client to tear down a moral framework and unleash sexual or aggressive behaviors that may lead to more losses. This fear of opening a Pandora's box without knowing how to recapture the unleashed woes comes, I think, from not understanding the nature of moral imperatives. Much of the training of therapists is remarkably silent on the subject of such imperatives—how they affect self-esteem and interpersonal relationships, and their links with gender and with culture. Despite reasons for resistance on the part of both therapist and client, moral themes provide an entry into the terrain of women's depression.

But focusing on moral themes is not enough. Depressed women tell us that they feel silenced. Remembering that dialogue is a form of relation, not just of speech, we are pulled to examine the therapy relationship itself. The therapeutic encounter must offer a quality of relatedness that hears the silenced "I" of a depressed woman and brings it into dialogue. This means that therapists need to *be with* the woman's "I." Instead of thinking that we, as clinicians or researchers, know how to interpret what she will say, our task is to be with her in attentive receptiveness for what *she* will uncover as she listens to her own self-knowledge within a safe relationship. In such a way, for both parties, listening can become a path to new wisdom.

In the Sumerian language, as Diane Wolkstein tells us, the word for ear and for wisdom is the same. "The ear, which is located mostly internally and is coiled like a spiral or labyrinth, takes in sounds and *begins to transform the imperceptible into meaning*" (Wolkstein and Kramer, 1983, p. 156, emphasis added). The ear, the path to wisdom, is a central metaphor in the myth of Innana, who has to travel to the underground to integrate the angry, destructive side of self in order to become whole. The opening line of the text foretells her path of healing: "From the Great Above the goddess opened (set) her ear, her receptor for wisdom, to the Great Below" (ibid., p. xvii).

The metaphors of dialogue, ear, and wisdom remove the objectivity and distance of the formal therapeutic encounter. "Unlike the eye, the ear requires closeness between subject and object. Unlike seeing, speaking and listening suggest dialogue and interaction" (Belenky et al., 1986, p. 18). As it currently exists, much of therapy reproduces a hierarchical relationship of (authoritative, male) therapist and (deferential, female) client. Bringing the hidden, fearful "I" back into active dialogue is not likely to happen within this arrangement. Or, if it does, the "I" is likely to repeat its attempts to please the more powerful authority in order to gain approval and love.

Recognizing that women have not been accepted as equal

partners in the cultural dialogue, that women's voices have been trained not to disrupt, not to challenge, not to assert, the therapy relationship must provide a different kind of dialogue, one that challenges prevailing interpersonal and intrapsychic patterns. As both parties attend carefully to the depressed woman's murmurings of feelings long condemned and silenced, the imperceptible can be recognized and transformed into meaning by being considered, and—perhaps—enacted, within a safe connection.

Acknowledging the truth of the feminist maxim "The personal is political," we come also to the issue of naming in therapy. Instead of exploring a woman's "depression," perhaps it is more effective to look together at the areas where a woman feels silenced, where she silences herself, where she is being inauthentic. Within the safety and attentiveness of a therapeutic dialogue, a woman may consider the risks of acting on her self-knowledge. What will it mean to listen to herself? To entertain seriously her own self-knowledge? To bring the "I" into relationship? What if that relationship is a specific intimate attachment, a company, a job, a profession? What if moving out of silence makes her an outsider, placing her beyond the conventional narrative of a woman's life while she attempts to find the vision, the words, and the actions that will allow authentic relationship?

A woman's social context is critical for its support or rejection of her newly emerging ways of seeing. Group work offers community support for a woman to form new interpretations and evaluations of interpersonal events. In groups, women can gain strength and support from one another through identifying, sharing, and reinterpreting (renaming) events together. Groups also allow movement beyond words to symbolism and ritual to help women break the destructive forms of relating they have learned. For example, within a group, Mary decided to present an outer, symbolic enactment of her inner changes. At 45, when she had been married for eighteen years and her three children were in school, Mary decided to go to college. On the evening of her first day of classes, her husband announced that he wanted a divorce. Mary had been depressed several times earlier in her marriage, but this event, his leaving just as she had decided to pursue her own development by going to school, threw her into a major depression. She was certain that the timing of his decision meant that her either/or understanding was true: either she had to sacrifice her identity and personal goals and live in his shadow, or she would be left alone.

After a year of working through the issues, Mary felt ready to symbolize with the group the passing of a set of beliefs that she no longer wanted to claim as hers. She designed two masks. One was gray and had no eyes and no mouth, to symbolize that she had been unable to see and unable to speak the truths of her own experience while living out the role of the "good wife." The other mask was brightly colored, smiling, eyes open, and symbolized her movement to claim choice and responsibility, and to see and speak her feelings. Wearing the gray mask, Mary burned pieces of paper with the following phrases or words written on them: "wife of——," "devalued," "silent," "pleasing." She then put on the brightly colored mask and spoke to the group about her new ways of perceiving and relating. She knew that this one symbolic act would have to be repeated countless times in concrete ways, but she had outwardly shared an inner transition with a community that supported her new images of self. Understanding the mythic, developmental dimensions of depression while supported by community allows a passage through the pain of loss and uncertainty to a healing transformation that holds new possibilities for relatedness.

Depression is both individual and social; it combines the personal and the political. The relational perspective asserts that the self *is* social. Mind and self come into being through communication with others. One cannot heal the self in isolation. Since the individual is in the deepest sense relational, and because women's vulnerability to depression lies in the quality of their relationships, it is the self-in-relation that begs for healing. A woman must work at this task herself and with others—perhaps in therapy, in group work, and with friends. But the fundamentally social nature of the healing implicates the cultural fabric. Each woman cannot seek these new forms of dialogue alone; they must come into being on a larger level, in ever widening circles. Women and men together must search for new forms of connection that transcend power differences and that allow for authentic dialogue and intimacy.

APPENDIXES
NOTES
REFERENCES
INDEXES

THE WOMEN IN THE
LONGITUDINAL STUDY

. APPENDIX A .

Before referral to the study each woman was diagnosed as depressed according to DSM III (1980) criteria by clinicians. Ten of the women were diagnosed as depressed under the 300.40 dysthymic disorder category, while two were diagnosed under 296.34, major depression, recurrent, with psychotic features.

The diagnosis of ten women under dysthymic disorder (or depressive neurosis), a category that first appeared in DSM III (1980), reflects, in my opinion, the *chronicity* of their symptoms rather than the absence of symptoms that would lead them to be diagnosed under major depression. In my interviews with the women, symptoms of major depression were clearly evident in all but one of the women (Julie). For at least two weeks, four of the specified symptoms of major depression were present: somatic aspects, such as weight loss, sleep disturbance, psychomotor agitation or retardation, loss of pleasure, energy, or sex drive; and/or other aspects of the symptom picture, such as feelings of worthlessness, self-reproach, guilt, problems in concentration, and suicidal feelings and attempts. I think that the following circumstances affected the referring therapists' diagnosis of these women's condition as dysthymia rather than as major depression: (1) therapists were using the DSM III in its first year of publication, and were still responding to the 300.40 category in the prior DSM II (1968). In the earlier 1968 version, the 300.40 category "was defined merely as 'an excessive reaction of depression due to an internal conflict or to an identifiable event . . .' For this reason, it was applied to a heterogeneous group of conditions" (DSM III, 1980, p. 377), including what DSM III calls major depression, single episode and recurrent (without melancholia, 296.22, 296.32); (2) the women were diagnosed only at intake, at which time all of them described *chronic* depression which, however, was not minor; (3) the tendency was to diagnose "down" in terms of severity.

In discussions of the DSM III category of dysthymic disorder, it is acknowledged that "the symptom set involved in dysthymia is very similar to that for major depression. The main boundary problem is with major depressive disorder, particularly the chronic form" (Klerman et al., 1987, p. 19). Further, the NIMH Collaborative Study has reported the phenomenon of "double depression," in which a substantial percentage of patients with dysthymia "have superimposed episodes of acute depression that meet the criteria for major depression" (ibid., p. 20). In this case, the authors suggest, "both diagnoses [major depression and dysthymic disorder] should be given." In my view, all of these women except Julie (see below) should receive the diagnosis of major depression, while some of them should have a diagnosis of both major depression and dysthymic disorder.

Age reported is at time of first interview, and subjects are presented in order of age, from youngest to oldest.

1.   *Rita*, age 19, was diagnosed 300.40, dysthymic disorder or depressive neurosis. She married shortly after graduating from high school and was physically and emotionally abused by her husband. She left him after a year and returned to live with her parents. She was a multiple substance abuser before and during her marriage. After attempting suicide twice, by an automobile accident and later by a drug overdose, she was required to be in therapy as a condition of release from hospitalization. At the time of her first interview she was divorced, living alone, involved with drugs, "overweight" (in her words), and very depressed. She had been concerned about her weight since 13, at which time she said she became "very heavy." By her last interview she was not depressed, had lost weight, was making plans for her future, had stopped using drugs, and was living with a man she was considering marrying. Her parents lived in the area and were still married. She had three interviews: two in March 1981 and one in September 1982.

2.   *Jan*, age 24, was diagnosed as 300.40, dysthymic disorder or depressive neurosis. She had completed four years of college and had been unhappily married for one year. At her first interview, she said she was depressed in her marriage and considering separation. Between her first and second interviews, she attempted suicide and then made the decision to separate from her husband. By the time of the second interview, she had enrolled in a masters program and was no longer depressed. Her parents were still married. Interviews occurred in September 1980 and September 1982.

3.   *Cindy*, age 26, was diagnosed 296.34, major depression, recurrent, with psychotic features. She was married with a girl, 5, and a boy, 2. She had graduated from high school and had not worked during her seven-year marriage. She was physically abused by her father when she was a child and abused her daughter during her second pregnancy. Reported to child

protective services, she received mandatory counseling. In her third pregnancy, she overdosed on Sinequan prescribed by her internist for treatment of depression at about the twenty-sixth gestational week and was hospitalized for three days. After the hospitalization, she had grave concerns about whether she had damaged the fetus. In the third pregnancy, her depression included auditory and visual hallucinations. During this time, she was involved in quarrels with her parents. In her last interview she was not depressed, though still taking Sinequan. Interviews were as follows: three during the last trimester of pregnancy, March and April 1981; two weeks after delivery, May 1981; five months after delivery, October 1981; and two final interviews, October 1982.[1]

4. *Julie*, age 30, was diagnosed 300.40, dysthymic disorder or depressive neurosis. Married to a recovering alcoholic, she had one girl, age 5. She had graduated from college and worked full-time until her daughter was born, then part-time until pregnant with the second child. She experienced a severe postpartum depression after the birth of her first child. She told the obstetrician she was worried about a recurrence of depression following the birth of the second child. Both her father and stepfather had died, and her mother was still living. Interviews were as follows: two during the last trimester of pregnancy, March 1981; two weeks after delivery, May 1981; approximately four months after delivery, September 1981; and the final interviews, September 1982.

5. *Laura*, age 30, was diagnosed 300.40, dysthymic disorder or depressive neurosis. At the time of her first interview, she was unhappy in her relationship of three years. She had been in one previous long-term relationship which included two pregnancies and abortions. She had completed two years of college and was attempting to make her living as a woodworker. At her second interview she had moved to another city, left her relationship, and enrolled in nursing school. She was no longer depressed. Her parents were still married and she remained in close contact with them. She was interviewed in June 1981 and twice in October 1982.

6. *Susan*, age 30, was diagnosed 300.40, dysthymic disorder or depressive neurosis. Married seven years to a wealthy man, she had two girls, ages 6 and 2. She had completed college but had never worked outside the home. At her first interview, she was unhappy in her marriage and considering divorce. She described occasional physical abuse from her husband. Two years later she was still depressed, unhappily married, and more actively considering divorce. A year after that (three years after first interview), she had separated from her husband and was no longer depressed. Her parents were still married. Susan was interviewed four times: September 1980, twice in September 1982, and September 1983.

7. *Diana,* age 30, diagnosed 300.40, dysthymic disorder or depressive neurosis, was married with a son, age 2, and was pregnant with her second child. She had completed one year of college and was working at home providing daycare for several children. She had been previously married and divorced. In that marriage, which lasted four years, she was emotionally and physically abused. She was in close contact with her still-married parents. Diana was interviewed six times over a period of seventeen months: three times during the last trimester of pregnancy, April and May 1981; two weeks after delivery, June 1981; four months after delivery, October 1981; and final interview, September 1982.

8. *Maya,* age 31, diagnosed 300.40, dysthymic disorder or depressive neurosis, was married to her first husband for seven years, had two children, and divorced. In her first marriage she and her son were repeatedly physically abused. She remarried and then separated from her second husband when she was three months pregnant. At first interview, her children were 7 and 3 and she was in the last trimester of her third pregnancy. She had five years of college and was certified as a teacher. At her first interview she was very depressed, and fifteen months later she was divorced from the second husband, on welfare, and depressed. At the follow-up a year after that, she was much less depressed and actively making plans to return to work. Her parents were still married and living close by. Tapes of four interviews were transcribed: last trimester of pregnancy, June 1981; four months postpartum, November 1981; and follow-up interviews in September 1982 and September 1983.

9. *Betty,* age 32, was diagnosed 300.40, dysthymic depression or depressive neurosis. Married fourteen years, she had a girl, 10, and a boy, 6. Betty's mother died when she was 3, and she lived in different foster homes until her father remarried when she was 7. Her stepmother occasionally physically abused her, and offered no emotional warmth. Betty graduated from high school and had one year of business school but did not work outside the home after she married. She described marital problems in her first interview, at which time she was very depressed, and by her second interview she had just filed for divorce and had begun work as a secretary/clerk. She was less depressed at this time. Interviews occurred in September 1980 and September 1982.

10. *Therese,* age 32, diagnosed 300.40, dysthymic disorder or depressive neurosis, graduated from high school, had some business school training, and worked for several years as a secretary after she married. She had been married fourteen years and ran a successful farm with her husband. At the time of the first interview she was separated from her husband and having an affair. She was very depressed, confused, and unsatisfied with her marriage. At the last interview she was divorced, was working as a clerk,

had moved out of the area, and was still depressed and confused. Drinking became a problem for her around the time of her first interview and had worsened by the follow-up interview. Her parents were still married and living nearby. Her three interviews occurred in October 1980 and October 1982.

11. *Cathy*, age 36, was diagnosed 300.40, dysthymic disorder or depressive neurosis. She had been married seventeen years and had a boy, 16, and a girl, 13. She had graduated from high school and had worked with her husband for many years managing a store. She became depressed on learning that her husband was having an affair. In her first interview she was deciding what to do and feeling very suicidal. At her second interview, he had discontinued the affair and she was not depressed. Her parents were still married but did not live close by. Interviews occurred in October 1980 and September 1982.

12. *Anna*, age 55, was diagnosed as 296.34, major depression, recurrent, with psychotic features. She was hospitalized in 1972 and 1980 for paranoia and depression and had been out of the hospital four months at first interview. She had been married thirty-six years and her husband was recently retired. Her two married sons lived elsewhere and visited occasionally with their children. Anna completed two years of college before she married but never worked outside the home. She was sexually abused by her grandfather for a number of years during latency and early adolescence, and her mother was physically abused by her father. Anna's depression worsened over the period of the study despite continuing therapy at the mental health clinic. She was interviewed three times: April and May 1980 and September 1982.

In addition to these subjects who were in the depressed women longitudinal study, I also draw from interviews with four women who were deciding whether or not to divorce. Alison, Linda, Sandra, and Kim were subjects in the Marital Decision Study (1985–1986), Carol Gilligan, Principal Investigator, for which I was a research associate and interviewer. In that study, 22 couples who were in the process of deciding whether or not to divorce were interviewed initially, and then reinterviewed one year later to look at their reasoning and language about the decision. The women I quote had all been diagnosed as depressed by therapists with whom they were in treatment.

Table A.1.   Characteristics of subjects: aspects of depression.

Name	Age	Depression outcome		In therapy for depression		Suicide attempt		Suicide ideation in interview		Ties problems to relationship with husband partner	
		Year 1	Year 2	Year 1	Year 2	Year 1	Year 2	Year 1	Year 2	Year 1	Year 2
Rita	19	300.40	better	yes	no	yes	no	yes	no	yes	—
Jan	24	300.40	better	yes	no	yes	no	yes	no	yes	—
Cindy	26	296.34	better	no*	no*	yes	no	yes	no	yes	—
Julie	30	300.40	better	no	no	no	no	no	no	yes	—
Laura	30	300.40	better	yes	no	no	no	no	no	yes	—
Susan	30	300.40	same	yes	no	no	no	no	no	yes	yes
Diana	30	300.40	better	no	no	no	no	no	no	yes	—
Maya	31	300.40	same	no	no	no	no	yes	no	yes	yes
Betty	32	300.40	better	yes	no	no	no	yes	no	yes	—
Therese	32	300.40	same	yes	no	no	no	yes	no	yes	yes
Cathy	36	300.40	better	yes	no	no	no	yes	no	yes	—
Anna	55	296.34	same	yes*	yes*	no	no	no	yes	yes	yes

*Taking antidepressant medication.

able A.2. Characteristics of subjects: selected social factors.

Name	Age	Depressive diagnosis	Education	SES*	Marital status** Year 1	Marital status** Year 2	Children's ages	Employed outside home Year 1	Employed outside home Year 2
Rita	19	300.40	HS	1	D	P	None	No	Service employment
Ian	24	300.40	B.A.	3	M	SE	None	No	Student
Cindy	26	296.34	HS	2	M	M	5 + 2	No	No
Julie	30	300.40	B.A.	2	M	M	5	No	No
Laura	30	300.40	2 yrs. college	2	P	SI	None	Yes	Student
Susan	30	300.40	B.A.	3	M	M	6 + 2	No	No
Diana	30	300.40	HS + 1 yr. college	2	M	M	2	No	No
Maya	31	300.40	B.A. +	1	SE	D	7 + 3	No	No
Betty	32	300.40	HS	2	M	SE	10 + 6	No	Clerical
Therese	32	300.40	HS + business school	2	M	D	None	No	Clerical
Cathy	36	300.40	HS	2	M	M	16 + 13	Self-employed with husband	
Anna	55	296.34	2 yrs. college	3	M	M	32 + 27	No	No

*SES is determined by the woman's husband or parent since none of the women were financially independent at the first interview. 1 = woman on welfare; 2 = indicates father or husband is blue-collar, farmer, and/or military; 3 = father or husband is professional or upper-middle-class.

**Marital status: M = married; SE = separated; D = divorced; P = partnered; SI = single.

THE SILENCING THE SELF SCALE

. APPENDIX B .

Please circle the number that best describes how you feel about each of the statements listed below.

Strongly disagree	Somewhat disagree	Neither agree nor disagree	Somewhat agree	Strongly agree

*1. I think it is best to put myself first because no one else will look out for me.

     1   2   3   4   5

2. I don't speak my feelings in an intimate relationship when I know they will cause disagreement.

     1   2   3   4   5

3. Caring means putting the other person's needs in front of my own.

     1   2   3   4   5

4. Considering my needs to be as important as those of the people I love is selfish.

     1   2   3   4   5

5. I find it is harder to be myself when I am in a close relationship than when I am on my own.

     1   2   3   4   5

6. I tend to judge myself by how I think other people see me.

     1   2   3   4   5

7. I feel dissatisfied with myself because I should be able to do all the things people are supposed to be able to do these days.

     1   2   3   4   5

*8. When my partner's needs and feelings conflict with my own, I always state mine clearly.

   1   2   3   4   5

9. In a close relationship, my responsibility is to make the other person happy.

   1   2   3   4   5

10. Caring means choosing to do what the other person wants, even when I want to do something different.

   1   2   3   4   5

*11. In order to feel good about myself, I need to feel independent and self-sufficient.

   1   2   3   4   5

12. One of the worst things I can do is to be selfish.

   1   2   3   4   5

13. I feel I have to act in a certain way to please my partner.

   1   2   3   4   5

14. Instead of risking confrontations in close relationships, I would rather not rock the boat.

   1   2   3   4   5

*15. I speak my feelings with my partner, even when it leads to problems or disagreements.

   1   2   3   4   5

16. Often I look happy enough on the outside, but inwardly I feel angry and rebellious.

   1   2   3   4   5

17. In order for my partner to love me, I cannot reveal certain things about myself to him/her.

   1   2   3   4   5

18. When my partner's needs or opinions conflict with mine, rather than asserting my own point of view I usually end up agreeing with him/her.

   1   2   3   4   5

19. When I am in a close relationship I lose my sense of who I am.

   1   2   3   4   5

20. When it looks as though certain of my needs can't be met in a relationship, I usually realize that they weren't very important anyway.

   1   2   3   4   5

*21. My partner loves and appreciates me for who I am.
     1   2   3   4   5

22. Doing things just for myself is selfish.
     1   2   3   4   5

23. When I make decisions, other people's thoughts and opinions influence me more than my own thoughts and opinions.
     1   2   3   4   5

24. I rarely express my anger at those close to me.
     1   2   3   4   5

25. I feel that my partner does not know my real self.
     1   2   3   4   5

26. I think it's better to keep my feelings to myself when they do conflict with my partner's.
     1   2   3   4   5

27. I often feel responsible for other people's feelings.
     1   2   3   4   5

28. I find it hard to know what I think and feel because I spend a lot of time thinking about how other people are feeling.
     1   2   3   4   5

29. In a close relationship I don't usually care what we do, as long as the other person is happy.
     1   2   3   4   5

30. I try to bury my feelings when I think they will cause trouble in my close relationship(s).
     1   2   3   4   5

31. I never seem to measure up to the standards I set for myself.
     1   2   3   4   5

If you answered the last question with a 4 or 5, please list up to three of the standards you feel you don't measure up to:

*Items with an asterisk are reverse-scored.

NOTES

1. PREPARING TO LISTEN

1. Using the specified diagnostic criteria of the DSM III (R) (1987) and the Diagnostic Interview Schedule (DIS), psychiatric epidemiologists are currently examining the incidence and prevalence of specific psychiatric disorders in the United States. The Epidemiologic Catchment Area (ECA) study, using the DIS in a five-site longitudinal study, is now analyzing data on the relationships among a number of variables, including gender, socioeconomic status, and familial patterns. The ECA study, based on probability samples of more than 18,000 adults age 18 and older, reveals sex differences in rates of major depression, with approximately twice as many women as men reporting major depressive symptoms (Wickramaratne, Weissman, Leaf, and Holford, 1989). See also Klerman and Weissman (1989). Though the ECA site studies are investigating the efficacy of therapeutic interventions, they are not conducting basic research on the psychology of female depression.

2. For research on women from a developmental perspective, see the work by Carol Gilligan (1977, 1982, 1990) and her colleagues at the Project on the Psychology of Women and the Development of Girls, Harvard University, particularly Brown et al. (1989); Brown and Gilligan (1990a, 1990b); Gilligan, Lyons, and Hanmer (1990); Gilligan, Ward, and Taylor (1988); and Gilligan, Brown, and Rogers (1990). New perspectives on women from a clinical orientation come from the Stone Center for Developmental Services and Studies, Wellesley College, particularly Kaplan (1984); Miller (1984); Stiver (1984); and Surrey (1984). For ideas about women's orientation to their relationships from a psychoanalytic perspective, see Chodorow (1978, 1989).

3. Throughout this book, the women's statements remain unedited. The

women's hesitation to state strongly their own point of view, their groping for words to express feelings, and their continual checking with me—the frequent "you knows" in their narratives—all help us understand their psychological state.

4. For clinical writings regarding sex differences in depressive response to loss, see Arieti and Bemporad (1978); Beck et al. (1979); and Mendelson (1974). Herman (1983) found that in college students, precipitating events for women were interpersonal, while for men they were achievement-related. Marital discord was the most common event in the previous six months reported by a sample of clinically depressed women (Weissman and Paykel, 1974).

G. W. Brown and colleagues are using the Life Event and Difficulty Schedule (LEDS) to investigate the association of certain life events with the development of depression. Brown and Harris (1978, 1989) summarize research findings regarding the importance of interpersonal events and onset of depression in women. Their (1978) study of low-income women in London describes issues of loss and disruption of relationship as the central features of most events bringing about clinical depression. In a prospective study of 400 working-class British women with children living at home, Brown et al. (1986) found that lack of support from a core relationship (defined as husband, lover, or someone "very close") at a time of crisis is strongly associated with increased risk of depression. Also at high risk were women who did not receive the support they expected.

A longitudinal study of depressed women (Birtchnell and Kennard, 1983a) found that marital maladjustment usually preceded the onset of depressive symptoms. Women experiencing marital violence were more likely to have been depressed, and to have had low self-esteem (Andrews and Brown, 1988). Finally, Dobson (1987) comparing depressed, nondepressed, and formerly depressed women, concluded that deficits in social and marital adjustment observed in women's depression were more likely to have precipitated the depression than to have been caused by it.

This is by no means an exhaustive review of the association of loss and disruption of relationship with female depression, but it provides a starting point for the interested reader.

5. Roger Gould emphasizes that adult development involves reworking assumptions about one's world that have been brought forward from childhood. He describes how ages 45 and over bring the challenge of creating a new way of being in the world based in the emerging adult assumption "I own myself" (1978, p. 310).

6. See also Gilligan's formulation of Freud's ideas about depression (Gilligan, Ward, and Taylor, 1988) and my earlier formulations of his thought (Jack, 1984).

7. A large body of work about the interpersonal nature of depression

already exists, though none of it takes into account the gender norms and the culture of inequality that powerfully affect women as they interact with others. It includes Bowlby's (1969, 1973, 1980, 1988) attachment theory and Coyne's (1976, 1985) examination of the interpersonal rejection that arises from the affect of depression. A theory of intervention and therapy, the "Interpersonal Psychotherapy of Depression" (IPT) described by Klerman et al. (1984), builds specifically on Sullivan's (1953, 1956) interpersonal theory and on Bowlby's attachment theory. While IPT goes far in tying depression to its interpersonal context, its authors do not bring a feminist analysis to the diagnosis of interpersonal problems, nor do they examine the ways gender affects a woman's sense of self, her self-esteem, and her behavior within relationships.

8. See the references cited in note 2 above. Also see the work of Mary Belenky and her colleagues on women's ways of knowing (1986) and Marcia Westkott's (1986) work on the "feminine type," which contains a penetrating analysis of how cultural forces affect women's psychology.

9. A study of daughters, mothers, and grandmothers (Cohler and Grunebaum, 1981) concludes that women's adult lives are not characterized by the concepts of autonomy and independence. A daughter is usually socialized into an undifferentiated and interdependent relationship with her mother that continues into adulthood. This relationship "becomes the model for the daughter's relational mode as an adult" (p. 331). The lives of women in this study were organized around relationships, leading the researchers to rename dependence as "normative," and to call for reconsideration of "the entire question of the significance for individual adjustment of this continuing affectional dependence across the life cycle" (p. 12).

10. Pollak and Gilligan (1982) elicited women's and men's fantasies about pictures of social intimacy and competitive success. Images of violence increased in men's stories as people were brought closer together in the pictures; violence in women's stories increased as people were set farther apart. Men see the danger of intimacy as "entrapment or betrayal, being caught in a smothering relationship or humiliated by rejection and deceit"; in contrast, locating danger in achievement, women describe a "danger of isolation, a fear that in standing out or being set apart by success, they will be left alone" (Gilligan, 1982, p. 42). Gilligan concludes: "Thus, it appears that men and women may experience attachment and separation in different ways and that each sex perceives a danger which the other does not see—men in connection, women in separation" (ibid.).

11. See research on female adolescence (Gilligan, Lyons, and Hanmer, 1990; Brown and Gilligan, 1990b); on depression in adolescence (Rutter, 1986); and on eating disorders in adolescence (Steiner-Adair, 1986).

12. See research by Coyne (1976, 1985); Bowlby (1980); and Klerman et al. (1984).

13. A large body of research on the impact of gender norms on socialization details interactional patterns that are beyond the scope of this discussion. For an overview, see Barry, Bacon, and Child (1957); Elder (1984); and Belle's (1987) review article.

14. Estimates are that one out of three girls and one out of seven boys are sexually abused before the age of 18. See Gallagher and Dodds (1985); Crewdson (1988); and Tower (1988).

15. Unlike object relations theorists, who derive the self from a social milieu and then write as if that self exists or operates more or less independently of current relationships (Mitchell, 1988), this perspective maintains a focus on the continuing social-interactional world. The presumption is that problematic interactions in the present are not caused by attributes in the depressed woman alone, but that social context fundamentally affects the self throughout the life span.

16. For definitions of dependency and overviews of the history of thought about dependence in psychoanalytic thought, see Mendelson (1974); Chodoff (1972); and critiques by Ainsworth (1969) and Bowlby (1969, 1973, 1979, 1980). See also feminist critiques of the concept by Lerner (1983) and Stiver (1984).

17. Recently, researchers with cognitive and psychodynamic perspectives on depression have distinguished between "dependent" and "autonomous" personality dimensions that relate to types of depressions. Sidney Blatt (1974; Blatt et al., 1976) labels these "anaclitic" (dependent) or "introjective" (self-critical), while Aaron Beck (1983) labels them "sociotropy" or "autonomy." Anaclitic/introjective and sociotropy/autonomy refer both to the types of personalities that are vulnerable to depression and to specific depressive states or "types" of depression. A "dependent" personality (in Blatt's terms) or the socially dependent personality (in Beck's terminology) "needs" people for safety, help, and gratification (Beck, 1983, p. 274) and is "especially vulnerable to negative interpersonal life events" (Blatt, D'Afflitti, and Quinlan, 1976, p. 383). Research testing the specificity of dependency and autonomy/self-critical dimensions as subtypes of depression or as personality types has not yielded consistent or promising results (Brown and Silberschatz, 1989; Hammen et al., 1989; Klein et al., 1988; Zuroff and Mongrain, 1987; see also review by Stoppard, 1989).

18. As the number of intimate ties decreases for any group, the prevalence of depressive symptoms increases (Birtchnell and Kennard, 1983a, 1983b; Gore, 1978; Gove, Hughes, and Style, 1983).

19. Bowlby outlines the following phases: (1) The protest phase, during which the person is acutely distressed, appears to search for the missing loved figure, and expresses anger, sorrow, and fear. (2) The despair phase, in which the person's behavior suggests increasing hopeless-

ness and includes monotonous or intermittent crying. Bowlby leaves no doubt in his descriptions that depression is the primary affect in this phase of disrupted attachment. (3) The detachment phase, character- ized by taking more interest in surrounding events and people. In children, when the loved person reappears, the child remains remote and seems to be uninterested, until a certain amount of time has passed, when clinging, anxious attachment behavior reappears in full force. These ideas, and the research that supports them, are presented in Bowlby's three-volume work on attachment (1969), separation (1973) and loss (1980). More recent studies appear in Bowlby (1988).

Within the relational model, John Bowlby's work on attachments, their formation and importance, and the predictable behaviors follow- ing their disruption or loss, contributes a theory to guide understand- ing of the interpersonal origin and nature of depressive symptoms. Attachment theory is "widely regarded as probably the best supported theory of socio-emotional development yet available" (Bowlby, 1988, p. 28). Combined with the feminist psychologists' analysis of gender differences in the sense of self and intimate interactions, this frame- work offers the possibility of developing a more accurate and less derogatory understanding of women's tendency to become stuck in depression at certain junctures in relationship.

20. Behavior labeled dependent by therapists often fulfills the hidden function of maintaining a marital system based on dominance/sub- mission (Lerner, 1983).

21. This quote was reported by Beatrix Campbell in "Model Female, or Female Role Model?" *The Times*, November 23, 1990, p. 20. It came from an interview with Thatcher by Miriam Stoppard.

22. For elaboration see Carolyn Heilbrun (1988), who made this point.

23. See research and conclusions by Jack (1987); Jack and Dill (in press), Lerner (1987); Miller (1976, 1984); and Pearlin (1980). See also the works cited in note 4 above. The importance of a supportive and intimate tie to offset a woman's depression has been confirmed in a number of studies (Brown and Harris, 1978; Belle, 1982b; Brown and Prudo, 1981; Campbell, Cope, and Teasdale, 1983; Parry and Shapiro, 1986).

In unhappy marriages, women are three times more likely to become depressed than men, and almost half of all unhappily married women are depressed. In happy marriages the incidence of depression is much lower, but here also, women are almost five times as likely as men to experience depression (Weissman, 1987). If depression stemmed from women's being excessively dependent on their relation- ships, then the loss of those relationships should precipitate depres- sion and we should find widows more often depressed than widowers. But Radloff's (1980) epidemiological study found that among the wid- owed, the men were usually more depressed than the women, while women were more depressed than men among the married and the divorced or separated. Examining responses to the death of a spouse, Bowlby (1980) found that the degree of conflict and ambivalence in the marital relationship, rather than dependence on the spouse, predicted disordering mourning and/or depression.

24. Brown and Harris (1978) designed a measure (the LEDS, see note 4) that asked women what events they saw as having caused their depressions, and what threat the events posed for them. They also designed an objective measure of provoking events, which included interviews with the depressed woman and her relatives and "threat" ratings of listed events by researchers and therapists (who knew nothing about how a particular woman experienced the events). In designing this measure, they coincidentally checked the women's subjective reports with "objective" corroboration and established the reliability of depressed women's descriptions of their lives: "It is perhaps worth adding that we had the strong impression that depressed women were remarkably accurate in describing their lives . . . This is supported by the interviews with a close relative . . . Patient and relative agreed 86% of the time about difficulties rated on the top three points of severity and . . . it was only difficulties of this severity that played an aetiological role" (1978, p. 133). Also, in Belle's (1982b) study of women in poverty, the accuracy of depressed women's descriptions of relationships was corroborated by other family members. And in another study, husbands who were reported by their wives as giving emotional support and as involved in child care were the fathers whom children rated as "nurturant" (Zur-Spiro and Longfellow, 1982).

25. These studies are reported in more detail in Jack (1984, 1987) and in Jack and Dill (in press).

26. The subjects in these three studies come from very different social classes, but almost all are white, though intense efforts were made to include minority women. In the longitudinal study, the women were referred from treating clinicians, and the all-white sample reflects the racially homogeneous rural community within which the study was done. Further, minority women in this county rarely use the community mental health services or the services of private therapists. In the study of approximately 140 battered women from three shelters in Washington state, a fourth shelter, which housed primarily minority women, was not willing to allow researchers in. In analyses of shelter data (Jack and Dill, in press), Diana Dill and I include subanalyses on the small sample of minority women studied. Finally, in the research that was part of the Cocaine: Pregnancy Use and Offspring Development study at the University of Washington, Ann Streissguth, Principal Investigator, the sample of women is all Caucasian. This racially homogeneous sample was selected for NIDA-funded study because most other research on drug-abusing women focused on minority women.

2. LOSS OF SELF

1. Belenky et al. also report on the centrality of the voice metaphor in women's narratives: "We found that women repeatedly used the metaphor of voice to depict their intellectual and ethical development; and that the development of a sense of voice, mind, and self were intricately intertwined" (1986, p. 18).
2. For men's talking while women listen, see Argyle, Lalljee, and Cook (1968); Thorne and Henley (1975); Zimmerman and West (1975); Aries (1976); Swaker (1976); Bernard (1972, 1981); Fishman (1983); Spender (1980); West and Zimmerman (1983). For the devaluation of the products of women's minds, see Jose and McCarthy (1988).
3. Catherine Keller (1986) has written beautifully of the myths that ensnare women in conventional heterosexual relationship.
4. See Mitchell (1988, pp. 104–109) for a sustained discussion of "object seeking" and intimacy from an object relations perspective.
5. For a study examining such situations, see Heard (1973, 1982).
6. Gottman (1990) summarizes other marital interaction patterns that predict change in marital satisfaction over time as follows: conflict engagement predicted current dissatisfaction with the marriage, but improvement over time. However, conflict that indicated defensiveness, stubbornness, and withdrawal of either party (this occurred most often in the husband) was dysfunctional over time. The husband's whining predicted deterioration in his marital satisfaction.
7. "Under the common law, which we inherited from England and which remains in force in each state until modified by statute or judicial decision, a husband is obliged to support his wife during marriage. In return, a wife is obliged to do housework and care for children" (Mansbridge, 1986, p. 92). It was also legal, in forty-two states, for whoever paid for property and assets within a marriage to own them. Thus if a wife was a homemaker and the husband the sole financial provider, he owned everything purchased during the marriage. The eight other states had community property laws, with managerial rights given to the husband. Not until 1982 did most of these laws change to a more equitable distribution of joint property (Mansbridge, 1986).
8. Marcia Westkott has detailed the nurturing imperative as "the cultural expectation that women should nurture men, not just children" (1986, p. 123). Adrienne Rich, in "Husband-Right and Father-Right" says, "The father's economic 'obligation to support' allows him right of access to and contact with a child almost without regard to the kind of person he is; 'mother-right' is legally the obligation to nurture, and can be stripped from a woman on the grounds of her personal fitness as mother" (1979, p. 219).
9. Weissman and Paykel (1974) compared depressed and nondepressed

women and found that acutely depressed women are more hostile than nondepressed women, and that children are the objects of the most hostility. See also Belle's (1982b) study of women in inner-city Boston.

3 IMAGES OF SELF IN INTIMATE RELATIONSHIP

1. See Rich's (1979) essay, "Women and Honor: Some Notes on Lying."
2. The belief that one can help another through love does not always indicate dysfunctional codependency (see Bowlby, 1980; Kotler, 1985).
3. "Even though some changes have occurred at a behavioral level, the old cognitive constructs and accompanying feelings still operate in contemporary people" (Arieti and Bemporad, 1978, p. 369). Moulton (1973) observes that "the unconscious of modern woman contains many remnants of . . . her grandmother . . . [The human being's] adaptive powers are remarkable for their ultimate versatility, but rarely for their speed. A culture in flux offers an apparent breadth of choices, but effects are unpredictable . . ." (quoted in ibid., p. 369).
4. The virtues prescribed for women in centuries past have been detailed by feminist historians (Kerber, 1986; Welter, 1973). The cost to women of their "moral superiority" was clear in the nineteenth century. Cott (1977) describes "marriage trauma," and Smith-Rosenberg (1972) recounts how the inconsistencies and contradictions between the ideal of womanhood and the actuality of women's lives created tensions that led to the formation of certain symptoms among women. The symptoms of hysteria that were prevalent among women at that time presented "an intensification of women's traditional passivity and dependence" (Smith-Rosenberg, 1972, p. 671). Yet these symptoms offered a woman the chance to restructure her place in the family, because they caused shifts in the work and roles she could occupy. The fact that more women than men were depressed in the nineteenth century (Weissman and Klerman, 1977) as well as now, supports the argument that women's socially defined roles and feminine "goodness" are central to their vulnerability to depression.
5. The fear that Horney is right, that men do more often choose women who do not pursue their own self-development, was powerfully demonstrated when a study of 1982 and 1985 census data showed that the more education a woman had and the longer she waited, the less likely she was to be married (Bennett and Bloom, 1986). More interesting than whether or not the statistical inferences were correct was the media response to the data. Newspaper headlines warned of a "spinster boom on the horizon" and shouted "Single-Minded College Girls Put on Shelf at 30!" "No M.R.S. Degree for Those Who Wait!" "Women Who Tarry May Never Marry!" (Bennett and Bloom, 1986, p. 27). The researchers interpreted their statistics as showing that "a woman's

status no longer derives primarily from the man to whom she is married" and that "there has also been a voluntary shift in marriage patterns resulting from women's greater economic and social independence and their liberation from the assumption of motherhood" (1986, p. 27). Many women, however, feared that the data showed men's preference for a child-woman who fit the ideologies over a woman who would bring her own agency and activity into relationship.

4. MORAL THEMES IN WOMEN'S DEPRESSION

1. See Kohut (1980), Kohut and Wolf (1978), Miller (1981), and Winnicott (1965).

2. The concept of the authentic self (which implies the existence of a false or ideal self) is not new. It appears in religious and philosophical writings (Kierkegaard, for example) and in psychological theories such as those of Karen Horney, Heinz Kohut, Alice Miller, and D. W. Winnicott. Most simply put, the idealized, false self develops as a defense, in order to gain the love of powerful parents who criticize and ridicule the authentic self. The child perceives that she must possess certain qualities in order to gain acceptance and emotional nourishment from parents. The idealized or false self develops these qualities to present them to parents. Most psychological theories stress that this occurs within the family in response to withholding or narcissistic parents. Accommodation to parental needs leads to the "as-if personality" (Miller, 1981), a self that protects the parents from the child's unacceptable, negative feelings.

3. Karen Horney proposed the concept of the idealized self that attempted to live up to the images of parents in order to gain love and approval. Marcia Westkott, writing about Horney's theory, says: "The shoulds that constitute the idealized self are not genuine moral ideals required for maintaining civilized life, but externalized abstractions and 'the neurotic counterfeit of normal moral strivings' " (1986, p. 147).

4. This lawyer was not depressed, and her example is used here to illustrate how these conflicting standards create difficulties for women. See also Westkott's (1986) analysis of Karen Horney's theory regarding conflicts between love and work faced by women.

5. Because men form a gender identity based on difference from the mother, their sense of self is based more on denial of relation and connection, and on a more fixed and firmly split inner self-other world (Chodorow, 1989). The necessity of defining the masculine self as "not female" contributes not only to a more defensively structured sense of self in males, but also to a generalized devaluation and fear of women. As Dinnerstein (1976) and Chodorow (1989) suggest, the need to control the powerfully experienced mother, internalized as an archetype or

a nonpersonal mother-image, "fuels male dominance in culture and society and creates systematic tensions and conflicts in heterosexual relationships" (Chodorow, 1989, p. 184).

6. Brown and Gilligan (1990b) discover in a longitudinal study of adolescent girls the appearance of the "Perfect Girl"—"the girl who has no bad thoughts or feelings, the kind of person everyone wants to be with; the girl who, in her perfection, is worthy of real praise and attention, worthy of inclusion and love" (p. 16). Significantly, this Perfect Girl surfaces in the narratives of girls who are standing on the brink of sexual maturity and entry into the world of adults. Striving to become the Perfect Girl holds the promise of inclusion, love, attention. These researchers' discovery of the appearance of the image of the perfect girl at the time of adolescent transition into sexual maturing reinforces the observation that cognitive schemas of the self-in-relation are influenced throughout the life span by gender norms that powerfully affect interpersonal interactions *and* interpersonal shoulds.

7. So far, researchers developing scales to measure cognitive correlates of depression have been more interested in universal distortions of thought processes and content than in gender-specific beliefs. Beck has not detailed gender-specific patterns of thought that may make women more vulnerable to depression than men. Scales developed from his cognitive theory of depression, such as the Hopelessness Scale (Beck et al., 1974), the Dysfunctional Attitude Scale (Oliver and Baumgart, 1985), and the Sociotropy-Autonomy Scale (hypothesized to discriminate depressions within domains of achievement and the interpersonal field; Beck et al., 1983) do not find gender differences. Perhaps one reason sex differences do not emerge in these studies is that researchers are not investigating the cognitive schemas most potent for women's depression—the beliefs about the self in intimate relationship.

   The Dysfunctional Attitude Scale (DAS) is the closest scale theoretically to the empirical measure I have developed, the Silencing the Self Scale (SSS). Both scales tap attitudes and beliefs associated with depression, but the SSS understands self-negating attitudes to be contained in the traditional female role imperatives, and the sentences in the SSS reflect a hypothesized dynamic of thought associated with the role. The DAS is broader in scope, and measures beliefs associated with approval, love, achievement, perfectionism, entitlement, omnipotence, and autonomy. It is considered to be gender-neutral. For an excellent review of the adequacy or inadequacy of existing cognitive theories to understanding depression in women, see Stoppard (1989).

8. The Beck Depression Inventory (BDI) correlates significantly with the SSS in the two populations for which data have been analyzed; see Jack and Dill (in press) for norms of the scale and particulars of the study. As part of the Cocaine: Pregnancy Use and Offspring Development study (NIDA study, University of Washington, Ann Streissguth, Principal

Investigator), the BDI and the SSS were given at four months after delivery. The examples reported in the text are representative of those gained from approximately 175 of the sample.

9. On the BDI the score is 32, and the SSS score is 146. Both scores are at the high extreme end of possible ranges. (In presenting responses to the questionnaires, I use subject numbers in order to facilitate identification of cases for future reference.)

10. On the BDI, this woman's score was 20; her SSS score was 109.

11. Many of the items on the SSS list conventional imperatives of the "good wife," so it is not surprising that only eleven of the women list additional standards under this category, or relist some mentioned in the questionnaire.

12. Catherine Steiner-Adair has tied the prevalence of eating disorders in women to their attempts to live up to the superwoman image and to a failure to formulate their own, personal image of self to combat the demeaning cultural concepts of femininity (see Steiner-Adair, 1986). Also, Ann Willard (1988), examining mothers of one-year-old infants, finds depression associated with attempts to live up to cultural images of motherhood without clearly formulated personal images to offset cultural dictates.

5. SILENCING THE SELF

1. Belenky et al. (1986) use George Eliot's quotation from *Middlemarch:* "If we had a keen vision and feeling of all ordinary human life, it would be like hearing the grass grow and the squirrel's heart beat, and we should die of that roar which lies on the other side of silence." They describe their book, *Women's Ways of Knowing,* as "about the 'roar which lies on the other side of silence' when ordinary women find their voice and use it to gain control over their lives" (p. 5).

2. Cognitive theory (Beck, 1976; Beck et al., 1979; Beck et al., 1983) details distorted, unrealistic cognitions associated with depression. Therapeutic interventions occur in cognitive therapy to facilitate the patient's recognition of faulty beliefs and to substitute more accurate beliefs. A therapist might respond to Cathy's statement that "a wife gives of herself a lot more than a man" by calling it overgeneralization, and by having Cathy identify the times she has given more of herself, whether the generalization is true, and if so, how she might break the pattern. A woman with Cathy's orientation would probably back down very quickly from this statement, and take her husband's point of view. A woman may need to question in this global, "overgeneralizing" way her habits of interaction and acknowledge the resentment that goes with them in order to stay with her pain so as to understand its sources.

   Further, thought stopping is used frequently as a behavioral tool in therapy for depression. It is suggested when troublesome ideas, feelings, or thoughts spring into mind. The person is instructed to interrupt negative thoughts by saying "Stop!" and replacing the negative thought with a positive one. Though it is important to disempower the annihilating criticism of the Over-Eye, in order to do so a therapist needs to help a woman to distinguish the authentic voice of the self from the restrictive, diminishing voice of the Over-Eye. Otherwise, the therapist aligns with the culture to encourage the woman to adapt to structures of thought and relatedness that keep her trapped. If, without distinguishing between the authentic self and the conforming, compliant self, a therapist encourages a woman to stop her negative thoughts when they are troublesome, that therapist brings the authority of psychology to a woman's own tendency to silence her feeling self. Frequently the barely audible voice of the authentic self needs encouragement in therapy, not thought-stopping techniques.

3. Feminist film critics, particularly Kaplan (1983) and de Lauretis (1984), write about the "male gaze" of the camera. Kaplan notes that "men do not simply look; their gaze carries with it the power of action and of possession which is lacking in the female gaze . . . Second, the sexualization and objectification of women is not simply for the purposes of eroticism; from a psychoanalytic point of view, it is designed to annihilate the threat the woman (as castrated and possessing a sinister organ) poses" (1983, p. 31).

4. As Harriet Lerner writes, "Feelings of depression, low self-esteem, self-betrayal, and even self-hatred are inevitable when women fight but continue to submit to unfair circumstances, when they complain but participate in relationships that betray their own beliefs, values, and personal goals, or when they find themselves fulfilling society's stereotype of the bitchy, nagging, bitter, or destructive woman" (1987, pp. 216–217).

5. Westkott's (1986) excellent presentation of the feminine type's anger contains similarities and differences to the analysis I put forth here. The feminine type, proposed by Horney (1934) and expanded by Westkott, is caught between "overvaluing male love and achievement and disparaging one's own real abilities (Westkott, 1986, p. 15). Such a woman's craving for relationship with men is "a secondary expression of an underlying rivalry with other women" (ibid.). Further, the feminine type "needs to destroy other women and to secure the love of men in order to convince herself that she is not the worthless creature that she believes herself to be" (ibid., p. 17).

The differences between Westkott's and my analyses lie not only in the fundamental assumptions regarding the relational nature of the self and what fuels the search for relationship, but also in the concept of "characterological dependency." This characterological dependency "involves submission as confirmation of a degraded sense of self, the need to merge with a powerful other, and attraction to intimate relationships as salvation," and it includes "the response of the female altruist who needs the appreciation of others to assure herself that she is not the contemptible and selfish person she fears she is" (ibid., p. 145). When describing the behaviors of compliance and acquiescence to others, I do not presume characterological dependency. I think the concept of dependency is confusing and misleading, and am attempting to replace the notion of characterological dependency with concepts of self-silencing, inner division, and cognitive activity required to be passive that are situationally specific, historically constituted, and *subject to change* in ways a characterologically based dependency is not. Through an analysis of the social forces that create interpersonal behaviors, including women's awareness of the "game" they play with men, I try to create an understanding of what have been seen as traditionally feminine behaviors based not on characterological dependency but on internalized social norms as they intersect with women's relational self.

6. Outside of particular relationship, this dynamic occurs in women whose depression centers more on achievement issues than on relational issues. They strive to work "perfectly" in order to gain recognition, success, and a feeling of competence. When rewards are not forthcoming, the response is often to blame the self first, before examining external structures that may be biased against women.

7. Battered women, through their example, teach their daughters these behaviors as ways to ensure safety and survival within brutal relationships.

8. These excerpts come from an unpublished paper, "Feminist Developmental Cycles," by Anita Milavec (1989). The paper was written in response to an assignment to explore how *Women's Ways of Knowing* (Belenky et al., 1986) and other materials for a class on the psychology of women related to the students' own development.

9. Because of an easy identification through the commonality of gender, mothers often see themselves in their own daughters. A mother can see in her daughter the spirit of what she might have been, a symbol of new beginnings and freedom. Particularly when a mother has not realized her authentic self, she may want to possess the freedom to begin again, and she may incorporate her daughter as a way to regain a self that already has been lost, or was never found.

10. R. D. Laing (1969) used the phrase "the divided self" to describe the existential phenomenology of the schizophrenic. His presentation of the inner world of the schizophrenic differs significantly from the one I put forth regarding depressed women. I use the same phrase because it seems to capture, more than any other, the experience of self-alienation and disconnection within the self revealed by depressed women's narratives.

11. Gilbert and Gubar (1979) write about how female authors create "dark doubles" for themselves.

12. Though I describe a specific content of depressed women's cognitions (thought patterns) about the self-in-relation and tie those cognitions to specific cultural patterns and beliefs about women, I agree with Beck's observations regarding the hypothesized relationship between cognition and depressive symptoms. According to Beck (1967, 1976), biochemical changes can be triggered by tendencies to interpret the self, environment, and future in negative ways, through the negative cognitive triad. Beck (1983) elaborates the relation of cognition to the symptoms of depression: "signs and symptoms of the depressive syndrome may be viewed as consequences of the activation of the negative cognitive patterns. Motivational symptoms (for example, paralysis of the will, escape and avoidance wishes) can be understood as consequences of negative cognitions. 'Paralysis of the will' may result from the patient's pessimism and hopelessness. If he expects a negative outcome, he will not commit himself to a goal or undertaking. Suicidal wishes can be explained as an extreme expression of the desire to escape from what appear to be insoluble problems or an unbearable situation. The depressed person may see himself as a worthless burden and consequently believe that everyone, including himself, would be better off if he were dead.

"Increased dependency is also understandable in cognitive terms. Because the patient sees himself as inept and helpless and also unrealistically overestimates the difficulty of normal tasks, he expects his undertakings to turn out badly. Thus, he tends to seek help and reassurance from others, whom he considers more competent and capable.

"Finally, the cognitive model may also explain the physical symptoms of depression. Apathy and low energy may be the consequence of the patient's belief that he is doomed to failure in all his experiences" (pp. 268–269).

13. When referred to the study, Therese had just started counseling, having had only one session. The language of her interior world was not supplied by her therapist.

14. See Brown et al. (1986), who, having followed depressed women's experience closely in a prospective study, speculate that in women, self-esteem is the internal representation of support from a core tie. They argue that either a lack of a supportive relationship or a lack of conviction that support is available constitutes a vulnerability factor for risk of depression. See also Bowlby (1988).

6. THE SELF IN DIALOGUE: MOVEMENT OUT OF DEPRESSION

1. Holub (1989) makes this observation, as does Perera (1985) writing about Inanna's descent to the underworld.

2. I draw from the edition of *Grimms' Fairy Tales* translated by Mrs. E. V. Lucas, Lucy Crane, and Marian Edwardes (New York: Grosset and Dunlap, 1945).

3. The language of conventional plot and assigned script come from Heilbrun, who says of women, "How are they to imagine forms and language they have never heard? How are they to live to write, and to write that other women may live?" (1988, p. 39).

4. A number of writers have detailed the "impostor syndrome" in women, notably Clance (1985). See also McIntosh (1985).

5. Gaile was part of the study of male and female lawyers that examined the moral conflicts they perceived in their work (Jack and Jack, 1989). Gaile was not diagnosed as depressed, and in these interviews no inquiries were made regarding depressive symptoms.

6. Researchers are uncertain about the relation of cognition to depression, particularly whether cognitive patterns reflect traitlike variables (stable factors) or are aspects of a depressive episode (statelike and transitory) (see Dohr, Rush, and Bernstein, 1989). "There have been few advances in the direct study of meaning, how best to measure it, and how it relates to individual responses to events" (Hammen et al., 1989, p. 154); so debate continues about the association of cognitive schemas with depressive episodes.

Although only suggestive, and derived from a small number of racially homogeneous subjects, data from the women I have studied suggest that cognitive schemas about the self in intimate relation create a vulnerability to depression by affecting the women's behaviors, self-evaluation, and vision of self in the past, present, and future.

APPENDIX A: THE WOMEN IN THE LONGITUDINAL STUDY

1. As part of the study, I examined and scored the newborns of subjects 3, 4, 7, and 8 using the Brazelton Neonatal Behavioral Assessment Scale (1973) twice: within forty-eight hours and fourteen days after birth. I also observed each mother with her infant at those times in the hospital and in her home. Three months after the infant's birth, I assessed development using the Bayley Scale of Infant Development (1969). I was interested in how a mother's depression affects her interaction with her infant as well as the infant's development. With such a small sample, remarks would be purely speculative and so will not be offered. But the contact with the mothers around their infants was important to two of the women. Cindy, who had overdosed on antidepressants during the twenty-sixth week of pregnancy, gained reassurance that her infant was normal by watching how he attended to voice and other social cues, and how he followed objects with his gaze. For Maya,

separated from her husband, the contact provided an opportunity to share her new infant, as well as her fears and concerns. She explored what options she had for herself with three young children and no financial resources. She made the decision to apply for welfare rather than work outside the home.

REFERENCES

Ainsworth, M. D. S. 1969. Object relations, dependency and attachment: A theoretical review of the infant-mother relationship. *Child Development* 40: 969–1025.

Anderson, K., and D. C. Jack. 1991. Learning to listen: Interview techniques and analyses. In *Women's words: The feminist practice of oral history*, ed. S. B. Gluck and D. Patai. New York: Routledge.

Andrews, B., and G. W. Brown. 1988. Marital violence in the community. *British Journal of Psychiatry* 153: 305–312.

Argyle, M., M. Lalljee, and M. Cook. 1968. The effects of visibility on interaction in a dyad. *Human Relations* 21: 3–17.

Aries, E. 1976. Interaction patterns and themes of male, female, and mixed groups. *Small Group Behavior* 7: 7–18.

Arieti, S., and J. Bemporad. 1978. *Severe and mild depression: The psychotherapeutic approach.* New York: Basic Books.

Barry, H., III, M. K. Bacon, and I. L. Child. 1957. A cross-cultural survey of some sex differences in socialization. *Journal of Abnormal and Social Psychology* 55: 327–332.

Bayley, N. 1969. *Manual for the Bayley scales of infant development.* New York: Psychological Corporation.

Beck, A. T. 1967. *Depression: Clinical, experimental and theoretical aspects.* New York: Harper and Row.

———— 1970. The core problem in depression: The cognitive triad. In *Science and psychoanalysis*, ed. J. Masseman. New York: Grune and Stratton.

———— 1976. *Cognitive therapy and the emotional disorders.* New York: International Universities Press.

———— 1983. Cognitive therapy of depression: New perspectives. In *Treatment of depression: Old controversies and new approaches*, ed. P. J. Clayton and J. E. Barrett. New York: Raven Press.

——— 1984. Cognition and therapy. Letter to the editor. *Archives of General Psychiatry* 41: 1112–1114.

Beck, A. T., N. Epstein, and R. Harrison. 1983. Cognitions, attitudes, and personality dimensions in depression. *British Journal of Cognitive Psychotherapy* 1: 1–16.

Beck, A. T., A. J. Rush, B. F. Shaw, and G. Emery. 1979. *Cognitive therapy of depression*. New York: Guilford Press.

Beck, A. T., C. H. Ward, M. Mendelson, J. Mock, and J. Erbaugh. 1961. An inventory for measuring depression. *Archives of General Psychiatry* 4: 561–571.

Beck, A. T., A. N. Weissman, D. Lester, and L. Trexler. 1974. The measurement of pessimism: The Hopelessness Scale. *Journal of Consulting and Clinical Psychology* 42: 861–865.

Becker, E. 1964. *The revolution in psychiatry: The new understanding of man.* New York: Free Press of Glencoe.

Belenky, M. F., B. M. Clinchy, N. R. Goldberger, and J. M. Tarule. 1986. *Women's ways of knowing: The development of self, voice, and mind.* New York: Basic Books.

Bellah, R., R. Madsen, W. M. Sullivan, A. Swidler, and S. M. Tipton. 1985. *Habits of the heart: Individualism and commitment in American life.* Berkeley: University of California Press.

Belle, D. 1982a. The stress of caring: Women as providers of social support. In *Handbook of stress: theoretical and clinical aspects*, ed. L. Goldberger and S. Breznitz. New York: Free Press.

——— 1982b. *Lives in stress: Women and depression.* San Diego: Sage Publications.

——— 1987. Gender differences in the social moderators of stress. In *Gender and stress*, ed. R. C. Barnett, L. Biener, and G. K. Baruch. New York: Free Press.

Bennett, N. G., and D. E. Bloom. 1986. Why fewer American women marry. *New York Times*, December 13, p. 27.

Bernard, J. S. 1971. The paradox of the happy marriage. In *Women in sexist society*, ed. V. Gornick and B. K. Moran. New York: New American Library.

——— 1972. *The sex game: Communication between the sexes.* New York: Atheneum.

——— 1981. *The female world.* New York: Free Press.

Bernstein, D. 1983. The female superego: A different perspective. *International Journal of Psycho-Analysis* 64: 187–201.

Bibring, E. 1953. The mechanisms of depression. In *Affective disorders: Psychoanalytic contribution to their study*, ed. P. Greenacre. New York: International Universities Press.

Birtchnell, J., and J. Kennard. 1983a. Does marital maladjustment lead to mental illness? *Social Psychiatry* 18: 79–88.

―――― 1983b. Marriage and mental illness. *British Journal of Psychiatry* 142: 193–198.

Blatt, S. J. 1974. Levels of object representation in anaclitic and introjective depression. *Psychoanalytic Study of the Child* 29: 107–157.

Blatt, S. J., J. P. D'Afflitti, and D. M. Quinlan. 1976. Experiences of depression in normal young adults. *Journal of Abnormal Psychology* 85: 383–389.

Blumstein, P., and P. Schwartz. 1983. *American couples*. New York: William Morrow and Company.

Bowlby, J. 1969. *Attachment and loss*, vol. 1, *Attachment*. New York: Basic Books.

―――― 1973. *Attachment and loss*, vol. 2, *Separation: Anxiety and anger*. New York: Basic Books.

―――― 1979. *The making and breaking of affectional bonds*. London: Tavistock.

―――― 1980. *Attachment and loss*, vol. 3, *Loss, sadness and depression*. New York: Basic Books.

―――― 1988. *A secure base: Parent-child attachment and healthy human development*. New York: Basic Books.

Brazelton, T. B. 1973. Neonatal behavioral assessment scale. Clinics in Developmental Medicine 50. Spastics International Medical Publications. Philadelphia: J. B. Lippincott.

―――― 1982. Joint regulation of neonate-parent behavior. In *Social interchange in infancy*, ed. E. Tronick. Baltimore: University Park Press.

Brown, G. W., B. Andrews, T. Harris, Z. Adler, and L. Bridge. 1986. Social support, self-esteem and depression. *Psychological Medicine* 16: 813–831.

Brown, G. W., and T. O. Harris. 1978. *The social origins of depression: A study of psychiatric disorders in women*. New York: Free Press.

―――― 1989. *Life events and illness*. New York: Guilford Press.

Brown, G. W., and R. Prudo. 1981. Psychiatric disorder in a rural and an urban population: 1. Aetiology of depression. *Psychological Medicine* 11: 581–599.

Brown, J. D., and G. Silberschatz. 1989. Dependency, self-criticism, and depressive attributional style. *Journal of Abnormal Psychology* 98: 187–188.

Brown, L. M., and C. Gilligan. 1990a. Listening for self and relational voices: A responsive/resisting listener's guide. Paper presented at the 98th Annual Meeting of the American Psychological Association, Boston, August.

―――― 1990b. The psychology of women and the development of girls. Manuscript, Harvard University, Graduate School of Education.

Brown, L. M., M. Tappan, C. Gilligan, D. Argyris, and B. Miller. 1989. Reading for self and moral voice: A method for interpreting narratives of real-life moral conflict and choice. In *Entering the circle: Hermeneutic investigation in psychology,* ed. M. Packer and R. Addison. Albany: SUNY Press.

Buber, M. 1970. *I and thou.* Trans. W. Kaufmann. New York: Charles Scribner's Sons.

Campbell, B. 1990. Model female, or female role model? *The Times* (London), November 23, p. 20.

Campbell, E. A., S. J. Cope, and J. D. Teasdale. 1983. Social factors and affective disorder: An investigation of Brown and Harris's model. *British Journal of Psychiatry* 143: 548–553.

Caplow, T. 1982. *Middletown families: Fifty years of change and continuity.* Minneapolis: University of Minnesota Press.

Chodoff, P. 1972. The depressive personality. *Archives of General Psychiatry* 27: 666–673.

Chodorow, N. J. 1978. *The reproduction of mothering: Psychoanalysis and the sociology of gender.* Berkeley: University of California Press.

——— 1985. Gender, relation, and difference in psychoanalytic perspective. In *The future of difference,* ed. H. Eisenstein and A. Jardine. New Brunswick, N.J.: Rutgers University Press.

——— 1989. *Feminism and psychoanalytic theory.* New Haven: Yale University Press.

Clance, P. R. 1985. *The imposter phenomenon: Overcoming the fear that haunts your success.* Atlanta: Peachtree Publishers.

Clance, P. R., and S. A. Imes. 1978. The imposter phenomenon in high achieving women: Dynamics and therapeutic intervention. *Psychotherapy Theory, Research and Practice* 15: 241–247.

Cohen, S., and G. McKay. 1984. Social support, stress and the buffering hypothesis: A theoretical analysis. In *Handbook of psychology and health: Social psychological aspects of health,* vol. 4. Hillsdale, N.J.: Erlbaum.

Cohler, B. J., and H. Grunebaum. 1981. *Mothers, grandmothers, and daughters: Personality and childcare in three-generation families.* New York: John Wiley and Sons.

Cott, N. F. 1977. *The bonds of womanhood: "Woman's sphere" in New England, 1780–1835.* New Haven: Yale University Press.

Coyne, J. C. 1976. Depression and the response of others. *Journal of Abnormal Psychology* 85: 186–193.

——— 1985. Studying depressed persons' interactions with strangers and spouses. *Journal of Abnormal Psychology* 94: 231–232.

Crewdson, J. 1988. *By silence betrayed: Sexual abuse of children in America.* Boston: Little, Brown.

DeLauretis, T. 1984. *Alice doesn't: Feminism, semiotics, cinema.* Bloomington: Indiana University Press.

Dinnerstein, D. 1976. *The mermaid and the minotaur: Sexual arrangements and human malaise.* New York: Harper and Row.

Dobson, K. S. 1987. Marital and social adjustment in depressed and remitted married women. *Journal of Clinical Psychology* 43: 261–265.

Dohr, K. B., A. J. Rush, and I. H. Bernstein. 1989. Cognitive biases and depression. *Journal of Abnormal Psychology* 98: 263–267.

DSM III: Diagnostic and statistical manual of mental disorders. 1980. Annotations by R. L. Spitzer and H. B. Williams. Washington, D.C.: American Psychiatric Association.

DSM III (R): Diagnostic and statistical manual of mental disorders, 3rd ed. 1987. Washington, D.C.: American Psychiatric Association.

Ehrenreich, B., and D. English. 1979. *For her own good: 150 years of the experts' advice to women*. Garden City, N.Y.: Doubleday/Anchor.

Elder, G. H., Jr. 1984. *Children of the great depression*. Chicago: University of Chicago Press.

Eliot, G. 1965. *Middlemarch*. New York: Penguin Books.

Fairbairn, W. R. D. 1952. *An object-relations theory of the personality*. New York: Basic Books.

Fishman, P. 1983. Interaction: The work women do. In *Language, gender and society*, ed. B. Thorne, C. Kramarea, and N. Henley. Rowley, Mass.: Newbury House.

Freud, S. 1917. Mourning and melancholia. In *The standard edition of the complete psychological works of Sigmund Freud*, vol. 14, ed. J. Strachey. London: Hogarth Press, 1957.

——— 1925. Some psychical consequences of the anatomical distinction between the sexes. In *The standard edition of the complete psychological works of Sigmund Freud*, vol. 19, ed. J. Strachey. London: Hogarth Press, 1961.

——— 1930. *Civilization and its discontents*. Trans. J. Strachey. New York: W. W. Norton, 1961.

Gallagher, V., and W. F. Dodds. 1985. *Speaking out, fighting back: Personal experiences of women who survived childhood sexual abuse in the home*. Seattle: Madrona Publishers.

Gaylin, W. 1978. *Doing good: The limits of benevolence*. New York: Pantheon.

Gilbert, S., and S. Gubar. 1979. *The madwoman in the attic: The woman writer and the nineteenth century literary imagination*. New Haven: Yale University Press.

Gill, M. M., and I. Z. Hoffman. 1982. *Analysis of transference*, vol. 2. Psychological Issues, Monograph 54. New York: International Universities Press.

Gilligan, C. 1977. In a different voice: Women's conceptions of self and of morality. *Harvard Educational Review* 47: 481–517.

——— 1982. *In a difference voice: Psychological theory and women's development*. Cambridge, Mass.: Harvard University Press.

——— 1990. Joining the resistance: Psychology, politics, girls and women. *Michigan Quarterly Review* 29: 501–536.

Gilligan, C., L. M. Brown, and A. Rogers. 1990. Psyche embedded: A place for body, relationships, and culture in personality theory. In *Studying persons and lives,* ed. A. Rabin, R. Zucker, R. Emmons, and S. Frank. New York: Springer.

Gilligan, C., N. Lyons, and T. Hanmer, eds. 1990. *Making connections: The relational worlds of adolescent girls at Emma Willard School.* Cambridge, Mass.: Harvard University Press.

Gilligan, C., J. V. Ward, and J. M. Taylor, eds. 1988. *Mapping the moral domain: A contribution of women's thinking to psychological theory and education.* Cambridge, Mass.: Harvard University Press.

Gilligan, C., and G. Wiggins. 1988. The origins of morality in early childhood relationships. In *Mapping the moral domain: A contribution of women's thinking to psychological theory and education,* ed. C. Gilligan, J. V. Ward, and J. M. Taylor. Cambridge, Mass.: Harvard University Press.

Gore, S. 1978. The effect of social support in moderating the health consequences of unemployment. *Journal of Health and Social Behavior* 19: 157–165.

Gottman, J. 1990. How marriages change. In *Depression and aggression in family interaction,* ed. G. R. Patterson. Hillsdale, N.J.: Erlbaum.

Gottman, J. M., and R. W. Levenson. 1986. Assessing the role of emotion in marriage. *Behavioral Assessment* 8: 31–48.

Gould, R. L. 1978. *Transformations: Growth and change in adult life.* New York: Simon and Schuster.

Gove, W. R., M. Hughes, and C. B. Style. 1983. Does marriage have positive effects on the psychological well-being of the individual? *Journal of Health and Social Behavior* 24: 122–131.

Greenberg, J. R., and S. A. Mitchell. 1983. *Object relations in psychoanalytic theory.* Cambridge, Mass.: Harvard University Press.

Grimm, Brothers. 1945. Rumpelstiltskin. In *Grimms' Fairy Tales,* trans. E. V. Lucas, L. Crane, and M. Edwardes. New York: Grosset and Dunlap.

Hall, N. 1980. *The moon and the virgin.* New York: Harper and Row.

Hammen, C., A. Ellicott, M. Gitlin, and K. Jamison. 1989. Sociotropy/autonomy and vulnerability to specific life events in patients with unipolar depression and bipolar disorders. *Journal of Abnormal Psychology* 98: 154–160.

Hartmann, H. 1960. *Psychoanalysis and moral values.* New York: International Universities Press.

Harvey, T. J., and A. Stables. 1986. Gender differences in attitudes to science for third year pupils: An argument for single-sex teaching groups in mixed schools. *Research in Science and Technological Education* 4: 163–170.

Heard, D. H. 1973. Unresponsive silence and intra-familial hostility. In *Support, innovation, and autonomy,* ed. R. Gosling. London: Tavistock.

——— 1982. Family systems and the attachment dynamic. *Journal of Family Therapy* 4: 99–116.

Heilbrun, C. 1988. *Writing a woman's life.* New York: Norton.

Henderson, S., D. G. Byrne, and P. Duncan-Jones. 1981. *Neurosis and the social environment*. New York: Academic Press.

Herman, J. 1989. Violence in the lives of women: Treatment and recovery. Paper presented at a conference entitled Women: Connections, Disconnection, and Violations, Harvard Medical School, Boston, Ma., June 10, 1989.

Herman, M. F. 1983. Depression and women: Theories and research. *Journal of the American Academy of Psychoanalysis* 11: 493–512.

Hochschild, A., and A. Machung. 1989. *The second shift: Inside the two-job marriage*. New York: Penguin.

Holub, L. 1989. Myth and the role of depression in women. Manuscript, Fairhaven College, Western Washington University, Bellingham.

—— 1990. Celie's ways of knowing. Manuscript, Fairhaven College, Western Washington University, Bellingham.

Horney, K. 1934. The overvaluation of love. In *Feminine psychology*, ed. H. Kelman. New York: Norton.

—— 1967. *Feminine psychology*, ed. H. Kelman. New York: Norton.

Jack, D. C. 1984. Clinical depression in women: Cognitive schemas of self, care, and relationships in a longitudinal study. Ed. D. dissertation, Harvard University.

—— 1987. Silencing the self: The power of social imperatives in female depression. In *Women and depression: A lifespan perspective*, ed. R. Formanek and A. Gurian. New York: Springer.

Jack, D. C., and D. Dill. In press. The Silencing the Self scale: Schemas of intimacy associated with depression in women. *Psychology of Women Quarterly*.

Jack, R., and D. C. Jack. 1989. *Moral vision and professional decisions: The changing values of women and men lawyers*. New York: Cambridge University Press.

Jacobson, E. 1971. *Depression: Comparative studies of normal, neurotic, and psychotic conditions*. New York: International Universities Press.

—— 1976. Ways of female superego formation and the female castration conflict. *Psychoanalytic Quarterly* 45: 525–538.

Jose, P. E., and W. J. McCarthy. 1988. Perceived agentic and communal behavior in mixed-sex group interactions. *Personality and Social Psychology Bulletin* 14: 57–67.

Kahn, R. L., and T. C. Antonucci. 1980. Convoys over the life course: Attachment, roles, and social support. In *Life-span development and behavior*, ed. P. B. Baltes and O. G. Brim. New York: Academic Press.

Kaplan, A. G. 1984. The "self-in-relation": Implications for depression in women. Wellesley, Mass.: Stone Center Working Papers Series, Paper #14.

Kaplan, E. A. 1983. *Women and film: Both sides of the camera*. New York: Methuen.

Keller, C. 1986. *From a broken web: Separation, sexism, and self.* Boston: Beacon Press.

Kerber, L. K. 1986. *Women of the Republic: Intellect and ideology in revolutionary America.* New York: Norton.

Klein, D. N., K. Harding, E. B. Taylor, and S. Dickstein. 1988. Dependency and self-criticism in depression: Evaluation in a clinical population. *Journal of Abnormal Psychology* 97: 399–404.

Klerman, G. L., R. M. A. Hirschfeld, N. C. Andreasen, W. Coryell, J. Endicott, J. Fawcett, M. B. Keller, and W. A. Scheftner. 1987. Major depression and related affective disorders. In *Diagnosis and classification in psychiatry: A critical appraisal of DSM-III,* ed. G. L. Tischler. Cambridge: Cambridge University Press.

Klerman, G. L., and M. M. Weissman. 1989. Increasing rates of depression. *Journal of the American Medical Association* 261: 2229–2235.

Klerman, G. L., M. M. Weissman, B. J. Rounsaville, and E. S. Chevron. 1984. *Interpersonal psychotherapy of depression.* New York: Basic Books.

Kohut, H. 1980. Reflections on advances in self psychology. In *Advances in self psychology,* ed. A. Goldberg. New York: International Universities Press.

Kohut, H., and E. Wolf. 1978. The disorders of the self and their treatments: An outline. *International Journal of Psychoanalysis* 59: 413–425.

Kotler, T. 1985. Security and autonomy within marriage. *Human Relations* 38: 299–321.

Krebs-McMullen, B. 1989. Depression and survival. Manuscript, Fairhaven College, Western Washington University.

Laing, R. D. 1969. *The divided self: An existential study in sanity and madness.* London: Penguin.

Lauter, E., and C. S. Rupprecht, eds. 1985. *Feminist archetypal theory: Interdisciplinary re-vision of Jungian thought.* Knoxville: University of Tennessee Press.

Lerner, H. E. 1983. Female dependency in context: Some theoretical and technical considerations. *American Journal of Orthopsychiatry* 53: 697–705.

Lerner, H. G. 1987. Female depression: Self-sacrifice and self-betrayal in relationships. In *Women and depression: A lifespan perspective,* ed. R. Formanek and A. Gurian. New York: Springer.

McIntosh, P. 1985. Feeling like a fraud. Wellesley, Mass.: Stone Center Working Papers Series, Paper #18.

Mansbridge, J. J. 1986. *Why we lost the ERA.* Chicago: University of Chicago Press.

Mead, G. H. 1956. *On social psychology: Selected papers,* ed. A. Strauss. Chicago: University of Chicago Press.

Mendelson, M. 1974. *Psychoanalytic concepts of depression.* 2nd ed. Flushing, N.Y.: Spectrum Publications.

Milavec, A. 1989. Feminist developmental cycles. Manuscript, Fairhaven College, Western Washington University, Bellingham.

Miller, A. 1981. *The drama of the gifted child*. New York: Basic Books.

Miller, J. B. 1976. *Toward a new psychology of women*. Boston: Beacon Press.

—— 1984. The development of the feminine sense of self. Wellesley, Mass.: Stone Center Working Paper Series, Paper #12.

—— 1986a. *Toward a new psychology of women*. 2nd ed. Boston: Beacon Press.

—— 1986b. What do we mean by relationships? Wellesley, Mass.: Stone Center Working Paper Series, Paper #22.

Mishler, E. G. 1979. Meaning in context: Is there any other kind? *Harvard Educational Review* 49: 1–19.

Mitchell, S. A. 1988. *Relational concepts in psychoanalysis: An integration*. Cambridge, Mass.: Harvard University Press.

Oliver, J. M., and E. P. Baumgart. 1985. The Dysfunctional Attitude Scale: Psychometric properties and relation to depression in an unselected adult population. *Cognitive Therapy and Research* 9: 161–167.

Olsen, T. 1978. *Silences*. New York: Delacorte Press.

Parry, G., and D. A. Shapiro. 1986. Social supports and life events in working class mothers: Stress-buffering or independent effects? *Archives of General Psychiatry* 43: 315–323.

Paz, O. 1987. *The collected poems of Octavio Paz: 1957–1987*. Ed. and trans. E. Weinberger. New York: New Directions.

Pearlin, L. I. 1980. Life strains and psychological distress among adults. In *Themes of work and love in adulthood*, ed. N. J. Smelser and E. H. Erikson. Cambridge, Mass.: Harvard University Press.

Perera, S. B. 1981. *Descent to the Goddess: A way of initiation for women*. Toronto: Inner City Books.

—— 1985. The descent of Inanna: Myth and therapy. In *Feminist archetypal theory*, ed. Lauter and Rupprecht.

Pfuetze, P. 1961. *Self, society, existence: Human nature and dialogue in the thought of George Herbert Mead and Martin Buber*, rev. ed. New York: Harper Torchbooks.

Pollak, S., and C. Gilligan. 1982. Images of violence in thematic apperception test stories. *Journal of Personality and Social Psychology* 42: 159–167.

A Psychiatric Glossary, 5th ed. 1980. American Psychiatric Association. Ed. A. Werner, R. J. Campbell, S. H. Frazier, and E. M. Stone. Boston: Little, Brown.

Radloff, L. S. 1980. Risk factors for depression: What do we learn from them? In *The mental health of women*, ed. M. Guttentag, S. Salasin, and D. Belle. New York: Academic Press.

Rado, S. 1968a. The problem of melancholia. In *The meaning of despair*, ed. W. Gaylin. New York: Science House.

—— 1968b. Psychodynamics of depression from the etiologic point of view. In *The meaning of despair*, ed. W. Gaylin. New York: Science House.

Rich, A. C. 1979. *On lies, secrets, and silence: Selected prose, 1966–1978*. New York: Norton.

Robins, C. J., and P. Block. 1988. Personal vulnerability, life events, and depressive symptoms: A test of a specific interactional model. *Journal of Personality and Social Psychology* 54: 847–852.

Rutter, M. 1986. The developmental psychopathology of depression: Issues and perspectives. In *Depression in young people: Developmental and clinical perspectives*, ed. M. Rutter, C. Izard, and P. Read. New York: Guilford Press.

Sadker, M., and D. Sadker. 1985. Sexism in the classroom. *Vocational Education Journal* 60: 30–32.

———— 1986. Sexism in the classroom: From grade school to graduate school. *Phi-Delta Kappan* 67: 512–515.

Slipp, S. 1976. An intrapsychic-interpersonal theory of depression. *Journal of the American Academy of Psychoanalysis* 4: 389–409.

Smith, A. 1937. *The wealth of nations*, ed. E. Cannan. New York: Modern Library.

Smith-Rosenberg, C. 1972. The hysterical woman: Sex roles and role conflict in 19th-century America. *Social Research* 39: 652–678.

Spender, D. 1980. *Man made language*. Boston: Routledge and Kegan Paul.

Steinem, Gloria. 1988. Quoted in M. Smilgis, The dilemmas of childlessness: Careers and indecision are leading many to bypass parenthood. *Time*, 2 May 1988: 88–90.

Steiner-Adair, C. 1986. The body politic: Normal female adolescent development and the development of eating disorders. *Journal of the American Academy of Psychoanalysis* 14: 95–114.

Stern, D. N. 1985. *The interpersonal world of the infant*. New York: Basic Books.

Stiver, I. P. 1984. The meanings of "dependency" in female-male relationships. Wellesley, Mass.: Stone Center Working Paper Series, Paper #11.

Stoppard, J. M. 1989. An evaluation of the adequacy of cognitive/behavioural theories for understanding depression in women. *Canadian Psychology* 30: 39–47.

Sullivan, H. S. 1953. *The interpersonal theory of psychiatry*. New York: Norton.

———— 1956. *Clinical studies in psychiatry*. New York: Norton.

Surrey, J. 1984. The "self-in-relation": A theory of women's development. Wellesley, Mass.: Stone Center Working Paper Series, Paper #13.

Swaker, M. 1976. Women's verbal behavior at learned and professional conferences. In *Proceedings of the conference on the sociology of the languages of American women*, ed. B. L. Dubois and I. Crouch. San Antonio: Trinity University.

Thorne, B., and N. Henley, eds. 1975. *Language and sex: Difference and dominance*. Rowley, Mass.: Newbury House.

Tower, C. C. 1988. *Secret scars: A guide for survivors of child sexual abuse*. New York: Viking.

Walker, A. 1982. *The Color Purple*. New York: Pocket Books/Simon and Schuster.

Walker, L. E. 1979. *The battered woman.* New York: Harper and Row.

Weissman, M. M. 1987. Advances in psychiatric epidemiology: Rates and risks for major depression. *American Journal of Public Health* 77: 445–451.

Weissman, M. M., and G. L. Klerman. 1977. Sex differences and the epidemiology of depression. *Archives of General Psychiatry* 34: 98–111.

——— 1987. Gender and depression. In *Women and Depression: A lifespan perspective,* ed. R. Formanek and A. Gurian. New York: Springer.

Weissman, M. M., and E. S. Paykel. 1974. *The depressed woman: A study of social relationships.* Chicago: University of Chicago Press.

Welter, B. 1973. The cult of true womanhood: 1820–1860. In *Our American sisters: Women in American life and thought,* ed. J. E. Friedman and W. G. Shade. Boston: Allyn and Bacon.

West, C., and D. H. Zimmerman. 1983. Small insults: A study of interruptions in cross-sex conversations between unacquainted persons. In *Language, gender and society,* ed. B. Thorne, C. Kramarae, and N. Henley. Rowley, Mass.: Newbury House.

Westkott, M. 1986. *The feminist legacy of Karen Horney.* New Haven: Yale University Press.

Wickramaratne, P. J., M. M. Weissman, P. J. Leaf, and T. R. Holford. 1989. Age, period and cohort effects on the risk of major depression: Results from five United States communities. *Journal of Clinical Epidemiology* 42: 333–343.

Willard, A. 1988. Cultural scripts for mothering. In *Mapping the moral domain: A contribution of women's thinking to psychological theory and education,* ed. C. Gilligan, J. V. Ward, and J. M. Taylor. Cambridge, Mass.: Harvard University Press.

Winnicott, D. W. 1958. *Collected papers: Through paediatrics to psychoanalysis.* London: Tavistock.

——— 1965. *The maturational process and the facilitating environment: Studies in the theory of emotional development.* New York: International Universities Press.

Wolkstein, D., and S. N. Kramer. 1983. *Inanna, queen of heaven and earth: Her stories and hymns from Sumer.* New York: Harper and Row.

Woolf, V. [1942] 1970. Professions for women. In *The death of the moth and other essays.* New York: Harcourt Brace Jovanovich.

Zimmerman, D. H., and C. West. 1975. Sex roles, interruptions, and silences in conversation. In *Language and sex: Difference and dominance,* ed. B. Thorne and N. Henley. Rowley, Mass.: Newbury House.

Zur-Spiro, S., and C. Longfellow. 1982. Fathers' support to mothers and children. In *Lives in stress: Women and depression,* ed. D. Belle. Beverly Hills: Sage Publications.

Zuroff, D. C., and M. Mongrain. 1987. Dependency and self-criticism: Vulnerability factors for depressive affective states. *Journal of Abnormal Psychology* 96: 14–22.

ACKNOWLEDGMENTS

Over the years, many people and institutions have supported my research and writing on depression. I wish especially to thank the depressed women whose voices fill these pages. Without their willingness to share their thoughts, confusion, and pain, this work would not have been possible. All of them participated in the studies out of a hope of helping others; I share their hope as the goal of this book.

I am grateful to the Whatcom Counseling and Psychiatric Clinic, which gave me access to women who agreed to be interviewed; to the battered women's shelters—Womencare, New Beginnings, and Skagit Rape Relief and Battered Women's Services—that opened their doors to this research; to the Northwest Women's Clinic, for referring depressed pregnant women to the study; to Northwest Pediatrics, for allowing me to examine infants' social responses; and to Ann Streissguth, principal investigator with the study "Cocaine: Pregnancy Use and Offspring Development," funded by the National Institute of Drug Abuse (#5 ROI DAO 5365), through whom I reached a large group of women who volunteered to participate in aspects of this research. My good friend Therese Grant was instrumental in linking this study of depression to the NIDA-funded project.

The inspiration to view depression from a different perspective grew directly out of my association with Carol Gilligan. Her work sparked my interest in exploring the moral themes in women's depression; her method of listening for the voice of the self has been a model for my own work. As my doctoral advisor at Harvard University, she generously offered ideas and encouragement, as she has continued to do throughout the years as a friend and colleague. I am also grateful to her for permission to quote from interviews from her Marital Decision Study, for which I was a research associate and interviewer.

The benefit of participating in the learning community of Harvard's Human Development program, surrounded by other students' diverse interests and lively minds, also contributed to this work and continues in importance to me. Mary Belenky, Nona Lyons, Ann Willard, Jane Attanucci, Kay Johnston, Diana Dill, and Sherry Langdale shared ideas and fostered growth. Deborah Belle has also been a warm supporter, particularly in urging me to develop a research instrument to supplement in-depth interviews. I profited from discussions with Mary Belenky regarding the differences between choice and dialogue, and from Mary's comments on an early version of a chapter of the book. I am also grateful to Marcia Westkott and Blythe Clinchy for helpful suggestions, and to Jean Baker Miller and others at the Stone Center for Developmental Services and Studies, Wellesley College, for their interest and responses to early versions of these ideas.

I have benefited immensely from the interdisciplinary, innovative atmosphere of Fairhaven College, Western Washington University. At Fairhaven, conversations over the years with Kathryn Anderson sharpened my awareness of historical themes in women's self-reflection, and Connie Faulkner introduced me to economic theory. The creativity of Fairhaven students has enriched my insight into the themes of this book. Drawings by Judith Wallen inspired the term "Over-Eye." For careful readings of drafts of chapters, I am particularly grateful to Lois Holub, whose comments, interest, and questions deepened this work. Elizabeth Harris, Candice Wiggum, Connie McCollum, and Robert Keller also read and commented on various chapters.

A previous version of some of these ideas, along with some of the quotes from depressed women, appeared in "Silencing the Self: The Power of Social Imperatives in Female Depression," in *Women and Depression: A Lifespan Perspective*, edited by Ruth Formanek and Anita Gurian (New York: Springer, 1987). The quotation from Octavio Paz appears in *The Collected Poems of Octavio Paz, 1957–1987*, edited and translated by Eliot Weinberger (New York: New Directions, 1987), copyright © 1986 by Octavio Paz and Eliot Weinberger, reprinted by permission of New Directions Publishing Corporation.

Financial support was given by the Harvard Project on the Psychology of Women and the Development of Girls, by a Depression Prevention Grant Award from the Stone Center, Wellesley College, and by grants from Western Washington University and Fairhaven College.

At Harvard University Press, Arthur Rosenthal encouraged me at critical times. Angela von der Lippe was a most supportive and helpful editor, and Camille Smith edited the manuscript with imagination, clarity, and nerves of steel. Working with both of these skilled editors has been a great pleasure.

Although I take a critical perspective on the institution of marriage, I rely upon my own. My husband, Rand, provided the secure base from which this work was launched and has maintained loving support throughout its long journey to completion. Many questions that we have discussed and shared in a daily way have been set down in some form here, and his editing has immeasurably improved my writing.

I also thank my children, Darby and Kelsey, who participated in the unfolding of these ideas, for their love, humor, and patience. My mother, Dorothy Beach, has given encouragement and instrumental help. Her series of watercolors depicting silencing of self and inner division were inspiring. Her oil painting embodying depression hangs in my office, with unknown effects on others, but as a continual reminder to me of the critical importance of facing what is dreaded in order to know and transcend it.

I have come to think of this book on depression as a weaving that has been on my loom for many years. The work is now completed, but it will not take its final form until it meets the hearts and minds of readers. My hope is that the meeting will promote a new understanding of the origins and treatment of depression in women.

INDEX OF STUDY PARTICIPANTS

INDEX

Abuse: sexual, 15, 201–202, 222n14; physical, 66–67, 99–100, 138, 155–157
Activity, to appear passive, 129–139
Adolescence, 14, 221n11
Alienation: from self, 5–6, 44, 132–135; from culture, 135–136
Angel in the House, 86–87
Anger, 83, 129, 137, 140–146, 168–169, 189–190; communication of, 41–43; and inequality, 41–43, 51–54; and anxiety, 49; mind rehearsals, 51–53; goal of, 52–53. *See also* Hostility
Arieti, S., 16, 112
Attachment, 3, 7, 10, 84; anxious, 18, 40–41, 46–47; theory, 18, 222n19; inequality within, 21–22, 39–49, 62–63, 80–84, 112–115; ways to secure, 55–84, 191; security of, 65, 66, 71–72
Attachment behaviors, 18, 46–47; culturally defined as feminine, 55–84
Authentic self, 32, 48, 60, 101, 141; defined, 94, 227n2; judged by Over-Eye, 95–99; in depression, 168–182, 191–192
Authority, 61, 104, 185–187, 196–199; male, 81, 127, 141–142, 175–176; of Over-Eye, 101–102, 130–133, 199; maternal, 109–112, 162–164, 172–175; of church, 117, 176–179

Beck, A., 2, 121–122, 123, 222n17, 229n2, 232n12

Becker, E., 84
Belenky, M., et al., 14, 33, 85, 136, 139, 196, 203
Bellah, R., et al., 85
Belle, D., 23, 224n24, 225–226n9
Bemporad, J., 16, 112
Bernard, J., 78–79
Bernstein, D., 114
Blatt, S., 108
Blumstein, P., 43
Bowlby, J., 7, 11, 14, 18, 40, 41, 149, 222n19
Brazelton, B., 91, 233n1
Brown, L. M., 14, 27
Buber, M., 190

Capitalism, 8
Caplow, T., 85
Care: forms of, 38–39, 151, 194–195; as selflessness, 49, 112–117, 120–121, 153–154
Children: as objects of hostility, 53–54; men as, 66–67
Chodoff, P., 17
Chodorow, N., 11, 12, 13, 149
Cognitive schemas, 15–16, 121–123, 197–199
Compliance in relationship, 39–49, 62, 68
Connection, 27; forms of, 19–20, 37–54, 126–127
Cott, N., 85